The Oxford C...... Development

Learning to Teach

RUNNING TUTORIALS AND SEMINARS

Training Materials for Research Students

David Baume and Carole Baume

© Oxford Centre for Staff Development 1996

Published by
THE OXFORD CENTRE FOR STAFF DEVELOPMENT
Oxford Brookes University
Gipsy Lane
Headington
Oxford
OX3 0BP

Learn to Teach: Running Tutorials and Seminars
ISBN 1 873576 44 7

British Library Cataloguing-in-Publication Data. A catalogue record for this book is available from the British Library.

Designed and Typeset in 10.5 on 14 pt Palatino and Helvetica by Ann Trew
Illustrations by Bob Pomfret

Printed in Great Britain by
Oxonian Rewley Press Ltd
Oxford

Printed on paper produced from sustainable forests.

First Printed 1996
Reprinted 2002

Contents

Introduction

You have been asked to run a tutorial or seminar on the topic of the lecture. You may have been told the learning outcomes, in which case your job is to design and run a session which will enable the students to achieve these. You may only have been told something like 'get the students talking about the subject.' In this case, you need to establish more clearly the learning outcomes and then decide how, for example, you are going to ensure that everyone talks, cover all of the topic, and prepare students for further reading and future contributions to seminars.

As you may remember, students can hide in a lecture. In a well-run small or large group, and especially when preparing and making a presentation, they find it much harder. This series of booklets stresses that activity is essential for learning. Groups, then, are places where students are active – alright, most students are active.

Activity doesn't of itself ensure learning. This booklet suggests kinds of student activities which are more likely to help students to learn, from you, and from one another.

Precisely because they involve student activity, groups, of whatever size, may seem to you to be a daunting prospect. This booklet suggests underlying principles and detailed techniques and scripts which will help you through these concerns, and assist you to develop your own techniques for the rewarding business of managing student learning in tutorials and seminars.

Aims and overall learning outcomes for this booklet

This booklet is intended to help you plan and manage small and large student groups, including tutorials, seminars, problem classes and student presentations. It will also help you to plan for, and deal with, any difficult incidents which may arise.

On completing it you should also be able to lay out rooms for various kinds of groups, use appropriate audio-visual aids and handouts, ask good questions and respond appropriately to student questions.

Running Tutorials and Seminars

Small Group Sessions

Why small group discussions?

Learning is an active process. Much valuable learning occurs in discussion. We learn by testing our ideas and testing the ideas of others. In discussion we make meaning. This is as true of undergraduate as it is of research students.

In providing effective support for discussion in small groups, you are helping some of the most powerful and effective learning which the students will experience. You already have many of the necessary skills, though you may not be conscious of having them.

This section will make some of these skills explicit. It will help you develop and extend your expertise in facilitating student learning in small groups. At the same time it will inevitably extend your own abilities for working in small groups, abilities which will be of use to you during and after your time as a research student.

Aims and learning outcomes for this section

This section aims to help you to conduct small group discussions which will enable your students to achieve the learning outcomes set by the course or module leader.

In order to achieve this aim, you will need to be able to:

- plan a small group session to help students achieve specified learning outcomes
    - lay out a room to facilitate small group discussion
    - choose or devise appropriate learning activities
    - collect or prepare necessary support materials
    - schedule a teaching session
- construct questions to encourage discussion and check students' understanding
- respond to student questions in an appropriate way.

Small Group Sessions

1.1 Planning a small group session

1.1.1 A checklist for you to use and add to

1 Research

Have you got the lecture outline, or can you go to the lecture on which the small group is based?

Have you read the key references, the course guide, handouts, problem sheets, past exam papers . . .?

Have you checked out the room you'll be using?

Have you asked the course or module leader what they would do in the session?

2 Learning outcomes

What are the learning outcomes for this small group session you are to conduct? That is, what should the students be able to do at the end of the session? (These may be in the course or module handbook, or you may need to ask the course or module leader or write them yourself.)

Are you clear what these outcomes mean? Could you explain to the students what the outcomes mean? (If not, ask someone else who teaches on the course.)

3 Assessment

How does the session you are planning contribute to the course or module assessment? For example, are seminar presentations assessed?

Does the discussion in the seminar inform the answering of exam questions? (If so, you could formulate 'exam type' questions for discussion in class.)

4 Learning activities

What learning activities might help the students to achieve the outcomes?

Do you need an 'icebreaker' activity to begin the session?

What review activity will you use at the end to help you plan for the next session?

5 Scheduling a session

What is the total session length? What time do students actually arrive?

Do the students (and you) need a break during the session?

Are there other things you have to do during the session? (For example, take register, give things out, remind about assessment, collect in work . . .)

Have you produced a timetable for the session? (See activity in section 1.1.3.)

Which activity can you ditch if the others overrun? Which additional activity will you have ready, just in case?

6 Planning the room layout

How many students are registered in your group? What is the likely attendance? (There should be a chair for each registered student, but lay out chairs only for the number you expect to turn up!)

Do students need tables to work on materials? (Discussion may flow better without tables.)

Will you (or the students) be using the white board/black board/flip chart/overhead projector? (If so, make sure everyone in the room can see it.)

7 Learning materials

What lecture notes/handouts/reading lists are students working from?

Which parts of the recommended texts work best for this session?

Are there additional articles or handouts which you want to use? Have you prepared them?

Have you prepared any overhead transparencies you plan to use?

Have you got the appropriate pens/flip chart paper/blank overheads for use 'live' in the session?

8 Additional particulars for your subject area

9 Additional particulars for your students

Student Presentations

Learning through teaching?

The increasing use of student presentations reflects a spreading view that learning is an active business. It also bears out the experience of many teachers that teaching something is a great way to learn it, or to consolidate and develop learning. However, for many of the same reasons you find your first few teaching sessions scary, students often find their first presentation to other students and a tutor scary.

Your recent or current experience as a student, and your current experience of giving, for example, presentations to your own peer group or papers to research seminars, makes you well able to understand how your students feel in delivering presentations. This means you are a good person to help them.

Aims and learning outcomes for this section

This section is intended to help you to:

- brief students on preparing and undertaking presentations

- support them during and after their presentation

- plan and manage student presentation sessions

- give feedback to student presenters, and manage the process of students giving feedback.

5.1 Briefing students

Most of what we say in the 'Making Presentations' booklet in this series about the way you should plan your presentations also applies to how your students should plan their presentations.

So, as you brief them, you should either be telling them or helping them to work out:

- the **purpose** of their presentation

- an appropriate **structure** for their presentation.

You will also need to tell them, or help them work out, some other things:

- the **audience** for their presentation (of course the audience will be other students and a tutor, probably you: but it can boost the value of a student presentation if they have another audience in mind – the chair of a public enquiry, other design team members, potential customers . . .)

- the **duration** of the presentation – and how this will be enforced, and maybe the consequence of them over- or under-running!

- your expectations about **questions from the audience** and how they will deal with them

- how and by whom their presentation will be **assessed**.

Student Presentations

5.2 Supporting students

5.2.1 Before the seminar series starts . . .

Most students will be nervous at the thought of making presentations. You could try telling them that they'll be all right and not to worry, but you may find it more helpful to give them time and space to share their concerns.

Previous experience

Ask each one to say if they have made a presentation to a group before. Define 'presentation' and 'group' broadly. Get them to talk about how it felt, what worked and what didn't, and how they knew.

Hopes and fears

Ask some of them them what it would feel like for their presentation to this group to be a complete success. Ask them what they, and everyone else in the group, would have to do to make their presentation a complete success. Ask some other people in the group what they think about what they've just heard.

Then ask the same three questions about an unsuccessful presentation. Prepare for laughter!

Resources

Inspired by your own excellent presentations and those of your colleagues, students will clamour for access to materials for using a flipchart, white-board or even overhead projector slides. Indulge and support them: these are useful skills and can greatly improve their presentations. Again, some of the guidance on audio-visual aids which we provide in the booklet in this series on 'Making Presentations' will apply to your students.

Planning, rehearsal, feedback

Encourage them to plan, to rehearse and to give each other feedback on their rehearsal performances.

5.2.2 . . . and as the seminar series proceeds

Find out what the seminar leader wants

Ask the leader what room layout they want, what audio-visual equipment they need, what they would like you to do (for example, look encouraging, discourage questions until they ask for them, keep quiet). Then provide and do what they want!

Chair the seminar

They may well find it easier to present if they know you'll take responsibility for timekeeping, for forming the questioners into an orderly queue, for dealing with people who arrive late or are likely to misbehave, and generally for everything but the actual presentation.

Help them if they get scared or stuck

It's difficult to know what to do when a presenter shows signs of distress. Do you let them flounder too long and suffer a serious loss of confidence? Or maybe ask them if now would be a good time for a few questions? You could recap – *'So what you've said so far is . . .'* Or you could simply reassure them – *'It's OK, you're doing fine, keep going.'*

Student Presentations

5.3 Planning and managing student presentations

5.3.1 Scheduling

You have 22 students in the class. Each of them should give one presentation. There are 12 sessions, each of one and a half hours. No problem – the first week is used for planning, and then there are two presentations each week for the rest of the course . . .

It's not quite that simple. Everyone wants to give their presentation as late as possible in the course, preferably in the last week. Students go sick, sometimes in the week they were due to present. Students leave the course; others join it. All of these things are foreseeable, in general at least. You know it; they know it.

You could take total responsibility for the scheduling and operation of the series of presentations.

Or you could form a joint venture with the students. Plan with the group how the group should decide on order of presentation, deal with sicknesses and absences and cope with new students.

5.3.2 Preparing and supporting the audience

We've discussed above ways in which you can help the student who is making the seminar presentation. It's also important to help the audience. The audience will (usually!) outnumber the presenter. What benefit should the audience derive from the seminar? What should the audience do in order to achieve this benefit? What can you do to make sure that these good things happen for the audience?

5.3.3 Managing questions

We stress throughout these materials that learning is an active process. We also stress the power of questions as a tool for learning. Seminars and student presentations are a particularly rich setting for questions. Everyone can ask everyone else questions.

Who can ask who what kinds of questions? Who can answer what kinds of questions from whom? Here are some suggestions. Think of others!

	Tutor asks . . .	Presenter asks . . .	Audience asks . . .
. . . the tutor	*How well is it going How could I improve it – now? – next time?*	(at the end) Is there anything you'd like to add? (later) How did I do?	What did you think about the presentation? How well did it represent . . .?
. . . the presenter	(during) Could you say a bit more about . . .? (after) How do you feel you did?	*How well am I doing against the criteria? How could I have improved it?*	[Questions about any aspect of the presentation and its content!]
. . . the audience	Who has a question? How does this presentation relate to [last week's]?	Any questions? Anything to add? Any disagreements? Any agreements? Anything?	*What am I getting from this? How could I get more – now? – next time?*

Running Tutorials and Seminars

"Yes, a sack of barley meal. And
 there was something else."
"Was it chicken food?" said the miller.
"Or flour?"
"Flour!" said Farmer Bungle. "Yes,
 a sack of flour."

But when he got back to the farm,
he fed the flour to the pigs and
took the barley meal to Mrs Bungle.
"This is barley meal," she said when
she opened the sack. "I can't bake bread
and make cakes with barley meal!"
"Oh dear," said Farmer Bungle. "I forgot
which sack was which."
"Well, I've forgotten to get you
any lunch," said Mrs Bungle sharply.

In the afternoon Mrs Bungle went out
to the hen-run to feed her hens and
collect their eggs.

She took a tray full of eggs
to Farmer Bungle, who was
rolling a field. She put them down
by the gate. "Take these up to the house
when you've finished," she said.
"Why, where are you going?"
asked Farmer Bungle.
Mrs Bungle said, "I am going to go
and buy some flour."
"Take the eggs up to the house,"
said Farmer Bungle to himself
when she had gone.
"I'll remember that or
my name's not Bill Bungle."

When he had finished rolling the field,
he drove out of the gate. Somehow
he had forgotten about the eggs.

When Farmer Bungle came in
for his tea, he found that
there was no bread on the breadboard,
no cakes on the cake stand and
no milk in his teacup.
There was an egg cup in front of him,
but there was no egg in it.

CHAPTER 1

People management: personnel management and human resource management

INTRODUCTION

Good managers are not only effective in their use of economic and technical resources, but when they manage people they remember that these particular resources are special, and are ultimately the most important assets. People are the only real source of continuing competitive advantage. Good managers also remember that these particular assets are human beings.

LEARNING OUTCOMES

On completion of this chapter you should:

- have a good appreciation of what the 'people management' function in contemporary organisations comprises
- know what we mean by the term 'human resource management' (HRM) and how this differs from the earlier 'personnel management' (PM) concept of the function
- have some appreciation of the theoretical development of HRM
- understand the relationship between HRM and business strategy
- have an appreciation of the practical application of HRM
- understand the impact of new working methods on HRM
- recognise some of the key themes of HRM in the twenty-first century.

The definition of terms such as 'personnel management' and 'human resource management' is one area of particular confusion and irritation to general managers, and we will discuss later the differences between what typically is meant by these terms. We will use the phrase 'people management' as a generic term to cover both 'personnel management' (PM) and 'human resource management' (HRM) in the absence of a specific definition of either.

But broadly, we can say that the 'people management' function – whether we wish to define it as 'personnel management' or as 'human resource management' – may be described as:

> All the management decisions and actions that directly affect or influence people *as members of the organisation rather than as job-holders.*

In other words, people management is not executive management of individuals and their jobs. Management of specific tasks and responsibilities is the concern of the employee's immediate supervisor or manager – that is, the person to whom his or her performance is accountable (sometimes this might be the person's team). So people managers – whether 'personnel managers' or 'human resource managers' – do not have line authority over employees.

The term 'human resource management' was being used by Peter Drucker and others in North America as early as the 1950s without any special meaning, and usually simply as another label for 'personnel management' or 'personnel administration'. By the 1980s, however, HRM had come to mean a 'radically different philosophy and approach to the management of people at work' (Storey, 1989; pp4–5) with an emphasis on performance, workers' commitment, and rewards based on individual or team contribution, differing significantly in all of these from the corresponding aspects of traditional personnel management.

One of the main characteristics of HRM is the devolution of many aspects of 'people management' from specialists directly to line managers. HRM itself has been called 'the discovery of personnel management by chief executives'. So line managers over the past ten years or so have frequently been confronted with HRM decisions and activities in their day-to-day business in a way that was not the case previously.

This process has been accelerated by a more recent development which adds to the burden of the line manager while increasing the effectiveness of the organisation as a whole. Outsourcing of large areas of the traditional personnel management department's routine functions has happened on a massive scale in the last decade. Outsourcing of non-core functions, allowing the organisation to concentrate on its core competencies, has been one of the single most important organisational factors in both business and the public sector in recent times. It is extremely unlikely that this will be set in reverse in the foreseeable future. In the case of HR services the 'dis-integrating' effects of outsourcing have been amplified by such related developments as 'e-HR', in which the use of new technologies allows the provision of 'self-service' HR to employees and managers, and 'HR business partnering', in which large organisations disperse 'HR partners' to constituent businesses (Caldwell and Storey, 2007).

This outsourcing does not remove the day-to-day burden of HR from line managers: it increases it. Nor does it remove the need for HR specialists, but these people are just that – highly specialised, technical experts who act as consultants, either internally in the case of larger organisations, or externally (eg as a specialised bureau service used by line mangers as required). This means that it will be more important than ever for line managers to communicate effectively with HR specialists and be able to weigh up their advice in an intelligent and knowledgeable manner – and to do that they have to speak the language and understand the concepts of the expert.

⁇ REFLECTIVE ACTIVITY

Write down what you think personnel or human resource managers are actually supposed to do.

WHAT DO PEOPLE MANAGERS DO?

Torrington *et al* (2008), an authoritative text widely used in teaching managers who are studying for the professional exams of the Chartered Institute of Personnel and Development (CIPD), describe the general role of people management as comprising specific objectives under four headings: staffing, performance, change management, and administration.

- *Staffing objectives* are firstly concerned with 'getting the right people in the right jobs at the right times' – ie the recruitment and selection of staff, but increasingly these days also advising on subcontracting and outsourcing of staff. Staffing also concerns managing the release of employees from the organisation by, for example, resignation, retirement, dismissal or redundancy.

- *Performance objectives*: people managers have a part to play in assisting the organisation to motivate its employees and ensure that they perform well. Training and development, reward and performance management systems are all important here. Grievance and disciplinary procedures are also necessary, as are welfare support and employee involvement initiatives.

- *Change management objectives* include employee relations/involvement, the recruitment and development of people with the necessary leadership and change management skills, and the construction of rewards systems to underpin the change.

- *Administration objectives* include the maintenance of accurate employee data on, for example, recruitment, contracts and conditions of service; performance; attendance and training; ensuring organisational compliance with legal requirements, for example in employment law and employee relations; and health and safety.

General managers are increasingly involved directly in all of the first three types of objectives. Other than in managerial oversight for legal compliance issues, administration objectives tend to remain the preserve of dedicated PM/HR support staff.

The above closely reflects the arguments in David Ulrich's highly influential *Harvard Business Review* article of 1998, 'A new mandate for human resources', which has helped to shape human resources (HR) in the new century. After acknowledging that some commentators had been calling for the 'abolition of HR' on the grounds of serious doubts about its contribution to organisational performance, Ulrich agreed (Ulrich, 1998; p.124) that:

> there is good reason for HR's beleaguered reputation. It is often ineffective, incompetent and costly.

His solution was for HR to be 'reconfigured' to focus on outcomes rather than on traditional processes such as staffing or compensation:

> HR should not be defined by what it does but by what it delivers – results that enrich the organisation's value to customers, investors and employees.

His recommendations were that:

- First, HR should become a 'partner' with senior and line managers in strategy execution.
- Second, it should become an 'expert' in the way work is organised and executed, delivering administrative efficiency to ensure that costs are reduced while quality is maintained.
- Third, it should become a 'champion for employees', vigorously representing their concerns to senior managers and at the same time working to increase employees' contribution – 'that is, employees' commitment to the organisation and their ability to deliver results'.
- Finally, HR should become an 'agent of continuous transformation', shaping processes and a culture that together improve an organisation's capacity for change.

Ulrich's model of the HR role has set the agenda for people management in the twenty-first century as being essentially about its contribution to organisational performance.

Linda Holbeche, the Director of Research and Policy for the CIPD, has written (Holbeche, 2007; pp10–11) that

> building organisational capability is HR's heartland,

and she added that HR managers

> can help make capitalism human.

These two statements more or less sum it all up.

SO WHAT IS HRM?

What exactly does this rather self-important-sounding phrase 'human resource management' actually mean? To many people it is seen as just a fancy or pretentious re-labelling of what used to be called 'personnel management'. But to many managers and management theorists it is vital to the survival and success of organisations in the twenty-first century. Why they think so really derives from one single, simple idea: that people – their skills, knowledge and creativity – are *the* key resource for economic and organisational success in what Peter Drucker (1993) called 'the knowledge-based economy'.

By the 1970s a settled idea of people management in large organisations had evolved in developed free-market economies, and this was typically termed 'personnel management' (PM) or sometimes 'personnel administration' (PA). It reflected the predominantly Taylorist[1] organisation of work, which in turn had developed to exploit the technology available for the mass production of industrial goods. It acknowledged and incorporated the institutions of collective industrial relations recognising the role and power of trade unions.

The extraordinary economic success of Taylorist industrial practices ensured that this became the standard model for all large organisations, even those in service industries and in the public sector, and PM techniques used in industry – eg in recruitment and selection – were usually assumed to be best management practice.

Something of a revolution in people management occurred in the 1980s which seemingly overturned the established paradigm[2] of personnel management in favour of 'human resource management' (HRM). If today, over a quarter of a century later, one surveys the academic and professional management literature on people management, whether aimed at specialists or at general managers, one would think the revolution had been total. Normative models[3] of HRM and examples of HRM 'best practice' abound, with little or no trace of traditional personnel management.

However, if in fact we look at the empirical evidence, we are forced to conclude that indeed there has been a revolution, but that it is not complete in terms of either organisational culture or management practice.

Few, if any, new techniques of people management have been developed within HRM. It is often the scope and manner of their use, and the intent behind their employment, that differs in the two approaches. For example, psychometric testing and personality profiling have been available for decades but in PM these were used only for executive and other highly paid appointments. Many firms adopting HRM now routinely apply such techniques to all appointments, the intention being not to predict whether one high-cost appointment will be successful in a particular role but rather to ensure that all employees can accept a strong common culture.

As we will discuss in some detail in the following section, it makes sense to talk of two paradigms in people management: 'personnel management' ('PM') and 'HRM', the latter being predominant, and increasingly so, but with most organisations still showing some mixture of the two.

We will first discuss the evolution of each of these paradigms.

THE EVOLUTION OF PEOPLE MANAGEMENT AND THE EMERGENCE OF 'PERSONNEL MANAGEMENT'

People management originated in the UK in the nineteenth century amidst the factory conditions of the first Industrial Revolution. The unrestrained capitalism of the initial industrialisation of the UK was restricted by the Factory Acts of the 1840s, which compelled factory owners to consider the well-being of their workforces, at least to some degree. Enlightened capitalists such as Rowntree and Cadbury, who were often motivated by religious convictions, appointed 'welfare officers' to monitor and improve the conditions and lives of workers. Their actions would often seem intrusive and paternalistic today – for example, they discouraged drinking out of work hours as well as during. Caring for the welfare of employees was thus the first true 'people management' role in the sense of organisational responsibility beyond that of specific job performance.

With the rise of industrial trade unionism in the twentieth century another role evolved in people management – that of negotiating and communicating with the collective representatives of the workforce (the workplace 'shop stewards' and the full-time paid trade union officials) on behalf of the organisation.

The rise of 'scientific management' and the organisation of industrial work along Taylorist lines also led to increased interest in more rigorous selection of personnel administered by management, instead of the haphazard traditional methods which often relied on the foremen or 'gangmasters' to pick men and women for work. It also led to management taking an interest in organising and providing skills training.

Following World War II, social science – particularly as employed in the Human Relations School – started to exert a direct influence on work in the areas of job design, attempting to ameliorate the worst side-effects of scientific management while still achieving its productive and economic benefits. Although such developments might not affect people management directly, they shaped the culture in which it was operating and evolving. The conscious application of social science also encouraged the use of more sophisticated techniques in recruitment and selection, which did have an impact on people management policies and practice.

By the 1970s a fairly consistent set of activities and roles had developed for people management, which in most large organisations was perceived as a specialist management function, usually termed Personnel Management and comprising the areas of recruitment and selection, pay and conditions of service, employee welfare, industrial relations, training and development, and employee exit (retrenchment, redundancy or retirement). Most day-to-day people management, especially in the area of employee relations, was handled by personnel specialists and not by line managers. In the UK the professional status of personnel managers was supported by the formation of the Institute of Personnel Management (IPM), which was later to evolve and become the present-day Chartered Institute of Personnel and Development (CIPD).

Of course personnel management was not without its critics. Peter Drucker (1955) thought that 'personnel administration', as he called it, was just a set of unrelated, albeit individually important, activities. The Drucker critique can be read now as an early plea for people management to be returned to line managers as later advocated by HRM models. The ambiguity of traditional personnel management was noted with the welfare role expected by employees but efficiency and cost-control increasingly demanded of it by management (Legge, 1995). Radical critics disliked it on principle (see below).

THE DEVELOPMENT OF HUMAN RESOURCE MANAGEMENT

The people management policies and practices which are usually termed 'HRM' originated in manufacturing industry in the USA during the late 1970s and early 1980s. These represented a significant break with the personnel management paradigm. A number of factors led to this new management thinking, principally loss of faith in the traditional approach to mass production, the example of Japanese work organisation and manufacturing processes, and the realisation of the impact of new technology on work practices (Gallie *et al*, 1998).

The remarkable success of Japanese manufacturers in the 1970s and 1980s in capturing Western markets for sophisticated products, such as electronics and cars, brought to a head long-standing concerns about traditional Taylorist/ Fordist models of work organisation. These models were characterised by low- or semi-skilled work, close supervision, pay being linked to quantity of output, and – at least in mass-production industries – assembly-line technologies in which the pace of work was controlled by machine. Academic studies had shown concern about some of the human effects of Taylorism and Fordism for decades, and this led to the rise of the Human Relations School, but by the 1980s it was recognised by business and managers as well that the costs of such systems were becoming unacceptable in terms of low levels of job involvement and weak commitment to the employing organisation. There was an increasing willingness on the part of employees to disrupt production to achieve higher financial or other rewards despite the damage such action could have on the long-term health of the organisation. Crucially, it had also become recognised that these traditional systems of work organisation were intrinsically unable to produce the quality output now required to compete in a global marketplace (Beer *et al*, 1984; p.viii).

The perceived superiority of the Japanese model was confirmed for many Western managers and academics by an influential MIT study in the 1980s which concluded that Fordist methods would inevitably be replaced in the car industry by the 'lean production' model of work organisation typified by Toyota's work methods. This approach to work organisation was seen to combine the best features of both craft-production and mass production (Kenney and Florida, 1993) and to achieve very high levels of employee commitment with resulting benefits in quality and flexibility.

Technology also played a part in shifting managerial concern towards human resources. Managers had become aware that the rapid development of new technologies in competitive markets meant that organisations faced continual technological change, which in turn implied the need for continuous learning by employees. Employers would have to be able to assess individual employees' training needs and provide the necessary investment in changing and upgrading skills.

All this implied the development of a much closer relationship between managers and employees, and therefore also changes in the work of managers as well as that of workers. In particular, it meant that the traditional approach of managing people – 'personnel management' or 'personnel administration', which had evolved to help manage Taylorist/Fordist organisations more effectively – was no longer viable. In an increasingly competitive global economy, with advancing technology and better-educated workforces, it was not enough to manage people reactively or passively. In the industries that mattered, competitive advantage now ultimately came not from capital investment but from human resources, and these had to be managed proactively and strategically if an organisation was to be successful.

The collectivised employment relationship, in which trade unions represented the workforce and bargained with employers on its behalf for wages and conditions of employment (often on an industry-wide basis), had come to be seen by management as a hindrance to the adoption of the new technologies and work practices which were necessary to compete with the Japanese. In fact most Japanese workers in the major exporting industries were unionised but the Japanese trade unions did not share the pluralist culture of their counterparts in the West (see below).

Initially, the new human resource policies were linked to non-unionised and greenfield sites (Foulkes, 1980; Kochan *et al*, 1994). Typically, these were in large-scale manufacturing, where the Taylorist/Fordist pattern of work organisation had been most dominant, but the new approach soon exerted influence in all sorts of organisations and in every part of the economy, including services and the public sector.

Theoretical and academic models of HRM signalled from the outset the importance of strategy in normative models of HRM. HRM was regarded as superior to personnel management or personnel administration partly because it was supposed to be 'strategic' in two senses: (i) the function itself was conceived of in strategic rather than reactive ways; and (ii) the HRM strategy would be intimately linked to, and consciously supportive of, overall business and corporate strategies.

PERSPECTIVES IN THE MANAGEMENT OF PEOPLE

As we will see below, managerial perceptions of how people view relationships within their organisations are important in our analysis of human resource management. Our 'frame of reference' will influence how we expect people to behave, how we think they *ought* to behave, and how we react to the behaviour of others. We are concerned here with three major perspectives: the 'pluralist', the 'unitarist' and the 'radical' or 'critical' (Fox, 1966).

THE PLURALIST PERSPECTIVE

Until relatively recently, this reflected the typical Western industrial workplace post-World War II. It rests on the assumption that society consists of various groups which will each have their own interests and beliefs. It is naive to pretend that the interests of workers and managers/owners can be fully reconciled, and so institutions such as trade unions and arrangements such as collective bargaining are needed to achieve workable compromises between these differing interests. In the pluralist view, conflict at work is seen as inevitable, because management and workers will not have identical interests, but conflict is not in itself 'wrong'. The issue is not to try to eliminate it, which would be impossible, but rather how it should be handled. In cases where conflicts seem to be insoluble at the workplace or industry level, third-party intervention – often through state agencies (eg ACAS: the Advisory, Conciliation and Arbitration Service, in the UK) – can provide solutions.

THE UNITARIST PERSPECTIVE

From this perspective a work organisation has a purpose (or set of purposes) common to all members of it – owners, managers and workers. So there should be no real conflict of interest between these groups. Everyone has the same ultimate interest in high levels of efficiency which will generate high profits and add to shareholder value – and allow the payment of high wages.

It is a win/win situation for all concerned. Managers and those they manage are really all members of the same 'team'. Management has special leadership responsibilities and should pursue policies which allow the organisation to achieve its goals and satisfy shareholders (and other stakeholders), but which are also fair to employees. On this view, conflict within the organisation between management and the workforce is perceived as being the result of some sort of failure; it is not regarded as necessary or inevitable – in principle, at least, it could be eliminated. From this perspective trade unions are often seen as competing for the loyalty of the employees, and collective bargaining may be regarded as unnecessary.

The unitarist perspective in its purest form was traditionally found in private, typically family-owned employers, but HRM is usually associated with unitarism (sometimes termed 'neo-unitarism' to distinguish it from the earlier, more paternalistic, family-firm version).

THE RADICAL/CRITICAL PERSPECTIVE

Quite different from both the other perspectives, this derived originally from the Marxist view of society and industrial capitalism. In essence this saw all work as inevitably being exploitative of workers. Conflict between management and labour was unavoidable as part of wider class conflict in society. Management always, and inevitably, represented the interests of capital. There may be few unreconstructed Marxists in the twenty-first century, but shades of post-Marxist thought persist, and there are cultural and social radicals of various types who reject the mainstream, free-market culture in which most organisations now operate. To such radicals, as to nineteenth- and twentieth-century Marxists, work organisations reflect the inherently unfair or oppressive structures of society (for example, to radical feminists they reflect the patriarchal nature of society) and help to buttress these same structures.

Postmodern intellectuals often share this view (see McKinlay and Starkey, 1998), and many writers on HRM and management within the Critical Management School hold a radical perspective in this sense (see, for example, Legge, 1995, and Thompson and McHugh, 2002).

From this perspective even 'enlightened' management practices and philosophies such as the Human Relations School, or employee 'empowerment', or profit-sharing are really either hopelessly naive and doomed attempts to overcome the inevitable exploitative nature of capitalism/existing society, or are conscious and cynical strategies to fool the employees. Even pluralistic industrial relations structures can be seen in this light.

REFLECTIVE ACTIVITY

In terms of the perspectives examined above, how would you describe:

a) your personal perspective?

b) the managerial culture of your own organisation?

HUMAN RESOURCE MANAGEMENT IN THEORY

We noted above the practical considerations such as quality, competition and technology which led to questioning of the traditional forms of people management. Management theorists were as concerned as practising managers and governments were about the evident failure of the Taylorist/Fordist approach and produced a number of academic models of HRM.

The theoretical heritage of HRM includes the managerial writings of Peter Drucker, the Human Relations School, human capital theory, and Organisational Development. Interest in HRM proceeded alongside other developments in economics, business strategy and organisational change. Many of these ideas revolved around the notion of the resource-based theory of the firm (Barney, 1991) and core competencies (Prahalad and Hamel, 1990), which argued that sustained competitive advantage ultimately derives from a firm's internal resources provided that these (i) can add value, (ii) are unique or rare, (iii) are difficult for competitors to imitate, and (iv) are non-substitutable. Of course, human resources fit such a list of criteria well (Storey, 2001).

One of the first, and most important, intellectual proponents of HRM was the Harvard Business School (HBS). The faculty and alumni of the School agreed in the early 1980s that a new course in HRM was required to equip general managers to deal with the changes that were occurring both in society and in the competitive environment in which business had to operate. Accordingly, in 1981, HBS introduced a course in HRM in its core MBA curriculum, the first new required course since Managerial Economics twenty years before (Beer *et al*, 1984; p.ix). The primary intention of Beer *et al* was to develop a framework for general managers to understand and apply HRM in their organisations. Figure 1 shows the Harvard model of HRM.

Figure 1 The Harvard model of HRM

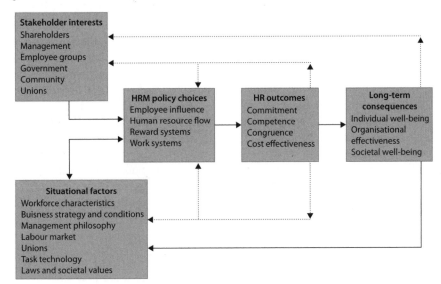

Source: Beer *et al* (1984; p.16 'Map of the HRM territory')

The central issue here is performance – managing human resources to achieve positive HR outcomes in terms of a committed workforce, working in harmony with the objectives of the organisation and achieving competence and cost effectiveness. These outcomes in turn lead to positive long-term consequences: firstly organisational effectiveness, but also individual and society's well-being.

We should note the emphasis on policy choice. This implies that managers have at least some degree of discretion in their HR policies. The situational factors and stakeholder interests identified in the model may impact on managerial decisions on HRM, but none of these will *determine* which HRM polices are followed. The choice made will have outcomes and long-term consequences both of which, as the model shows, may feed back into policy choices, and, in the longer term, also into the stakeholder interests and situational factors.

The Harvard model has been influential worldwide. Hollinshead and Leat (1995) used the model as a framework to examine HRM in Germany, France, Italy, the Netherlands, Sweden, the UK, Japan, Australia and the USA. However, as these authors acknowledge (1995; p.27), although the fundamental principles and relationships identified by the model are pretty much universal, it is always necessary when applying it in a specific country, or in making comparisons between countries, to give due weight to specific cultural factors.

For instance, in the UK from the end of World War II to the 1980s trade unions were unusually powerful, and while their power is now much diminished, that era has left a legacy of a pluralistic industrial relations framework, especially in the public sector. In Germany and Scandinavia trade unions remain relatively powerful, whereas in the USA their influence has been waning for a generation and is practically non-existent in many industries, especially high-technology and other 'knowledge-based' ones. The wide degree of applicability of the Harvard model is one of its most useful aspects.

Of course, there have been significant developments in management practice and theory since the 1980s when the Harvard model was first conceived – for example, in areas such as knowledge management, talent management, ethics and corporate governance, the details of which often transcend the limits of the Harvard model. Technological advances also have had an obvious major impact on work including HRM (eg online recruitment, teleworking, the use of virtual teams). Nonetheless, the model has proved to be remarkably durable because, as its authors intended, it still serves as a wide-ranging 'map of the HRM territory'. It is still probably the best single model to give general managers an initial picture of what HRM entails and what it tries to achieve. The biggest single omission from the Harvard model is the neglect of learning and development.

UNIVERSALIST VERSUS CONTINGENCY

One of the faultlines in the theoretical debates on HRM has been an argument that in one form or another has run through all of management literature from the time of Taylor's 'scientific management' to the present day. This is whether there is one best way to manage – ie is there a set of principles which if applied correctly will always bring better performance, or does it depend on the particular circumstances and factors such as the nature of the work and technology that is employed? This is sometimes referred to as the 'universalist versus contingency' debate.

Somewhere between the two extremes lies the 'best fit' view: there may or may not be eternal, universally applicable management techniques but experience (sometimes supported by theory) shows that, given similar structures and contexts, successful organisations tend to employ the same methods or policies.

At the time of writing we see this debate in the arguments over whether there are specific 'bundles' of HRM which enhance performance. In reality, the debate in HRM is usually about the range and choice of techniques rather than one of absolute principle. There probably are some generic HR processes and general principles of people management common to all successful organisations (Boxall and Purcell, 2006; p.69). No one really doubts that it is best to be as systematic and accurate as possible in selecting people for work, for example, but there is much less certainty as to whether it is effective or even ethical to screen employees' personality profiles to select only those whom the organisation believes will conform to the company culture.

On the other hand, Huselid (1995) argues that there is sound evidence, gathered from over 1,000 firms in various (US) industries, for a universalist case for specific high-performance work practices impacting on firms' financial performance.

The framework presented by the Harvard model is clearly in the contingency camp, but can accommodate a variety of 'best fit' practices in various specific environments (eg industries, technology groups or cultures) as determined by the situational factors and stakeholder interests.

Critical and postmodernist interest has always been high in academic treatments of HRM, especially in the UK – for example, Legge (1995), Blyton and Turnbull (1992), du Gay and Salaman (1992), and Kennoy (1999). As might be expected, such commentators tended to be hostile to the HRM model and were often opposed to its adoption, fearing that it represented continuing or even enhanced exploitation of ordinary employees.

On the other hand, even non-radical critics have pointed out that the specific practices associated with HRM are actually rather varied in nature, even in the theoretical models, and some have questioned whether they really can be regarded as making up a coherent approach to the management of people. For example, performance-related payment systems on the one hand seem to represent an individualisation of the employment relationship, whereas the promotion of team involvement – eg quality circles and total quality management (TQM) – represent the opposite (Gallie *et al*, 1998; pp6–7).

HARD AND SOFT MODELS OF HRM

Two main variants of HRM were identified early in academic discussions of HRM: 'hard' HRM with an emphasis on the strategic, quantitative aspects of managing human resources as an economic factor in production, and 'soft' HRM rooted in the Human Relations School and emphasising communication, motivation and leadership (Storey, 1989). All models of HRM are concerned with strategic issues, but 'hard' models typically have a stronger focus on ensuring that the HRM strategy 'fits' and is driven by the overall corporate strategy (Keenan, 2005). This is a matter of degree, however, since all HRM models stress the importance of taking a strategic view of the human resource, but in the Harvard model, for example, the link to business strategy is implied rather than explicit. Table 1 shows a simple typology of HRM models with classification according to (i) the degree of emphasis on strategic fit, and (ii) a 'hard' or 'soft' model of HRM.

Table 1 A typology of HRM models: hard/soft, and strategic fit

	'Hard' HRM model	'Soft' HRM model
High emphasis on strategic fit	Fombrun *et al* (1984)	Mabey and Salaman's 'open approach' (1995)
Low emphasis on strategic fit	Schuler and Jackson (1987) Huselid (1995)	Beer *et al* (1984) [the Harvard model] Guest (1987)

SUMMING UP THEORETICAL HRM: KEY DIFFERENCES BETWEEN PERSONNEL MANAGEMENT AND HUMAN RESOURCE MANAGEMENT

At this stage the reader might plausibly ask, 'Why bother with personnel management? Haven't you just shown us how it has been replaced by HRM?' Well, not quite. As we shall see below, the empirical evidence is that the adoption of HRM in practice has been incomplete when compared to theoretical models. At the time of writing it can make sense to talk of two 'traditions' in people management: one largely following the 'personnel management' (PM) paradigm and the other the HRM paradigm – most organisations showing some aspects of each in their management of people, and few following either completely. Table 2 on page 16 contrasts theoretical PM with theoretical HRM along a number of key characteristics.

ARE MODELS USEFUL?

Before we look at this comparison we should deal with another question the sceptical reader might have. We acknowledge that both the HRM and PM descriptions above may never be found in their entirety in real life. So the sceptic may reasonably ask: why bother with them? The work of the great social scientist Max Weber provides an answer with his concept of 'ideal types' (Weber, 1949; p.90).

An ideal type is formed by simplifying the description of complex reality to accentuate its most important features and ignore less relevant ones, so that what is really vital about the subject under study can be identified and understood. Weber did not mean that the ideal type is some completely hypothetical entity, but rather that it possesses all of the relevant features of the type exhibited in extreme clarity. Ideal types exist, but you cannot expect to find them empirically in their purest states.

For example, no actual coin in circulation meets perfectly all the requirements of its design because of imperfections in manufacture and wear in use, yet we have complete knowledge of what the coin ideally should be like – an 'ideal type'. By comparing any actual coin to this 'ideal type' an expert can grade or classify the condition of a rare coin in terms of, for example, wear and damage, and so estimate its worth to a collector (Bailey, 1994).

The concept of ideal types is very useful in social science. For instance, an economist will not expect to find examples of 'pure competition' in any actual market in real life but by having an explicit model of pure competition he or she can make comparisons between the actual and the ideal and come to a reasoned judgement as to whether improvements in the degree of competition in the market should be pursued.

So, bearing in mind the dictum of the anonymous statistician that 'all models are wrong, but some are useful', we can regard the descriptions of PM and HRM in Table 2 as representing 'ideal types' of PM and HRM respectively. We could then study the characteristics of the people management function in a real firm or organisation, and use the descriptions in Table 2 to help us to assess whether this was closer overall to the HRM model or the PM one.

In some contexts ideal types might seem to be similar to 'normative models', as discussed in this chapter's Endnote 3. They are not identical, however. The author of a normative model may expect it to be fully realisable in practice, whereas for the reasons given above, ideal types are not.

We can consider the differences in the characteristics of the two models.

Strategic nature: traditional PM was usually expected to work on a short time-scale – 'fire-fighting' (ie dealing with immediate problems such as local industrial relations issues, or urgent staff shortages) rather than taking a long-term, strategic view of people management issues. Note the implications for this longer-term perspective for all HR issues, and the necessity for an articulated strategy for HRM, which should not only be coherent in itself but should be informed by, and support, the business strategy of the organisation.

The psychological contract is not to be confused with the legal contract of employment, or any written statement of terms and conditions of employment. As the term implies, it exists purely in the mind of the employee and his or her managers, and so is unwritten and never clearly articulated. It has been described by Armstrong (2009; p.297) as follows:

> The psychological contract expresses the combination of beliefs held by an individual and his or her employer about what they expect from one another.

There will always be some sort of psychological contract between the employee and the organisation, but David Guest concluded (Guest, 1996) that:

> a positive psychological contract is worth taking seriously because it is strongly linked to higher commitment to the organisation, higher employee satisfaction and better employee relations.

The PM model assumed that the basis of the psychological contract was compliance – the employee would do as he or she was told and the employer in turn expected this. Management should be able to determine exactly what is required of the employee and enforce at least minimal compliance. The HRM model, on the other hand, assumes that the employee shows positive, willing

Table 2 'Ideal types' of personnel management and human resource management

Characteristics	Personnel management (PM)	Human resource management (HRM)
Strategic nature	• Predominantly dealing with day-to-day issues • Ad-hoc and reactive in nature: a short-term perspective rather than strategic	• Dealing with day-to-day issues; but proactive in nature and integrated with other management functions • A deliberately long-term, strategic view of human resources
Psychological contract	• Based on compliance on the part of the employee	• Based on seeking willing commitment of the employee
Job design	• Typically Taylorist/Fordist	• Typically team-based
Organisational structure	• Hierarchical • Tendency to vertical integration	• Flexible with core of key employees surrounded by peripheral shells • High degree of outsourcing
Remuneration	• Collective base rates • 'Pay by position' • Any additional bonuses linked to Taylorist work systems	• Market-based • Individual and/or team performance • 'Pay for contribution'
Recruitment	• Sophisticated recruitment practices for senior staff only • Strong reliance on external local labour market for most recruitment	• Sophisticated recruitment for all employees • Strong internal labour market for core employees. Greater reliance on external labour market for non-core
Training/ development	• Limited and usually restricted to training non-managerial employees. Narrowly job-related. Management development limited to top executives and fast-track candidates	• Transformed into a learning and development philosophy transcending job-related training. An ongoing developmental role for all core employees including non-management. Strong emphasis on management and leadership development • A learning organisation culture
Employee relations perspective	• Pluralist: collectivist; low trust	• Unitarist: individualistic; high trust
Organisation of the function	• Specialist/professional • Separated from line management • Bureaucratic and centralised	• Largely integrated into line management for day-to-day HR issues • Specialist HR group to advise and create HR policy
Welfare role	• Residual expectations	• No explicit welfare role
Criteria for success of the function	• Minimising cost of human resources	• Control of HR costs, but also maximum utilisation of human resources over the long term

Source: adapted and developed from Guest (1987)

commitment. Because more is expected from employees, management cannot always specify exactly what is required, and so employees must use their own judgement and initiative to a much greater extent than in the past. They must also extend and upgrade their skills and knowledge-bases.

Job design: the compliance sought in Taylorist organisational culture is reflected in the low degree of autonomy workers typically have in such a context. We would expect the PM model to be followed where jobs tend to be designed under scientific management principles (see Endnote 1). The search for greater commitment in the HRM approach implies that employees should be allowed and encouraged to use self-control in matters of work and organisational discipline, rather than be driven by a system of compliance and direction imposed upon them by management. Teamworking and similar initiatives would be much more common under HRM than PM.

Organisational structure: reflecting the higher-commitment working associated with HRM we would expect to find less hierarchical and more flexible organisational structures, with the team as the 'organisational building-block' and with fewer management levels. Organisations featuring PM will tend to be hierarchical, pyramid-shaped and bureaucratic. Those following HRM will typically be flexible with a core of key employees surrounded by peripheral shells of other workers. Note that the core employees are not all senior executives – the core is defined as comprising those members of the organisation who possess the skills, knowledge and competence necessary for the organisation's success. Core workers will possess considerable market attractiveness and will consequently enjoy better remuneration and terms of employment than others. In return, they will be expected to provide high levels of performance and flexibility in working, and accept the need for continuous learning and re-skilling to support incessant technological and process improvement. The peripheral shells of employees act as buffers against short-term market fluctuations and can be relatively easily shed or reinforced. Thus employees in those parts of the organisation will tend to be employed on short-term or temporary contracts. HRM organisations also tend to feature considerable outsourcing of non-core work.

Remuneration: PM is usually associated with traditional approaches to remuneration, long pay scales characterising the hierarchical organisational structure mentioned above, reflecting length of service rather than current contribution. Pay structures are usually agreed via collective bargaining, at least for non-managerial employees. The HRM approach to remuneration is more focused on rewarding contribution and is likely to be individually or team-based. This implies both the use of performance management and appraisal and the setting of base rates from the market rather than by means of collective agreements.

Recruitment: sophisticated techniques such as the use of psychometric testing, psychological profiling and assessment centres have often been used with PM for recruitment and selection into senior executive posts, while much simpler and less costly methods usually suffice for non-managerial employment. With HRM these sophisticated tools are much more likely to be used for all employees, or at least core ones.

Training and development: when employees are viewed mainly as a cost (which should be minimised), commitment to training is usually negligible, employers fearing that employees will be 'poached' by free-loading competitors who do no training themselves, and this would be the typical position in the PM paradigm. An exception was often made, however, in industries with collective agreements on apprentice training. Except for large PM organisations, management training and development would be virtually non-existent. When two UK academics, Iain Mangham and Mick Silver, surveyed management development in the mid-1980s, they reported a surprisingly high proportion of firms which seemed to do no management training at all, on the grounds that, as one respondent put it, 'We only employ managers who can do the job' (Mangham and Silver, 1986).

In HRM there is a culture of continuous development of all core employees who are seen as the originators and possessors of the organisation's strategic competencies necessary for sustainable competitive advantage. Senior managers are not exempt, the directors and CEO receiving 'executive development'. This commitment would not be expected in the peripheral shells surrounding the core.

Employee relations perspective – ie the dominant managerial perspective within the organisation: personnel management typically operates in a unionised, pluralistic environment. This can be contrasted with the HRM model in which the employment relationship is much more individualised than when dealing with the workforce collectively. This is reflected in, for example, the absence of trade unions and the introduction of performance-related rewards systems.

The unitarist nature of HRM would seem to discourage the formation of a pluralist organisational culture, but in practice there have been examples where HRM has been successfully adopted within a previously pluralist culture while maintaining the pluralist style of collective bargaining in employee relations. See for example Tayeb's account of the Scottish division of the American firm NCR (Tayeb, 1998). But see also the empirical evidence from the Workplace Industrial/Employment Relations Surveys in the UK (referred to below in this chapter) on the long-term decline of trade unionism in the UK.

The organisation of the function differs in the two models. In the PM model the function tends to be seen as a specialist function which, in many important respects such as dealing with employee relations issues, is separate from line management. This often leads to the creation and maintenance of large, rather bureaucratic, personnel departments. The HRM model instead stresses that most people management, even employee relations, is actually just part of normal management, at least in its day-to-day aspects. Accordingly in the HRM model, where there are specialist HR departments, they will be small and highly specialised and their function is (i) to formulate HR policies and (ii) act as internal consultants to line managers. The line managers will implement most HR policy, only seeking the involvement of HR in particularly difficult issues.

Welfare role: there are at least residual expectations under PM of a welfare role, the personnel manager being the member of the management team who could be approached with personal problems (at least if these impacted on work). This always led to ambiguous perceptions of PM. By the time the PM paradigm had become fully established, there was no doubt that it was a management function with the primary objective of reducing and controlling labour costs (see 'Criteria for success' below) but many employees expected a fuller welfare aspect than was often given, and this was a principal reason for the ambiguity with which PM was often viewed. Unreconstucted finance managers sometimes viewed PM in similar terms albeit negatively as an unnecessary cost on the organisation. So personnel managers often felt themselves to be 'the meat in the sandwich' caught between dissatisfied employees and unsympathetic management colleagues, neither of whom really understood what they were supposed to be doing. Marxist critics always saw PM as in any case reflecting the perceived contradictions of capitalism (Legge, 1989), but even dyed-in-the-wool free-marketers could see the possibility of perceived inconsistencies in the role of PM and unreconciled expectations here.

There is no explicit welfare role in HRM although proponents might argue that with its unitarist culture it is no longer necessary. Critics would not agree.

The two models also show very different *criteria for success of the function* – ie how the organisation judges the performance of the people management function. In the personnel management model, the organisation will judge the effectiveness of the function by how well it minimises unit labour costs; in the HRM model by how well it maximises the use of the organisation's human resources (while still maintaining proper control of costs).

REFLECTIVE ACTIVITY

Taking each of the people management characteristics listed in Table 2 to be represented by a seven-point scale in which 1 corresponds to 'pure PM' and 7 to 'pure HRM', profile your own organisation. Is it predominantly PM or HRM? Why is that, do you think?

It can be a useful exercise to discuss your results first with a senior line manager and then with a senior HR manager.

HRM IN PRACTICE

In addition to the theoretical literature, empirical studies have shown that significant changes in the practice of managing people in modern organisations have occurred in recent years. Interpretations may sometimes be controversial, but that there have been changes is not in doubt.

The late 1980s and early 1990s saw a transformation in the vocabulary of management in the UK, as in the USA, concepts such as 'empowerment', 'teamworking' and 'commitment' becoming widespread, along with 'human resource management' itself. Substantial survey evidence shows the adoption of a range of new practices which reflected HRM ideas: McKersie (1987); Storey (1992); Fernie *et al* (1994); Osterman (1994); Wood and Albanese (1995) – even if these studies found less evidence of integrated adoption of the whole HRM programme, or of Walton's (1985) assumed transformation of the employment relationship 'from control to commitment' (Gallie *et al*, 1998; pp9, 57).

Evidence of the adoption of a number of key HRM practices in the UK has been authoritatively established by the series of Workplace Industrial Relations/ Workplace Employment Relations Surveys. These surveys provide a nationally representative account of the state of employment relations, working life and the management of people inside British workplaces, and of how these have all been changing over a quarter of a century. The surveys were jointly sponsored by the Department of Trade and Industry (DTI), the Advisory, Conciliation and Arbitration Service (ACAS), the Economic and Social Research Council (ESRC) and the Policy Studies Institute (PSI), and were conducted in 1980, 1984, 1990, 1998 and 2004. These were all large-scale, representative surveys. The fieldwork for the 2004 survey, for example, was conducted between February 2004 and April 2005: face-to-face interviews were conducted with around 3,200 managers and almost 1,000 worker representatives. Over 20,000 employees completed and returned a self-completion questionnaire.

The 1990 survey found evidence of a shift from collectivism to individualism, with a marked decline in trade unionism, and a significant increase in the sort of approaches to participation and communication that are embraced by HRM, such as team briefings, quality circles and newsletters. There was also evidence of organisational changes such as the increasing involvement of line managers in personnel activities (Millward *et al*, 1992).

The 1998 survey found that human resource matters were often incorporated in wider business plans. They concluded that there was evidence that a number of practices consistent with a human resource management approach were 'well entrenched in many British workplaces' (Cully *et al*, 1999).

The preliminary findings of the 2004 survey showed that most of the HR practices which the earlier surveys had identified had become consolidated or were increasing in use (Kersley *et al*, 2006).

These findings reinforced the view that many organisations operated a 'flexible organisation' with a 'core' of key employees and a 'peripheral' workforce of other workers who typically enjoyed less secure and less attractive terms and conditions of employment. A large majority (83%) of workplaces had part-time employees (up from 79% in 1998). In 30% of all workplaces more than half of the workforce were part-time employees. Just under one third (30%) of workplaces had employees on temporary contracts. The use of temporary agency staff, although less prevalent than fixed-term contracts, was still quite widespread, 17% of all workplaces employing 'temps'. About one fifth (22%) gave preference to internal applicants when recruitiung, and the proportion was higher for the private sector (25%).

The selection process usually involved the use of interviews, application forms and references. Personality or competency tests, although used less frequently, had gained in importance in the search for greater objectivity in selection, even though their validity and reliability continued to be subjects of debate. Among workplaces using personality tests, three-fifths (61%) of managers said that they used these tests when recruiting core employees. Performance or competency tests were routinely used in 46% of workplaces. Performance tests were also more likely to be used when recruiting core employees, irrespective of their occupation, even more so than personality tests. Overall, one third (34%) of all workplaces used such tests for these recruits.

The use of performance appraisals had increased, 78% of managers in workplaces reporting in 2004 that performance appraisals were undertaken, compared with 73% in 1998. Two-thirds (65%) of all workplaces conducted regular appraisals for most (60% or more) non-managerial employees (48% in 1998).

Most workplace managers (84%) reported that off-the-job training had been provided for some of their experienced, core employees over the previous year – an increase since 1998, when 73% of workplaces provided training for some of their experienced core employees.

The authors of the 2004 survey noted that in recent years much of the discussion about methods of work organisation had concerned 'high-performance', 'high-commitment' or 'high-involvement' work practices. These were practices that were intended to enhance employee commitment and involvement, often by increasing employees' participation in the design of work processes and the sharing of task-specific knowledge. The most commonly cited practices included teamworking, cross-training (or 'multi-skilling') and the use of problem-solving groups.

Teamworking was the most common, almost three-quarters (72%) of workplaces having at least some core employees in formally designated teams. The incidence and operation of teamworking had changed little since 1998. Where teamworking was in place, it was 'usually embedded among staff': four-fifths (80%) of workplaces with teamworking extended it to at least three-fifths of core employees. In 83% of workplaces with teamworking, teams were given responsibility for specific products and services, and in 61% they could jointly decide how work was done. However, in just 6% they were allowed to appoint their own team leaders.

Cross-training involves training staff to be able to undertake jobs other than their own. Two-thirds (66%) of workplaces had trained at least some staff to be 'functionally flexible'; again, this proportion had changed little since 1998 (69%). Around one-fifth (21%) of workplaces had groups of non-managerial employees that met to solve specific problems or discuss aspects of performance or quality. The equivalent figure in 1998 had been 16%. Almost half (48%) of all workplaces had trained at least some core employees in teamworking, communication or problem-solving skills in the previous year.

These new methods of working are at once the effects of development in HRM and the cause of further changes in HRM practice.

Additionally, the 2004 survey found that the UK trend for work culture to become more unitarist and less pluralistic was unremitting. Trade unionism continued to decline, particularly in the private sector; almost two-thirds of workplaces (64%) had no union members (compared to 57% in 1998), and union members made up a majority of the workforce in only one-sixth (18%) of all workplaces (22% in 1998).

Subsequent empirical research such as the 2009 European Company Survey (Eurofound, 2010) confirms the picture.

SUMMING UP HRM PRACTICE

So the empirical evidence seems clear. In most UK workplaces the management of people has been progressively moving closer to the HRM model and away from the PM model over the last 20 years (see Table 2), and the most recent evidence suggests strongly that this is continuing. We can assume that the UK is not unique in this, and that giving due weight to local cultural and contextual factors, similar changes in the management of people have been happening worldwide in the developed and developing economies.

KEY THEMES IN HUMAN RESOURCE MANAGEMENT IN THE TWENTY-FIRST CENTURY

The authors of the 2004 Workplace Employment Relations Survey (2004 WERS) referred to above (Kersley *et al*, 2005) identified many of the key themes current in HRM.

The survey noted the interest in the UK in 'high-performance', 'high-commitment' or 'high-involvement' work organisation and practices. This was confirmed by a study funded by the UK government Department of Trade and Industry (DTI) and conducted in association with the CIPD. *High-Performance Work Strategies: Linking strategy and skills to performance outcomes* (DTI/CIPD, 2005) comprised detailed case studies of a sample of 10 firms drawn from the *Sunday Times* 100 Best Companies to Work For 2004, and a survey of nearly 300 firms.

In addition to reinforcing the findings of the 2004 WERS survey this report provided further empirical evidence on present managerial interests in the management of people in the UK. The case studies established good practice in a range of 'high-performance work practices' (HPWPs), these being defined as:

- a set of complementary work practices covering three broad areas or 'bundles' of practices covering:
    - high employee involvement practices – eg self-directed teams, quality circles and sharing/access to company information
    - human resource practices – eg sophisticated recruitment processes, performance appraisals, work redesign and mentoring

– reward and commitment practices – eg various financial rewards, family-friendly policies, job rotation and flexi-hours.

It was found from the case studies that leadership was regarded as crucial in creating, shaping and driving these high-performing organisations. Skills development was focused on achieving specific business outcomes and levels of performance. In most of the case studies, high levels of training and continuous development were regarded as fundamental to success, and tacit skills and institutional knowledge were perceived as relatively more important than technical skills. Employees could learn all the time as part of their normal work and were encouraged to innovate and improve performance (individual, team and organisational).

High-performing organisations tended to be leaders in their industries and they set the standards for best practice. In most of the case studies HPWPs had been used to create business success from the founding of these companies, but to ensure their continued success, these practices were subject to constant modification in line with the requirements of business objectives.

The wider survey of CIPD members established how far the high-performance work practices identified in the case studies were adopted by other UK organisations, and examined the relationship between the level of adoption of high-performance work practices and a range of organisational outcomes. It was found that many of the HPWPs had been adopted by UK organisations, and there was evidence that the level of HPWP adoption, as measured by the number of practices adopted, was positively correlated with better organisational outcomes. For example, those adopting more HPWPs identified had greater employee involvement, and were more effective in delivering adequate training provision, in motivating staff, in managing change and in providing career opportunities. These organisations also had more people earning over £35,000 and fewer people earning less than £12,000.

THE INTERNATIONAL CONTEXT

The importance of high-performance working for organisational performance was confirmed in the international context by an earlier joint study from the International Federation of Training and Development Organizations (IFTDO) – of which the CIPD in the UK is a member – and the International Labour Organisation (ILO). This examined high-performance working in nine organisations around the world (ILO/IFTDO, 2000): the *Laiki Bank* (Cyprus), the *Mandarin Oriental Hotel* (Hong Kong), *SATS Security Services* and Comfort Driving Centre (Singapore), *W.H. Smith & Sons* and Thorn Lighting (UK), South African Breweries, and Motorola and the *Social Security Administration* (United States).

High-performance working was understood (ILO/IFTDO, 2000; Appendix B) to be associated with:

the achievement of high levels of performance, profitability and customer satisfaction by enhancing skills and engaging the enthusiasm of employees.

The report also cited an Organization for Economic Co-operation and Development (OECD) definition of the characteristics of HPW organisations as:

flatter non-hierarchical structures, moving away from reliance on management control, teamworking, autonomous working based on trust, communication and involvement. Workers are seen as being more highly skilled and having the intellectual resources to engage in lifelong learning and master new skills and behaviours.

The report concluded:

Increasing evidence is becoming available about the connections between people management and development and 'the bottom line'. Researchers have identified three ways in which this occurs: through the use of best HR practice; getting the right 'fit' between business strategy and HR practices; and using specific 'bundles' of practices, varied according to organisational context. The case studies used in the ILO/IFTDO research show significant evidence of the use of all these approaches. They bear witness to the search by organisations for an alignment between practices and outcomes and active searching for examples of good practice.

The report thus also illustrates how HRM now has a global relevance beyond the US/UK industrial cultures in which it first developed.

Of course the concept of high-performance working has not been without its critics in terms of both its theoretical base and its practical effects – eg Guest (1997); Guest *et al* (2003); MacDuffie (1995); Applebaum *et al* (2000); Legge (2001); Purcell (1999) – but the International Labour Organisation (ILO) could acknowledge the validity of many of the criticisms and, while calling for more research to clarify contested areas, conclude (ILO/IFTDO, 2000) that:

Increasing evidence is becoming available about the connections between people management and development and 'the bottom line' . . . The seamless application of people management and development and line management leadership, expertise and vision provides the strategy and powerhouse for high-performance working. Finding out how to manage and develop people so as to generate freedom to learn and contribute will be a major challenge in the early part of the twenty-first century.

So the empirical evidence is mounting up to support the commonsense view that the idea that 'better' management of people should lead to 'better' performance at individual, team and organisational level – everything else being equal – is probably true. Common sense would also suggest it is wise to take what management theorists call a 'contingency' approach to this question. That is, instead of looking for a universally applicable set of HR practices that will inevitably lead to better performance in all cases, the specific circumstances of the situation should be taken into consideration. For example, individual performance-related pay might boost performance in some cases, such as sales personnel, but not others (policemen, say). This does not alter the underlying key principle that reward should reflect contribution. It just means that the principle may be applied in different ways according to the circumstances. It is worth remembering here the policy choice aspect of the Harvard model (Figure 1).

In fact, the DTI/CIPD (2005) report cited above found that different 'bundles' of high-performance work practices seem to be effective in different industry sectors (p.71):

> There is no 'one best way' or 'one best set of practices': this is not a tick-box approach. The crucial component is the business strategy, because this underpins the choice of practices, the way they are implemented and their effectiveness in improving performance. It is the business strategy that gives the high-performance working practices their dynamism and provides the framework against which performance can be evaluated and improved. ...

> The choice of which bundle of practices to use in order to achieve a given organisational outcome or objective is influenced by the type of sector in which the organisation or company is operating. Some bundles of practices are more effective in particular industrial sectors than others.

KEY THEMES IN HRM

The findings of these reports, together with those of the WERS series, especially the 2004 survey, allow us to build a picture of the key themes in HRM in the twenty-first century.

- The adoption of 'high-performance work practices' – also known as, 'high-commitment' or 'high-involvement' work practices' – which are intended to achieve better individual, team and organisational performance by increasing employee commitment and involvement. These are typically thought of as comprising 'bundles' of sophisticated HR practices in the areas of employee involvement, resourcing (eg in recruitment), and rewards and commitment.

- A 'flexible organisation' with a 'core' of key employees (including non-managerial employees) with greater investment in these human resources; and a 'peripheral' workforce of other workers who typically enjoy less secure and less attractive terms and conditions of employment and less HR development. But in efficient organisations the barriers to the core will be permeable to hard-working and capable employees on the periphery.

- The organisation of work at a micro-level – teamworking, cross-training, multi-skilling, and problem-solving groups to increase functional flexibility, participation in the design of work processes, and the sharing of task-specific knowledge.

- Sophisticated HR practices in recruitment and selection – eg the use of psychometric testing and personality profiling and competency and performance tests for a wide range of key or core employees including non-managerial ones.

- Employee relations in a unitarist environment – trade unions are in a historically precipitate decline in most advanced economies, and especially in new industries, but all but the smallest employers have to find means of communicating with their employees and achieving perceptions of fairness and legitimacy in pay rates and conditions of employment agreement.

- Change management: 'the only constant is change' has become a cliché but reflects the acknowledgement now that the competitive global economy and continuous increasing technological advances are realities. Physical resources are relatively easy to change; human ones are much more challenging. HRM is often tasked with taking the lead and coordinating change across the organisation.

- The 'learning organisation', defined as an organisation which encourages learning at all levels and thereby brings about continuous (and by definition often unpredictable) change to itself. This is a consequence of the realisation that employees are expected and encouraged to learn all the time, and should employ their learning by being innovative and enhancing performance; that 'to pay someone to work is to pay them to learn'.

- Knowledge management: 'using the ideas and experience of employees, customers and suppliers to improve the organisation's performance', in the words of a managing editor of the *Financial Times* (Skapiner, 2002).

- Leadership to initiate and effect change and to achieve high-performance working.

In all of these areas it will usually be the line or general manager who initiates action and carries responsibility to make it happen, but he or she will increasingly rely on HRM specialists, who may have a lead role within the organisation in coordinating activities across the organisation.

SUMMING UP: WHAT IT'S ALL ABOUT

In July 2006, in an article entitled 'Technology dinosaurs', *The Economist* reported that exactly 25 years after the launch of the IBM 5150 – the famous IBM PC which led the personal computing revolution – many of 'Silicon Valley's former high-fliers' were in trouble. Dell's share price had hit a five-year low following a profit warning; Intel was still losing ground to AMD; Silicon Graphics had filed for bankruptcy; and Borland had laid off a fifth of its staff and was about to sell the best-known part of its business. Even Microsoft had just announced that it would buy back 8% of its shares for some $20 billion – 'a sign that its high growth days are behind it', according to *The Economist*. Noting that companies which start off with a successful product often fail to stay the course, the article concluded that having a great business idea often creates a false sense that the firm is stronger and more successful than it really is, and that 'failure to evolve leads to extinction'. Evolution means managing and developing people.

In today's and tomorrow's world, sustainable competitive advantage can only come from the skills, experience, creativity, imagination and brainpower of people. In the modern economy it is relatively easy to raise capital to fund a bright idea, but managing the human resources of an organisation to turn that idea into a business and achieve *sustainable* competitive advantage – how to create and build the next BMW or the next Apple – is the single most important management challenge in the twenty-first century, and that's what ambitious MBAs want to be involved in.

To do this, managers have to know about people. Of course they need to know about other things like strategy, finance and marketing as well, and they really do need to understand the technology underlying their businesses, but they *must* know about people. They have to understand HRM and be able to work with specialists in that field.

KEY ISSUES

A consensus has evolved that post-Taylorist organisations require a new approach to managing people because in a technologically advancing, global economy sustainable competitive advantage ultimately can only come from the talents and efforts of an organisation's core employees. This approach is usually termed human resource management (HRM) and differs from more long-established personnel management (PM) in taking a strategic view of the use of human resources; in seeking to harness the willing commitment of employees rather than their coercion; and in favouring an individualistic rather than collective employment relationship.

All models of HRM should be regarded as 'ideal types' or 'normative models' which are unlikely ever to be found in entirety in real life. The Harvard model – one of the earliest such, which links situational factors and stakeholder interests to HR policy choices and outcomes – remains a useful first 'map of the HRM territory' for general managers, although it ignores crucial aspects of learning and of employee development.

Almost certainly no organisation practises absolutely pure HRM or PM. It can be helpful to think in terms of two traditions in people management: the older personnel management one, which tends to be pluralistic, bureaucratic and Taylorist; and the newer human resource management one – unitarist, non-bureaucratic and post-Taylorist. Many firms will have some mixture of these two traditions – but HRM is in the ascendant.

There has been considerable academic interest in HRM, much of it hostile both to its intent and its effects, but there is well-established empirical evidence that in the UK and other countries many HRM initiatives have become well established, without perhaps attaining the comprehensive changes in management philosophy and action that many early champions of HRM predicted. We may safely conclude that in the twenty-first century people management in developed economies in general far more closely resembles the HRM model than the PM one. One important consequence of this is that line and general managers are more directly involved in people management issues than previously.

We identified the current areas of key interest in HRM for managers as being:

- the adoption of 'high-performance' (or 'high-commitment' or 'high-involvement') work practices to increase employee commitment and involvement to achieve better individual, team and organisational performance

- a 'flexible organisation' with a 'core' of key employees and a supporting 'peripheral' workforce

- the organisation of work at a micro-level – especially teamworking and associated initiatives

- the use of sophisticated HR practices in recruitment and selection

- a unitarist environment in which trade unions have limited influence or are non-existent

- change management

- the establishment of a 'learning organisation' culture

- knowledge management

- leadership.

CASE STUDY

AN HRM STRATEGY FOR CALEDONIAN HEALTHCARE

You have been retained as a management consultant for Caledonian Healthcare (CH), one of the largest health insurance companies in the UK, insuring 435,000 lives and with a 6% market share. Following the acquisition of Acme Health Limited in June 2002, Caledonian Life renamed itself in April 2003 to become Caledonian Healthcare. It now employs 770 staff – 450 people in Guildford and 320 in Stockport. The ratio between female and male staff is roughly 60:40, and 20% of company employees are part-time staff. CH offers a range of products from traditional private medical insurance to self-pay options, which reduce premiums. It has also recently started providing healthcare solutions that aim to prevent health problems before they occur and manage absence for corporate customers.

The organisation is in major financial difficulties and has lost money in the financial year 2005/6. There is no clear business strategy and business focus has been entirely on sales. This has resulted in poor customer service, with increasing numbers of complaints. Supporting the failing business is a poor culture characterised by 'siloed' management, poor leadership, blame and power struggles. Staff turnover is running at 20% a year. As a result, the HR strategy is simply focused on survival and is mainly reactive (focusing on recruitment). There is no support or resources for new initiatives, like job evaluation or appraisal systems. In 2006, a new chief executive joined the company with ideas to turn the business around. In particular, he sees an opportunity for HR to work closely with him to help achieve desired business outcomes and he has hired you to produce an HR strategy aligned to the business needs of the company.

Case study question

What would you recommend?

CALEDONIAN HEALTHCARE: GUIDANCE

Resolution

The new chief executive in fact did not hire a management consultant but instead worked with the existing HR team from the outset. He sought to combine commercial ideas with HR corporate values, including customer and quality focus, teamwork, communications and integrity.

The business needed, first, cost-cutting and then profitable growth. Changes were made at director level to 'refresh' the top team and create a new start. The chief executive and his new team quickly decided that the people needed were for the most part already in the organisation, but that they had not been supported, nurtured or encouraged to use their potential. Aligning HR and business strategy was focused on building trust and engagement with staff. As the chief executive put it,

> We expect a lot from our people and expect them to have their own demands in return. People want to be valued for what they do.

The business aim was to increase market share from 6% to 15% over the next five years by differentiating through customer service, and HR had an important role to play in this. To make sure HR became, and continued to be, aligned with business objectives, HR staff were taken through business strategy documents at quarterly briefings.

There was an initial review of turnover and absence management policies, reward and recognition practices, and the company's approach to learning and development. There was also continual appraisal of HR policies and procedures in order to make sure that the policies supported the ethos of a 'great place to work' and did not inadvertently work against it.

The HR strategy focused on specified activities, with a designated member of HR to lead each one. The areas were: staff engagement; resourcing and retaining staff; reward and recognition; creating a learning organisation; and establishing a partnership with staff.

The company promoted staff engagement and created a staff consultative committee designed around the European Works Council model.

The chief executive and head of HR hosted two coffee mornings a month at which employees could speak frankly about any issues from any area of the business. People were encouraged to speak out if they thought their jobs were limited by business processes. It was the head of HR's responsibility to take notes and get back to individuals by email or letter with actions for improving the situation or an explanation of why the situation could not be changed. There was a 'back-to-the-floor' scheme where directors worked in all different parts of the organisation. The chief executive instituted a policy of meeting every new employee when they started, and to support this there was also a presentation, through which they were told three key messages:

1 Everyone's job is important to the success of the business.

2 Everyone is encouraged to contribute ideas.

3 It's important to enjoy work and get on well with colleagues, and a work–life balance is necessary to perform well.

Outcomes

Two years on, the business had moved into profit, and was looking sustainable with new business up by 26%. Staff turnover was at less than 10% at both sites (reduced by 60%), and sickness absence was around 3%. The company was in the top 25th percentile of companies in the UK for staff engagement and was finding that ex-staff were returning. Customer satisfaction was measured at 97% overall and customer retention was up by 2.2%.

The head of HR felt that the improvements were a 'virtuous circle' and the company was increasingly 'a great place to work'. The most positive outcomes for HR were showing how important it was as a function and the difference it could make to the company. The HR policies were now taken seriously. For example, when HR recommended that the company should only recruit the best people, the organisation stuck to this, even if it meant not filling a vacancy.

Based on the case of Standard Life Healthcare described in the Work Foundation Report *Achieving Strategic Alignment of Business and Human Resources* (2005).

ENDNOTES

1 The main elements of Frederick Taylor's *Principles of Scientific Management* (1911) were time and motion studies of work processes; standardisation of tools, implements and methods; and increased division of labour. This approach is often termed 'Taylorism'. Henry Ford pioneered the modern model of mass production by combining scientific management and moving assembly lines, and this was first put into operation at Ford's Model T plant at Highland Park, Michigan, in 1914. 'Fordism' displaced a largely craft-based production process in which skilled workers exercised substantial control over their conditions of work.

2 'Paradigm' is a term that was popularised by Thomas Kuhn in his study of scientific revolutions and has become widely used in the social sciences. Kuhn defined it as 'the entire constellation of beliefs, values, techniques, and so on shared by the members of a given community' (1970; p.175).

3 Normative models – In the social sciences we have two types of description. One is the 'normative', which is prescriptive, telling us what *ought* to be; the other is the 'positive', which describes what *actually is*. Understandably, much of management literature is normative – readers want to know the 'best' way to do something. But if the nature of such descriptions is not made clear, confusion results when we assume that what the author is saying ought to happen is really happening.

EXPLORE FURTHER

Armstrong, M. (2009) *Armstrong's Handbook of Human Resource Management Practice*. 11th Edition. London Kogan Page.

Chapter 1, 'Human Resource Management'. A brief overview, useful for quick reference and starting exam revision.

Boxall, P. and Purcell, J. (2006) *Strategy and Human Resource Management*. Basingstoke: Palgrave Macmillan.

Chapter 1. 'Human resource management and business performance'. A scholarly introduction to HRM which makes explicit linkage to business performance.

Boxall, P., Purcell, J. and Wright, P. (eds) (2007). The *Oxford Handbook of Human Resource Management*. Oxford: Oxford University Press.

Not to be confused with a practitioners' handbook such as Armstrong's (2010). This, like Storey (2007), is a collection of specialist chapters all by leading academics in the field, with a wider disciplinary and international scope than Storey.

Chapter 2. P. Boxall. 'The development of HRM in historical and international perspective'. A concise but thorough account.

Chapter 7. D. E. Guest. 'HRM and the worker: Towards a new psychological contract'. A discussion of how HRM helps to shape workers' attitudes and behaviour, especially their satisfaction and well-being. Optimistic about the potential of HRM to improve the workers' lot.

Chapter 8. P. Thomson and W. Harley. 'HRM and the worker: Labor Process Perspectives'. Something of a counter- argument to Guest's optimism in the previous chapter, an analysis from the Critical Management School.

Chapter 26. J. Purcell and N. Kinnie. 'HRM and business performance'. A sceptical evaluation of the case that HRM's impact on organisational performance can be measured.

Kersley, B., Alpin, C., Forth, J., Bryson, A., Bewley, H., Dix, G. and Oxenbridge, S. (2006) *Inside the Workplace: Findings from the 2004 Workplace Employment Relations Survey*. Abingdon: Routledge.

Chapter 3, 'The management of employment relations'. The definitive empirical evidence of the move in UK management practice from the traditional Personnel Management (PM) model to (at least some elements of) the Human Resource Management (HRM) model. As with other chapters which we recommended below, this also serves as a useful corrective to some of the more highly flown theoretical discussions in the HRM literature.

Storey, J. (ed.) (2007) *Human Resource Management: A critical text*, 3rd edition. London: Thomson Learning. The 3rd edition of a collection of essays by leading academics. This edition also has some useful short illustrative case studies.

Chapter 1. J. Storey. 'Human resource management today: an assessment'. Another scholarly introduction, this time with a flavour of the critical management school. Especially sceptical of the universalist approach.

CHAPTER 2

Looking ahead: HRM and strategy

INTRODUCTION

One of the key findings of Chapter 1 was the importance of strategy to HRM. Ulrich's first recommendation for the HRM function was that it should become a partner with senior and line managers in strategy execution (Ulrich, 1998; p.124). We also noted in that chapter that one of the reasons why HRM was supposed to be a better model for people management than either personnel management or personnel administration was because it was supposed to be 'strategic' – not only in itself but also in the sense that the HRM strategy would be consciously designed to support the overall business strategy.

LEARNING OUTCOMES

On completion of this chapter you should have acquired an understanding of:

- the importance of managers' taking a strategic view of HRM
- the elements of corporate strategy which are relevant to HRM
- the relationship between organisational strategy and organisational structure, and the relevance of this for HRM
- some implications of organisational macro-structure for strategy and HRM
- 'best-practice' models of HRM and strategy
- 'best-fit' models of HRM and strategy
- the HRM strategy process
- corporate social responsibility, and the role this has for HRM
- the significance of ethics for HRM.

We saw also in Chapter 1 that strategy was important in underpinning the choice of high-performance work practices (HPWPs) which were best suited to the organisation, how these work practices would be implemented, and how effective they would be in improving performance – according to the DTI/CIPD (2005) survey:

> It is the business strategy that gives the high-performance working practices their dynamism and provides the framework against which performance can be evaluated and improved.

There seems little doubt then of the importance of the topic. What might be less obvious to the reader is the role of organisational structure in the relationship between strategy and HRM. Not only are corporate strategy and corporate structure inextricably linked, however, but structure itself can affect HRM. For example, in a large company separate divisions might pursue different HR practices and policies as their particular business conditions demand – but this may then lead to difficulty in coordinating HRM strategy for the company as a whole.

The intimate relationship between strategy and structure was first clearly identified by Alfred Chandler.

> A company's strategy in time determined its structure … the common dominator of structure and strategy has been the allocation of the enterprise's resources to market demand.

And the importance of the human resource was evident in Chandler's account (Chandler, 1962/1991; p.383):

> Of these resources trained personnel with manufacturing, marketing, engineering, scientific and managerial skills often became even more important than warehouses, plants, offices and other physical facilities.

No MBA student will need to be reminded that the academic literature on business strategy is vast, complex, and contentious. HRM has a particular perspective, of course, and it is this that we shall follow. We will not be reviewing the whole of the management literature on strategy.

THE UNIVERSALIST VERSUS CONTINGENCY ARGUMENT (AGAIN)

As we remarked in Chapter 1, the *universalist* ('one-best way') versus *contingency* ('it all depends on the circumstances') debate runs through all management literature, and HRM is no exception. So we should not be surprised to see this appear in discussions of HRM and strategy. There are three main positions:

- the 'best-fit' school of thought, which suggests that certain HRM polices and practices work best with particular company strategies (or in some cases specified strategy–structure combinations). Examples are Miles and Snow (1984) and Schuler and Jackson (1987)

- the 'best-practice' school is universalist and states that specified HRM policies and practices always give best results (ie best organisational performance) regardless of strategy or structure or any other factor. Pfeffer (1994) and Huselid (1995) are instances of this school

- strategic choice – the view that is implied in the Harvard model described in Chapter 1 and the one adopted in this text as the most useful for managers. The managers of an organisation can make choices in HRM and these may be *influenced* by contingent factors and prior decisions, but are not *determined* by either.

CORPORATE STRATEGY

A widely accepted definition of strategy in business and management is that given by Johnson and Scholes (1997):

> The direction and scope of an organisation over the longer term, which ideally matches its resources to its changing environment, and in particular to its markets, customers and clients to meet stakeholders' expectations.

Armstrong (2009; p.29) describes 'strategic HRM' as:

> An approach that defines how the organisation's goals will be achieved through people by means of HR strategies and integrated HR policies and practices.

The term 'strategy' is usually associated with long-term decisions and is distinguished from short-term 'tactics' or 'operations' (Purcell and Ahlstrand, 1994; p.27). The principle is clear, but as Boxall and Purcell note, it is usually unhelpful to make too hard a distinction in practice between strategy on the one hand and either tactics or operations on the other (2006; p.28).[1] In real business life the distinction is often somewhat blurred.

But we can say that strategic decisions in management are likely to be concerned with:

- the long-term direction of the organisation
- the scope of the organisation's activities
- matching the organisation's activities to its business-social-political-technological environment, and/or seeking to modify that environment
- matching the organisation's activities to its resources, and/or seeking to change or enhance its resources.

Most strategic decisions will differ from operational ones in that they will involve more uncertainty – and they will primarily be concerned with the organisation as a whole, or at least a significant part of it: a division or strategic business unit.

Echoing Miles and Snow's earlier concept of the adaptive cycle (discussed below), Boxall and Purcell (2006) argue that the strategies of firms are their attempts to deal with the strategic problems that they face – most fundamentally, their initial viability (ie survival) and thereafter sustaining competitive advantage – and that strategic management is best viewed as a process that is continually evolving and changing as the firm survives.

In their concepts of the adaptive cycle and the associated strategic typology, Miles and Snow (1978) produced two of the most elegant and economical ideas in the literature of business strategy. The 'adaptive cycle' is the process by which firms seek a fit between their markets, their technologies and their structures. The strategic typology identified four distinct outcomes to the adaptive cycle problem, three of which were particular, successful solutions while the fourth represented failure to achieve the necessary fit.

Miles and Snow saw the process of organisational adaptation as central to successful organisations. Not only must the organisation respond to its environment, it must where possible adapt the environment. In creating their own concept of the 'adaptive cycle', Miles and Snow embraced both Thompson's image of top management continually 'shooting at a moving target of co-alignment' (Thompson, 1967; p.148) and Child's idea of 'strategic choice' (Child, 1972; 1997). This complex and dynamic process of adaptation was seen as being capable of analysis into three major problems which management needed continually to 'solve': 'entrepreneurial' (ie domain definition), 'engineering' (technology) and 'administrative' (structure-process and innovation) (Miles and Snow, 1978; p.21).

The authors acknowledged that a huge number of possible organisational strategies and strategy–structure relationships theoretically existed, but argued (Miles and Snow, 1978; p.29) that

> Patterns of behaviour begin to emerge which suggest that these organisational forms can be reduced to several archetypes. We have identified four types: the Defender, the Reactor, the Analyser and the Prospector.

'Defenders' were organisations which had narrow product-market domains. Top managers were highly expert in the organisation's limited area of operation but tended not to search outside their domain for new opportunities. Attention was mostly devoted to improving the efficiency of their existing operations rather than making major adjustments in their technology, structure or methods of operation.

'Reactors' were organisations in which top managers usually perceived change and uncertainty but were unable to make the organisation respond effectively. Lacking a consistent strategy–structure relationship, such organisations seldom made any kind of adjustment until forced to do so by external pressures.

'Analysers' operated in two types of product-market domain, one relatively stable, the other changing. Formalised structures and processes allowed the organisation to operate routinely and efficiently in the stable domain, while in the more turbulent one top managers scanned their competitors closely for new ideas, appropriating those which appeared to be useful.

'Prospectors' continually searched for market opportunities. They created change and uncertainty to which their competitors had to respond, but operating efficiency was often sacrificed in their strong concern for product and market innovation.

The primary and secondary literature on the Miles and Snow typology argues that strategic type will affect a firm's performance and its human resource management policies and practices (Miles and Snow, 1984).

Although the conclusion that Miles and Snow reached about the primacy of 'strategic choice', based on the work of John Child (1972, 1997), is widely accepted in the HRM-strategy literature (see, for example, Boxall and Purcell, 2006), and although their strategic typology of Defenders, Reactors, Analysers and Prospectors is very well known, the underlying logic demonstrated in the adaptive cycle is curiously neglected in the literature.

COMPETITIVE STRATEGIES

Michael Porter is arguably the most influential figure in business strategy. His book *Competitive Strategy*, which was first published in 1980, is, at the time of writing, reportedly in its 53rd printing (!) and is available in 17 languages.

The need for organisations to find sustainable competitive advantage is central to Porter's work. He distinguished three 'generic' competitive strategies: differentiation, cost leadership and focus.

- *differentiation* – setting the company's products or services apart from those of its competitors through, for example, advertising, features or technology to achieve a product or service which customers perceive as unique; and so achieving a premium price
- *cost leadership* – being the lowest-cost producer while achieving normal prices
- *focus* – concentrating on one or more niche markets and pursuing either differentiation or cost leadership in each niche.

Somewhat controversially, Porter maintains that a firm must choose one and only one of these strategies (or any rate each strategic business unit must) or it risks being 'stuck in the middle' with no sustainable competitive advantage and will be vulnerable to competitors.

Porter has his critics, of course, but an evaluation of his work is outside the scope of the present text. His relevance to strategic HRM is that one of the most influential 'best-fit' models of HR policies and practices – that of Schuler and Jackson (1987) – is based directly on his strategic prescriptions.

BEST-PRACTICE MODELS OF STRATEGY AND HRM

Best-practice models of HRM are universalist in nature and assert that regardless of context or internal factors there is one best way of managing human resources which, if applied, will lead to better organisational performance.

Pfeffer identified a set of seven HR practices that would lead to what he termed 'competitive advantage through people' (consolidated from an original list of 16). These were: employment security, selective recruitment, self-managed teams or teamworking, high pay contingent on company performance, extensive training, reduction of status differentials, and the sharing of information (Pfeffer, 1994; 1998).

In a large-scale study of US manufacturing companies across a range of industries and firm sizes Huselid (1995) reported evidence that the use of specified high-performance work practices (HPWPs) was reflected in better firm performance as measured by reduced employee turnover, increased productivity and enhanced corporate financial performance. The HPWPs which were identified were in the areas of personnel selection, performance appraisal, incentive compensation, job design, grievance procedures, information-sharing, attitude assessment, labour–management participation, intensity of recruitment (as measured by the selection ratio), average number of hours training per employee per year, and promotion criteria.

Huselid also specifically looked for evidence for internal and external fit in HR strategy (ie a coherent HR strategy for the former and a link between the HR strategy and the corporate strategy for the latter) but reported (1995; p.667) that

> despite the compelling theoretical arguments that better internal and external fit will increase firm performance, I found only modest evidence for such an effect for internal fit and little for external fit.

However, he acknowledged that the theoretical arguments in favour of both internal and external fit remain 'compelling', and he called for further research before a firm conclusion could be reached. It must be said that we still await such conclusive evidence that would close the debate on best-fit or best-practice for good one way or the other.

Huselid also made a final comment (1995; p.68) of significant interest, although it is seldom referred to in the HRM literature:

> Although traditional economic theory would suggest that the gains associated with the adoption of high-performance work practices cannot survive into perpetuity (because the returns from these investments will be driven toward equilibrium as more and more firms make them), the substantial variance in the HRM practices adopted by domestic [US] firms and the expectation that investment in such practices helps to create firm-specific human capital that is difficult to imitate suggest that at least in the near term such returns are available for the taking.

These are perhaps the two most widely known best-practice models, but there are many others, the most important of which is US Dept of Labor (1993), which Huselid based his work upon. Dyer and Reeves (1995), Becker and Gerhart (1996) and Youndt *et al* (1996) reviewed the field.

We can see from the above that best-practice models are typically universalist prescriptions for high-performance work practices. These models typically emphasise the importance of employee selection, training, flexibility, performance management and incentive-based pay, but they neglect issues of collective employee relations. This perhaps reflects their North American origins and arguably decreases the possibility of true universalism when applied to countries such as those of Scandinavia or Northern Europe which still enjoy a more vigorous tradition of employee representation and trade union influence than does the United States.

BEST-FIT MODELS FOR HRM AND STRATEGY

SCHULER AND JACKSON

Schuler and Jackson identified a set of twelve behaviours that were needed to make competitive strategies work. For each, the differentiation strategy required the opposite from that needed for cost leadership. These behaviours were: the degree of creative, innovative behaviour; the focus on long-term behaviour; the degree of independent, autonomous behaviour; concern for quality; concern for quantity; capacity for high risk-taking; concern for results; preference to assume responsibility; flexibility towards change; tolerance of ambiguity and unpredictability; range of skill application; and degree of job or firm involvement.

Schuler and Jackson then explicitly linked these HR characteristics of the workforce to Porter's generic competitive strategies (Porter, 1980).

According to Schuler and Jackson (1987), if a firm pursues a cost leadership strategy in Porter's terms it will be sufficient that the employees show a preference for predictable and repetitive behaviour with a low degree of flexibility and a narrow application of skill. They need only have a low concern for quality of the product. Employees need show little desire for responsibility and will probably have low feelings of involvement with their jobs or organisations. To support these employee behaviours and attitudes the firm's human resource practices can exhibit low employee participation, with little job security and minimal training.

Conversely, if a firm follows a differentiation strategy, the employees will have to exhibit a high concern for quality and be creative and innovative, with a high degree of flexibility and wide application of skills. They will have to be willing to assume responsibility and will experience a high level of involvement with both job and organisation. To support these employee characteristics, human resource management practices will have to maintain a much higher level of employee participation. Employee relations will be co-operative rather than hostile, and job security is likely to be high. Reward systems will be geared to individual and group performance.

One might almost say that for Schuler and Jackson a cost leadership strategy requires only personnel management whereas a differentiation strategy needs HRM.

MILES AND SNOW

Miles and Snow examined the sorts of HRM activities associated with their strategic types (Miles and Snow, 1984). They claimed to find quite consistent and distinct patterns of HRM in each of the Defender, Prospector and Analyser strategic types which in each case amounted to successful HR strategies. As might be expected, no consistent pattern could be found in Reactors.

According to Miles and Snow, the key HR strategy of Prospectors is to 'buy in' the personnel they require. They are 'poachers' who do not have time to undertake long-term training or development, so they attempt to lure experienced personnel from competitors. Similarly, they cannot afford bureaucratic management systems and so their HR practices tend to be informal and their reward strategies are highly geared towards performance. Employee relations will be unitarist and formal recognition of trade unions is unlikely.

Defenders, on the other hand, are doing very well out of the current business situation and so their HR strategies are geared to maintaining the status quo. With deep pockets they can afford to offer job security and long-term policies on development and training. Defenders aim to 'make' rather than 'buy' the talent they need. Their reward systems are less likely to be performance-oriented, being geared instead to reinforcing loyalty and long-term commitment to the firm. Defenders are more able to afford pluralistic employee relations, and long-established Defenders are probably happy to recognise trade unions.

Analysers share characteristics of both Prospectors and Defenders, and their HR strategies and practices will reflect this.

Reactors by definition fail to achieve consistent and effective business strategies, and similarly with their HR strategies. Constantly reacting to crises and unforeseen events, their people management will be short-term and inconsistent and unlikely to be successful. Reactors are prone either to neglect HR or to be subject to shortlived fads and fashions.

HR AND PORTFOLIO ANALYSIS

Purcell (1989) combined the concepts of divisionalisation and those of portfolio analysis using the Boston Consultancy Group (BCG) Growth–Share Matrix. This matrix places firms (or each of their divisions or strategic business units) in a quadrant according to (i) their relative market share compared to their nearest competitors, and (ii) the rate of market growth. Each firm (or SBU) is classified as either a 'cash cow', a 'star', a 'dog' or a 'problem child'.

'Cash cows' enjoy a high relative market share in a low-growth market. Low-growth markets are usually mature, so the cash cow is similar to Miles and Snow's Defender – a large, mature, successful firm whose priority is to preserve the status quo. As the name implies, cash cows are very profitable and they provide funds for the wider corporation. They seek order, stability and predictability to continue to enjoy their dominant market position. They will tend to have well-established, rather bureaucratic HR systems and in older industries may well cling to the personnel management paradigm with a highly unionised workforce, structured systems of collective bargaining and traditional reward systems.

'Stars' have a high relative share of a high-growth market. They are young firms in new markets. Although they have a good market share, they may not be immediately profitable for two reasons: the market, being new, may still be small in absolute terms and investment costs for the firm will still be high. But stars are the hope for the future, and as the market continues to grow and mature, the successful star may become tomorrow's cash cow. Stars are akin to Miles and Snow's Prospectors. This is the category of firm most likely to use sophisticated HRM.

'Dogs' have a low relative share of a low-growth market. They may be burned-out cash cows of yesteryear. Dog status does not mean that the firm or SBU cannot be profitable in the short term, but their future is bleak and good management will sell them or close them before they slip into unprofitability. With little prospect of increasing market share, profit margins can only be improved by constantly cutting costs – including those for people. With low rewards and no development the people management in this category will be the opposite of the HRM model.

Firms classed as 'problem children' have low relative shares of fast-growing markets. Typically, they are young firms in new markets which are not fulfilling their potential. Better management might turn then into stars. They require a flexible operation with employees willing to be adaptable and who possess a range of skills. They cannot afford the high overheads associated with formal HR procedures and structures.

We can see that this analysis implies that because each quadrant of the BCG matrix requires a different business strategy, each also requires a different HR strategy. This has obvious implications for a large divisionalised business which seeks a consistent HR strategy.

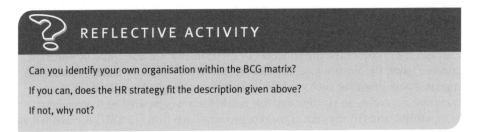

REFLECTIVE ACTIVITY

Can you identify your own organisation within the BCG matrix?

If you can, does the HR strategy fit the description given above?

If not, why not?

Of course we should be sceptical of too mechanistic a 'fit' between HR practice and strategy (see Chapter 1 on HPWP bundles), but we can see in the match between HR practices and Porter's competitive strategies, in those with Miles and Snow's strategic typology, and in Purcell's matching of HR with strategic business units that there is some plausibility in these correlations. Perhaps it is best to regard these prescriptions as starting points in selecting appropriate HPWPs for a particular organisation.

THE HRM STRATEGY PROCESS AND STRATEGIC CHOICE

Boxall and Purcell (2006) are probably right to hold that neither the best-practice nor the best-fit approach is completely correct. Their solution – which seems sensible in principle – is to think in terms of (a) some underlying general or generic processes of managing human resources that are universal and that can be applied regardless of context; while there is also (b), a 'surface layer' of policies and practices in any organisation which are influenced by contingent factors. The difficulty, of course, is in identifying the generic processes. Boxall and Purcell suggest recruitment as an example of the generic processes – but they do not proffer a definitive list.

The empirical studies we cited in Chapter 1 – eg DTI/CIPD, 2005 – certainly imply that the optimum selection of HPWPs for any organisation is influenced by, and dependent on, the business strategy, and that both are the consequence of managers' making choices.

Purcell and Ahlstrand (1994) examined the relationship between corporate strategy and human resource management in multi-divisional companies, the organisational form which dominates large organisations in developed economies. According to Purcell and Ahlstrand (1994), three levels of strategy formation can be identified in the multi-divisional firm:

- first-order strategy – ie decisions on long-run goals and the scope of activities
- second-order strategy – decisions on the way the enterprise is structured to achieve its goals
- third-order strategy – decisions regarding the development of functional strategies (for example, those regarding human resource management).

These authors were, as we have said, principally concerned with strategy-making in multi-divisional firms, but the logic of their argument – that strategy decisions ultimately operate at three interlinked levels – can be applied to any firm large enough to have an explicit HRM strategy, whether it is divisionalised or not. We can take their account as a general model of the HRM strategy-making process.

We should not make the mistake of regarding this process as being overly mechanistic. The three-stage process features 'political' bargaining and trading between power groups (usually groups of senior managers) in an unclear and uncertain environment.

Of course, not all strategies are the product of wholly rational and objective evaluation – they may 'emerge' from streams of actions within the organisation (Minzberg, 1978). Indeed, increasingly so, one might think, in 'knowledge economies'. However, even emergent strategies have to become articulated and visible, at least to some degree, at the point at which resources must be mobilised to support them. Business strategies will almost always be pretty fully articulated in terms of the first two levels of the Purcell and Ahlstrand model, and so will be largely a 'given' by the time the HR strategy is being planned or articulated itself. This is not to contradict the possibility of feedback from the third level to these higher levels. For example, a business strategy which requires certain HR resources may have to be modified or rejected if these resources prove to be too scarce or too expensive to obtain.

CORPORATE SOCIAL RESPONSIBILITY

There is as yet no single, universally accepted, definition of corporate social responsibility (CSR) but that of McWilliams and Siegel (2001; p.117) is as good as any to start with:

> CSR [comprises] actions that appear to further some social good, beyond the interests of the firm and that which is required by law.

The CIPD (2009b; p.1) offers a more extensive definition:

> CSR covers all aspects of corporate governance. It is about how companies conduct their business in an ethical way, taking account of their impact economically, socially, environmentally and in terms of human rights. This moves beyond traditional business stakeholders such as shareholders or local suppliers. CSR includes social partners such as local communities, and global responsibilities such as protecting the environment and ensuring good labour standards in overseas suppliers. CSR also includes relationships with employees and customers. It inevitably involves working in partnership with other organisations or groups. It can be seen as a form of strategic management, encouraging the organisation to scan the horizon and think laterally about how its relationships will contribute long-term to its bottom line in a constantly changing world.

Contemporary concerns about companies' activities beyond merely keeping to the letter of the law and making profits stem from debates in the USA in the 1960s and 1970s about firms' social responsibilities. These debates opened the way to thinking about multiple interests or stakeholders, not just shareholders or owners. Johnson stated that 'A socially responsible firm is one whose managerial staff balances a multiplicity of interests' (Johnson, 1971; p.50).

The idea of multiple interests emerged strongly in the UK in the mid-1990s with the notion of a 'stakeholder economy'. This was partly in reaction to Thatcherite economic policies which had been widely acknowledged to have worked, at least in narrow terms of economic success, but, in the view of many, only at an unacceptable social cost. A 'third way' which embraced both market economics and social polices was offered by New Labour under Tony Blair, and this was immensely popular – for a time.

Yet despite this, by the early 2000s the interest in a stakeholder society had rather diminished in the UK. Ironically, this was at least partly due to the fact that those European economies in which a social agenda had been more explicit than in the UK were perceived to be performing less well economically than those following the 'Anglo-Saxon' model (Roberts and Kynaston, 2001; Eurofound, 2003).

However, notorious cases of company scandal such as Enron, and spectacularly mismanaged environmental disasters such as the 2010 BP 'deepwater' oil spill in the Gulf of Mexico have kept the notion of CSR on social and managerial agendas. This has increased demands from customers, employees, statutory bodies and the general public for detailed information about whether companies are meeting acceptable standards.

As we will see in Chapter 3, what is now widely regarded as 'best practice' in organising work and the people who do it has evolved from Taylorist ideas of scientific management to the greater involvement of employees in the planning and organising of the work. It is one of the key themes of this text that this is central to and supported by human resource management. But at least in the Anglo-American system there has been no comparable development in ideas of corporate governance (Konzelmann *et al*, 2006).

We can see from the above why CSR should be of general strategic interest to an organisation – but what has CSR to do with HRM and strategy? The CIPD (2009b) argues that the HR function is crucial to effective CSR:

> Successful CSR strategies depend on building relationships with a range of stakeholders and getting buy-in across the organisation. Enlightened people management practices are key in delivering this, and CSR offers HR professionals many opportunities to make a strategic contribution to their business. This may mean reviewing existing policies and practices on, for example, internal communications, recruitment, induction, health and safety, diversity or training. One of the main conclusions from [CIPD research] was that CSR became an instrument of change in an organisation's behaviours, attitudes and performance, and this was where the HR function made its greatest contribution to the success of CSR initiatives.

HRM DILEMMA

Should *everyone* have a say?

Are there limits to how far we should extend stakeholding?

In one academic study it was found that although commitment-based HRM systems did generally have a positive impact on corporate performance, this could be constrained by corporate governance regimes which privileged 'remote' stakeholders, such as institutional shareholders in large plcs or the Treasury in public sector organisations (Konzelmann *et al*, 2006).

Yet these parties would seem to be legitimate stakeholders.

ETHICS AND HRM

The CIPD Code of Professional Conduct for HR practitioners makes the standard declaration expected from a professional body:

> In the public interest and in the pursuit of its objectives, the Chartered Institute of Personnel and Development is committed to the highest

possible standards of professional conduct and competency. To this end members:

- are required to exercise integrity, honesty, diligence and appropriate behaviour in all their business, professional and related personal activities

- must act within the law and must not encourage, assist or act in collusion with employees, employers or others who may be engaged in unlawful conduct.

But, in a residual echo of the welfare role of traditional personnel management, HRM is often expected to be something of a guardian of organisational ethics, and to act as a guarantor of organisational fairness and justice for all employees.

'While HRM does need to support commercial outcomes ... it also exists to serve organisational needs for social legitimacy' (Boxall *et al*, 2007). This means something more than just ensuring compliance with legal protection for employees with respect to heath and safety at work and against discrimination in employment.

CASE STUDY

CORPORATE SOCIAL RESPONSIBILITY IN TESCO

Background

Tesco is the UK's, and one of the world's, largest food retailers. The company operates more than 900 stores worldwide, with the majority – over 750 – in the UK. It employs over 240,000 people worldwide, over 190,000 of them in the UK. It was founded in 1932 by Sir Jack Cohen, and grew rapidly, largely through the acquisition of other grocery chains. During the 1990s the company expanded into other European and Asian markets, and has opened over 200 stores since 1993. Sales continue to expand: in 2001, group sales grew by 12.7% to £25,654 million, and 55 new stores were opened in the UK alone. Group profits increased in 2001 by 14.1% to £1,221 million.

CSR in Tesco

The company shows a CSR awareness across a range of external and internal activities. External activities include local regeneration and employment projects, a long-running initiative to link sales to donating computers for schools, and establishing ethical trading practices with different suppliers. In part this external CSR activity can be seen as a counter to past criticism of the supermarket sector in the UK that it was forcing suppliers (particularly farmers) to accept very low prices for produce, and then making unreasonably high profits from the sale of that produce in the supermarkets. Although subsequent reports have not supported these continuing allegations, supermarkets have taken a variety of steps to gain greater public support.

Internal CSR activities are noted in such areas as employment diversity, health and safety and the increased availability of an occupational pension scheme.

In terms of handling any issues relating to restructuring, a central mechanism for this is the partnership agreement that Tesco signed in 1998 with its recognised trade union USDAW (the Union of Shop, Distributive and Allied Workers). At the time, Bill Connor, USDAW's General Secretary, called this agreement 'the start of a partnership which will offer them the opportunity for more involvement and more consultation than ever before' (*Northern*

Echo, 14 March 1998). Likewise, the General Secretary of the TUC, John Monks, declared that poor employers should 'come to Tesco and learn that good partnership relations between a union and employer can add value' (*The Times*, 14 March 1998). Examples of this partnership approach have been evident in relation both to health and safety and assistance for the unemployed. In 1999 Tesco was praised by the TUC for a health and safety partnership with USDAW which cut staff accidents and sickness.

It was the first retailer to sign up to the TUC's safety initiative. More recently, the focus has been on providing jobs and regeneration through partnerships between local authorities, USDAW and Tesco to guarantee jobs in new stores to local unemployed people who completed specially run training courses. Under this partnership agreement, staff forums have been created in each of its over 700 stores, the forums comprising store management (the store manager and personnel manager), union representatives and elected employee representatives (elected on the basis of one employee representative per 50 employees, with a minimum of five representatives per store).

Elected representatives receive training in, for example, holding effective meetings and giving briefings. The forums meet four times a year and discuss local store issues but not terms and conditions. The individual store forums in turn send representatives to one of three regional forums, who in turn elect a national forum. The Tesco UK workforce includes over 100,000 USDAW members (up from 80,000 at the time the Partnership Agreement was signed in 1998). This represents the largest unionised workforce of any UK company.

Management thinking behind the agreement was to create greater staff co-operation, resolve local problems, and create a more open style of communication. The five key aspirations it had for the agreement were:

- to secure high-quality representation for staff

- to enable USDAW to understand and promote Tesco's business goals

- to guarantee co-operation

- to enable USDAW to challenge management, and

- to enable Tesco to remain flexible enough to retain its leading market position.

The union presence is seen by management to give greater legitimacy to the process, and the union has been highly supportive of the agreement.

Although partnership relations have not been without criticism – particularly criticism of union incorporation (see for example comments in *People Management*, 27 April 2000) – other commentators have seen advantages in replacing traditional union–management relations with the multi-level forums, particularly in terms of allowing a broadening of the union–management agenda to take more account of issues such as job security, training and career prospects. For some commentators the result has been an overall increase in trade union and employee input into business decision-making.

The company does not communicate extensively on the nature and activities of the workplace forums. Their existence is noted on its website but is not communicated in the company's Annual Reviews or CSR report.

Views on the workplace forums

The functioning of the workplace forums was discussed with managers and employee representatives at two stores, and in addition with a sample of employees not directly involved in the forum activity. Among those involved there was general satisfaction expressed that the partnership model, based on the staff forums, was a good idea and fitted well with the company's overall policy towards employee relations (although an even more tangible aspect of the partnership model was seen to be the significant bonuses paid to staff reflecting the annual profits made by the company). Among the trade union representatives a feeling was evident that the consultative style of employee relations was the only relationship the company was prepared to countenance with USDAW, and that the consequence for the union of not accepting a partnership approach would probably have been de-recognition by Tesco. However, all parties expressed the view that the forums worked reasonably well as an open exchange of views on store-level matters.

At the same time, a number of problems were identified with maintaining the level of forum activity. Two were most evident:

1   Maintaining an adequate agenda – The forum meetings are typically quarterly in frequency, and this was widely seen to be too infrequent for day-to-day issues to be adequately covered. These shorter-term issues are more likely to be covered in regular five-minute briefings by managers – referred to as 'Team 5s' within Tesco. These briefings have been introduced on a weekly basis and aim to cover all staff. According to the company, currently around two-thirds (65%) of staff say that they are getting a Team 5 briefing each week, and the company's target is to extend this to cover all staff (Tesco CSR Review, p.25). Further, there are certain subjects – notably issues relating to employees' terms and conditions of employment – that cannot be discussed in the forums. This again appeared to concentrate forum discussion on a store management rather than employee agenda.

2   The agenda of the workplace forums appeared also to have been restricted to a degree by the company's success and continued expansion. Thus, since their introduction in 1998, there had been very little in the area of restructuring for the forums to be concerned with. As a result, emphasis in the forums had been on work arrangements, store organisation, training, customer relations and so on, rather than employees' internal working conditions. Only if at a future date the company undergoes significant restructuring will the forum system, along with the broader partnership relationship with the union, be tested on its robustness in dealing with the consequences of restructuring. If this arises, however, both company and union representatives will have enjoyed a significant period of building relations under relatively conducive conditions.

Among the employees not directly involved in the forum process, there was some feeling that the forum activity was not a prominent source of information or consultation for them. The feeling appeared to be that these employees learned more about what developments were occurring from the management briefings, or informally from their union representative, than from the forums.

Conclusions from the Tesco case

The partnership agreement was welcomed by both the company and the union as a means of developing employee relations within Tesco. During a period which has seen considerable decline in union membership and the coverage of union recognition in the UK, this agreement with USDAW has proved symbolic in illustrating how companies and unions can develop collective relations. At the time, Tesco's retail manager, Michael Wemms, maintained that this partnership agreement showed 'that a unionised company should always be able to do better than a non-unionised set-up given a sensible structure' (Glasgow Herald, 14 March 1998). Since the late 1990s, a series of other companies in the UK have likewise forged partnership relations with their main union(s). The fostering of relations with unions rather than seeking to minimise their presence in the company represents an area of CSR that has not to date been adequately considered.

The discussions with those involved in the workplace forums indicated a generally supportive response to this method of social dialogue. Currently in the UK there is no legal requirement to consult with employees at workplace level, other than to deal with specific issues (such as collective redundancies and a transfer of undertakings). This will change in the coming period as the European Directive on Works Councils takes effect. What the Tesco case indicates, however, is that such forums can play a useful consultative role within organisations. But what the case has also demonstrated is the problem (also evident in other studies of consultative mechanisms) of maintaining an adequate agenda for such consultative bodies, particularly where the meetings are held relatively infrequently, where certain issues (such as terms and conditions) are deemed not suitable for discussion, and where other management briefing systems exist which allow more regular communication of locally relevant issues. As the discussions with those not directly involved in the forums also highlighted, a persistent difficulty with such representative mechanisms is how to keep the constituency informed and involved with the consultative process, rather than this becoming an activity more or less separate from the workforce.

Overall, however, although the company appears to make little of this activity as a form of CSR – indeed, primarily showcases its external, much more than any internal, CSR activity in its communications to its various stakeholders – the forum structure, and more broadly its partnership relationship with its trade union, represent an example of good practice CSR in the field of social dialogue.

Source: Eurofound (2003)

KEY ISSUES

The HRM function should be a partner with senior and line managers in strategy execution. The HRM strategy has to be internally consistent and must support the overall corporate strategy.

We took the model of strategy-making in divisionalised firms which was developed by Purcell and Ahlstrand, featuring three interlinked levels of decision-making to be a general model of the HRM strategy-making process in all firms. This model recognises the overriding importance of business strategy and the influence of structure.

'Best-practice' models probably contain a core of generic HR processes that are universal to all well-performing organisations, but these have not been definitively identified at other than a very general level. Best-practice models seem to miss important strategic, structural and contextual factors that in reality must be taken into account.

'Best-fit' models tend to be too mechanistic but probably offer a good first step in identifying strategies and HPWPs that firms should adopt.

Corporate social responsibility is seen as a vital strategic issue for organisations in the twenty-first century. HRM can play a crucial role in helping to build relationships with the various stakeholders involved and in getting buy-in across the organisation. Many key HR policies and practices can be vehicles for effective CSR, such as recruitment, induction, health and safety, diversity, employee relations and talent development.

HRM is often expected to act as a guarantor of organisational fairness and justice for all employees.

HRM in action

It is all about getting people to realise they can change things.

People Management, 20 September 2007

Among his many talents, Sir Gerry Robinson is a master of understatement. 'I've generally found things reasonably easy to sort out,' says the boss who masterminded the turnarounds of Coca-Cola UK and Granada, where he is credited with stemming the TV company's losses in a year and posting returns 10% higher than expected.

> 'I think I get bored too early in jobs and I really enjoy something that requires a huge shake-up. My strength has been the capacity to sort out messes.'

Along the way, he has notched up chairmanships at Allied Domecq, The Arts Council, BSkyB and ITN, as well as snatching the Forte group from under its founders' noses. He is now chairman of Moto service stations. Not bad going for a boy who led a cloistered life in a Catholic seminary in Lancashire until he was 17, before deciding not to become a priest.

After his first job at Lesney Products, makers of Matchbox toys, Robinson moved to Lex Service Group, then owners of the Volvo franchise, because, he says, he 'wanted a car'. From there he was promoted, then headhunted to Grand Met as finance director of Coca-Cola UK, ending up as chief executive of Grand Met's contract services division, before staging a management buy-out – the largest ever seen at that time – to create Compass Group.

A clue to Robinson's success may be his relentless enthusiasm for the nuts and bolts of business and for getting things right. Alongside an open and approachable charm, he is a stickler for efficiency and radiates a cut-to-the-chase, no-nonsense attitude to management that many have described as ruthless. He is impatient with those who believe management is complex or take a 'philosophical' approach.

'Business is essentially simple,' he says. 'The more you allow people to feel that things are complicated – and it's very tempting because it makes them feel clever – the less they are able to find out the answers. At the sharp end, people almost always know how to do it better. Good management is allowing them to find the answers and do it.'

Robinson is similarly dismissive of HR theories. 'I don't subscribe to over-sophisticated HR,' he asserts. 'In many ways it does itself a disservice. A genuinely important part of getting an organisation right is having people who know how to find the right people and having systems to encourage people to contribute. If you get into unbelievably complex philosophical analysis, or theoretical training, then it can become very costly and unhelpful.'

Robinson rejects the recent trend for management based on 'values'.

'There's no doubt that if you run an organisation that doesn't have decent values, you will be worse off,' he concedes. 'But everyone ticks the boxes and it begins to reveal a reverse correlation: the more talk there is, the less it is happening.'

Yet he is clear about HR's value to the business. 'It's the most important function to get right,' he says. 'You stand almost no chance of getting things right if you have the wrong people,' he adds. 'I cottoned on to that very early on.'

Consequently, he believes that the real task of HR is helping to choose the right people for the job and having the expertise to make sure they do the job they are meant to do. 'It is a skill that is much under-estimated,' he points out. He is committed to training – nothing fancy, just 'good, solid, reliable training' for functional quality. It is a refreshingly pragmatic, straight-talking approach to HR.

Robinson can be equally disarming about his setbacks, citing the launch of the doomed ITV Digital project as his biggest mistake. 'In my heart of hearts, I knew it was wrong,' he admits. He is even on good terms with Greg Dyke, despite his leaving to take over LWT. 'I tried to persuade him to stay on,' says Robinson. 'And it was a disaster when he left the BBC. He's a good people person.'

Known as a supporter of the Blair government, Robinson denied he had any political ambitions under the new Brown regime. But there seems to be one task he is itching to get his hands on. Having recently returned to filming at the hospital in Rotherham, Yorkshire, where he controversially tackled waiting lists for a BBC2 TV series *Can Gerry Robinson Fix the NHS?*, it's clear there is more he would like to be able to do.

'If someone asked me to run the NHS, the first thing I'd do would be to bring accountability back,' he says. 'People need to be held accountable directly for what they do.' As he warms to his theme, you begin to see how he must operate when tackling the thorny business crises he is renowned for sorting out.

'There are 600 hospitals. I'd have one person responsible for six hospitals. I'd build a management structure and get truly excellent people and pay what it takes. Running the NHS is the hardest job in the country. But have we really gone out and got [Tesco CEO] Terry Leahy? Have we, hell! I don't think management is taken seriously as a skill. If we got the right person to lead the NHS, they could release efficiencies of billions. The pay-off would be phenomenal.'

You can almost hear him rubbing his hands with relish as he continues. 'I'd take it out of government and create an independent health service – although it can never be completely independent because of funding. And I'd abolish the Department of Health – I'm not sure what it does, but there are a lot of people, and it is damned expensive. I heard that only 20p in the pound reaches operating level. If that's true, it is appalling. If you want something to happen, you have to manage it. It frustrates me.'

In Rotherham General Hospital, his trick to cutting waiting lists was to get the chief executive, Brian James, to walk around the floors and get a feel for what the issues really were. 'I think he thought I would come in with some amazingly clever idea – some sort of magic – and I think it was a disappointment to him to hear that if you want to change something you have got to do things,' Robinson says. 'But having people know that what they do is noticed is such a powerful thing. It's not very different from a family. There are rules and boundaries and everyone wants to have the security that people care about them and are following through.'

He is full of praise for staff who can see where change is needed. 'People in the NHS feel unhappy despite being totally committed. I believe it is all about people management,' he says. 'It is recognising people's need to contribute and be part of something. Over the years, instead of promoting people who have achieved things, I think they have promoted people who told a good story, not those who took a risk and had ideas. You can see it in any government organisation.

'[At Rotherham] people weren't allowed to feel they could influence a damn thing. You had a management divorced from day-to-day operations. It is all about getting people to realise they can change and influence things. Success breeds success. If people start to see that things can happen, it's amazingly encouraging,' he says.

Making a difference in business, Robinson says, involves two things: 'One is being absolutely clear about what the hell you are trying to do. And then it is about the people.'

You can see why Sir Gerry is an inspiring leader. But you can also see why he has developed a fearsome reputation as an axe-wielder. Yet he complains that this image is unjustified. 'I have only ever fired five people, and only one [David Plowright, see below] was high-profile,' he claims. It seems Gerry Robinson would have you believe he is really a pussycat – but, as everyone knows, even pussycats have sharp claws.

Robinson's highlights

£17m profit in two years. Led management buy-out of Compass Group from Grand Met in 1987. Joined Granada in 1991 and stemmed its losses in a year. Knighted in 2003 for his services to arts and business.

Career low points

In the early 1990s, was widely criticised for his role in ousting the late David Plowright from the post of Granada TV chairman, after Plowright had completed 35 years' service and secured Granada's franchise. There was also ITV Digital (launched as ONdigital in 1998). Following a series of problems, including a disastrous £315 million deal with the Football League, it went into administration in 2002.

REFLECTIVE ACTIVITY

What HR strategy would *you* recommend for the NHS?

FINAL CASE STUDY

Read through the Hennes & Mauritz case study in the Appendix (p.238).

How would you assess the company's policy on corporate social responsibility? How can HRM assist the company to fulfil this policy?

ENDNOTE

1 Although I do not agree with all of their conclusions on the subject I am indebted to Boxall and Purcell's (2006) review of strategy and HRM, and in particular their discussion of 'best-practice' and 'best-fit' models, and recommend their text to any reader who wishes to undertake further reading on the topic.

EXPLORE FURTHER

Armstrong, M. (2009) *Armstrong's Handbook of Human Resource Management Practice*. 11th Edition. London: Kogan Page.

Chapter 2. A useful outline.

Boxall, P. and Purcell, J. (2006) *Strategy and Human Resource Management*. Basingstoke: Palgrave Macmillan.

Chapter 2. 'Strategy and the process of strategic management'. A good general introduction to the notion of strategic management.

Chapter 3 'Strategic HRM best fit or best practice?' One of the best introductions to this debate.

Chapter 4. 'Strategic HRM and the resource-based view of the firm'.

Boxall, P., Purcell, J. and Wright, P. (eds) (2007). *The Oxford Handbook of Human Resource Management*. Oxford: Oxford University Press.

Chapter 5. M. R. Allan and P. Wright. 'Strategic management and HRM'. A good treatment from the perspective of the Resource Based View (RBV) of the firm.

Kersley, B., Alpin, C., Forth, J., Bryson, A., Bewley, H., Dix, G. and Oxenbridge, S. (2006) *Inside the Workplace: Findings from the 2004 Workplace Employment Relations Survey*. Abingdon: Routledge.

Chapter 9 'Equality, diversity and work–life balance'.

Chapter 10. 'Workplace climate and performance'.

Storey, J. (ed.) (2007) *Human Resource Management: A critical text*, 3rd edition. London: Thomson Learning

Chapter 4. J. Storey. 'What is strategic HRM?'. A good academic introduction.

Chapter 5. K. Sisson. 'Facing up to the challenges of success: putting "governance" at the heart of HRM'. Argues that since the HRM model is now dominant its focus should be 'the governance of the employment relationship'.

Chapter 8. G. Salaman. 'Managers' knowledge and the management of change' [maybe].

CHAPTER 3

Designing work: organising jobs and people for efficiency and flexibility

INTRODUCTION

Of course there has been division of labour in some sense since at least the Stone Age, with women having to mind the home and hearth while the men and boys went hunting and warring. Only Robinson Crusoe did everything himself – and as soon as Man Friday appeared, it was the newcomer who found he was doing all the servant stuff.

LEARNING OUTCOMES

On completion of this chapter you should:

- have an appreciation of the concept of division of labour
- know what is meant by job design
- understand the principles of 'scientific management'
- know about developments in job design following scientific management, and especially the principles of the autonomous work group and the Toyota production system
- understand the principles of team formation
- appreciate the team roles required for effective teamworking
- see why organisations seek flexibility in work patterns
- have some appreciation of the organisation of work beyond the team level: by function, by product, the use of the matrix structure, and divisionalisation
- understand the role of HRM in change management.

What do we mean by 'designing' work? In HRM the term 'job design' is frequently used. Michael Armstrong defined it (Armstrong, 2009; p.10) as follows:

> Job or role design: deciding on the content and performance and competency requirements of jobs or roles in order to provide a basis for selection, performance management and reward and to maximise intrinsic job satisfaction.

The recognition of the importance of organisation in the efficiency and effectiveness of work can be traced back at least to Adam Smith in his concept of the division of labour. The first sentence of Smith's great work of 1776, *The Wealth of Nations*, reads:

> The greatest improvement in the productive powers of labour and the greater part of the skill, dexterity, and judgement with which it is anywhere directed or applied, seem to have been the effects of the division of labour.

The necessity of the division of labour has naturally been hugely multiplied by the enormous technological advances which have been made, and the resulting complexity of products and services which are now possible, since Smith observed his simple pin-makers in eighteenth-century Kirkcaldy. For example, the modern motorcar is composed of more than 20,000 individual parts many of which require computer-assisted design and manufacture, while the computers and machines themselves each consist of many, many parts and software which needed many engineers and programmers to produce – and so on.

But, as the example of the car shows, to make anything work after division of labour must come reintegration or synthesis. The 20,000 odd parts of the modern car have to be assembled absolutely correctly if the car is to function at all.

So we can see that organisation of work is really fundamental to the modern technological world.

One of the principal tasks of management in any enterprise is to achieve the most effective combination of division and synthesis of work. That is why the organisation of work matters to executive management and investors. Why it matters to HRM is that unless the whole process, from conception through design to production, can be completely computerised, the division and synthesis crucially depends on, and intimately affects, human beings.

In this chapter we are concerned, first, with the 'micro-organisation' of work, from the level of the individual job to that of the group or team of related workers. We then examine the organisation work at levels above the team or group. After that we look at patterns of work and flexibility, and finally at some aspects of change management.

MICRO-ORGANISATION OF WORK: THE TASK, JOB AND TEAM

SCIENTIFIC MANAGEMENT

The best known, and perhaps most influential, managerial initiative to achieve efficient division of labour and synthesis of work following the Industrial Revolution was what become known as 'scientific management', and was pioneered by an American industrial engineer, Frederick Winslow Taylor.

Taylor presented a paper called 'A piece-rate system' to the American Society of Mechanical Engineers in 1895, giving him a claim to be the world's first management guru. He certainly became one of the most notorious. He is probably the only management writer whose works were the subject of an examination by a US House of Representatives Special Committee, which occurred in 1911 (Aitken, 1960).

Taylor (1911) established the following principles of what he himself called 'scientific management':

- a clear division of tasks and responsibilities between management and workers – management studying the work methods for each job, establishing the most efficient, and then dictating these to the workers
- 'scientific' selection and training of workers: matching suitable employees to the scientifically designed jobs
- the 'enthusiastic co-operation' of management and workers, secured by the use of economic incentives.

The use of this approach combined with high-speed, high-volume assembly lines at Ford's Highland Park plant in the USA led to typical work cycles of one to two minutes. This machine-driven variant of 'Taylorism' came to be known as 'Fordism'. Scientific management produced remarkable increases in productivity, but was usually deeply resented by the workforce. It became associated with poor industrial relations and increased absenteeism, ill-health, employee turnover, and sabotage. The 1911 House of Representatives hearing came about because of concerns that the intended use of scientific management techniques at a new US Navy arsenal would result in unacceptably hostile industrial relations in a vital military facility. In the event, Taylor's methods were not employed.

Despite these drawbacks scientific management was widely accepted and applied throughout the twentieth century. Braverman (1974) demonstrated how Taylor's approach had been extended to clerical work. Recent analyses of Japanese car assembly methods ('Toyota-ism') reveal some similarities with Taylorism, as we shall see later in this chapter.

CRITICISMS OF SCIENTIFIC MANAGEMENT

At least since the time of the Hawthorne Studies (Roethlisberger and Dickson, 1939) scientific management has been subject to criticisms that it assumed that the only motivation of the worker was economic; that it ignored workers' needs for feelings of achievement, job satisfaction and recognition; and that it neglected the importance of social relations and group psychology in the workplace.

However, it has been said (Buchanan, 1994) that:

> Modern techniques of work design have been developed and applied in the second half of this century as antidotes to Taylorism. The impact of these alternative techniques has not been as powerful or pervasive as the influence of scientific management on management practice.

THE INFLUENCE OF MOTIVATION THEORY ON THE DESIGN OF WORK

Psychologists have been studying the motivation of workers for over 100 years, and the theories that have sought to explain employees' motivation have reflected the dominant psychological theories of their day. The earliest theories were based on the assumption that people had an 'instinct' to work. Later theories such as those of Maslow (1943) and Herzberg (1966) introduced the concepts of 'needs', 'drives' and 'motives'. Behavioural psychology brought an emphasis on reinforcement of behaviour – ie in this context, job performance.

The 'cognitive revolution' in psychology has been influential more recently. This approach reacted to extreme behaviourism, which had held that mental states were irrelevant to behaviour, by insisting that people's behaviour was affected by their conscious states and intentions. Goal theory provides managers with a workable technology to structure work – including more abstract and complex work such as management and professional activities – in a way that can apply the general lessons learned from the body of motivation theory.

It is fair to say that there is still no comprehensive and universally accepted theory of motivation, and our current understanding and practice of motivation and commitment are influenced to some degree by all of the various principal schools of thought since the time of Maslow at least. However, we must not doubt the immense influence that motivation theory has exercised on the organisation of work. Buchanan could comment (Buchanan, 1994; p.93) that:

> Maslow's influence is clearly stamped across the work design theories and practices of the latter half of the twentieth century.

For instance, the concept of the 'composite autonomous work group' or 'self-managing multi-skilled team', which was first developed by the Tavistock Institute of Human Relations in London, explicitly reflects Maslow's ideas.

A comprehensive discussion of motivation theory is beyond the scope of the present text. The interested reader may be directed to Landy and Conte (2007) for an up-to-date and accessible treatment of these theories.

SOME PRACTICAL CONCLUSIONS FROM MOTIVATION THEORY

Some useful general principles have been derived from the body of motivation theory:

- We should set goals whenever we can, and, where it is possible and sensible to do so, we should involve the employee(s) concerned in designing and agreeing the goals.
- Establishing agreed, specific and difficult goals ('stretch goals') leads to significant increases in employee performance.
- We should link rewards to performance wherever we reasonably can. The actual scheme or schedule of rewards is usually less important than having a clearly perceived link to performance.
- We should seek to increase employees' sense of self-confidence ('self-efficacy') that they can successfully perform the job or task.
- We should let employees know the level of performance that is expected of them, and give them accurate and timely feedback on their actual work performance.
- Giving positive rewards for good performance is more effective in motivating people then punishing them for poor performance.
- Perceived fairness or equity is important to the motivation of employees.

Practicalities of goal-setting

One of the first and best-known systems of goal-setting at work was 'management by objectives' (MBO). The phrase was coined by Peter Drucker. MBO was initially developed for organising managerial work, but it is now extensively used at all levels of organisations. When used properly it facilitates both the performance of management and the development of individual employees.

Drucker stressed the importance of involving employees in the setting of goals for themselves rather than managers simply imposing goals upon them. From the manager's point of view the art of goal-setting is obtaining genuine employee input into the setting of goals which can 'stretch' the employee to improve their performance.

There is a widely known acronym that is helpful in reminding us how goals should be set at work: they should be 'SMART' – that is, they should be:

- **Specific**
- **Measurable**
- **Assignable**
- **Realistic**
- **Time-bound.**

In other words, people should know exactly what they are being asked to achieve (ie their goal is 'Specific'). Their performance should be capable of being assessed

- Develop a shared vision of how to organise and manage the change.
- Foster consensus, competence and commitment to a new shared vision.
- Spread the word about the change.
- Institutionalise the change through formal policies, systems and structures.
- Monitor and adjust strategies and policies as needed.

THE ROLE OF HUMAN RESOURCES IN CHANGE

The CIPD recommends (CIPD, 2009a) that HRM specialists be involved from the initial stages in any major change initiative and be represented in the main project team. Their specialist expertise is useful in the following areas:

- advising project leaders on the skills available within the organisation – identifying any skills gaps, training needs, new posts, new working practices, etc
- negotiating and engaging with employee representatives
- understanding employee concerns and anticipating problems
- advising on communications with employee groups
- helping people cope with change.

REFLECTIVE ACTIVITY

Describe a recent organisational change that affected you. What was your role in it?

Did HR have a role? *Should* HR have had a role?

How might you have improved the management of the change?

KEY ISSUES

Except for the case of the single self-employed person, it is always necessary for people and work to be organised in some way in order to (i) achieve division of labour, and (ii) achieve the necessary synthesis of the outputs of that division. This is the basis of job design. 'Scientific management' represents the first systematic attempts at modern job design.

The autonomous work group developed from attempts to humanise work while still achieving technical efficiencies. The Toyota production system of 'lean manufacture' is highly influential and it combines both the teamwork and elements of Taylorism. We understand quite a lot about how teams develop and the roles that are necessary for effective teamworking.

Organisations seek flexibility and are increasingly structured with a core of key employees that is surrounded by peripheral shells of non-core workers.

Effective change management is vital for all successful organisations and HRM should have a crucial role in achieving effective management of change.

HRM in action

Waiting times drop thanks to 'Toyota treatment'

The Scotsman newspaper (Monday 25 June 2007) reported that the National Heath Service in Edinburgh had adopted the Toyota production system in a pilot study which had resulted in significant improvements in services for patients. These included:

- Waiting times for patients needing CT scans were reduced from 21 weeks to four, which also allowed 20 extra patients a week to receive the service.

- The waiting time for a routine colonoscopy fell from 29 weeks to 18 weeks.

- A computer-based system to manage hospital beds saved more than 80 hours of staff travel time.

- And the 11 forms required to document rehabilitation patients were replaced with just one.

Following the principles of 'lean production', staff who dealt with patients 'on the front line' were asked to suggest improvements. These were not just doctors but included porters, nurses and drivers. The pilot has been so successful that the Health Service is to extend the programme to other areas of patient care.

A Health Service spokesman was quoted as saying: 'Our philosophy is that the person who is doing the job is the expert. They are the ones who know if something could be changed to make their job more efficient.'

Source: article available online at http://edinburghnews.scotsman.com/ index.cfm?id=992312007

CASE STUDY EXERCISE

Read the following case study and try to answer the question asked at the end.

When you have finished the task, look at the author's notes and guidance to potential answers that is presented beneath the case study.

CASE STUDY EXERCISE

The Betterlife Charitable Foundation

John Smith was depressed as he looked out of his office window into the open-plan area and saw yet another *ad hoc* team meeting taking place among the 10 members of his staff. He'd always adopted a participative management style, and when his team asked if they could have more autonomy and be more of a self-managed team he had agreed without question. However, he was now concerned at the number of meetings they were having, and felt this was beginning to interrupt the team's work with its client base.

Betterlife was a not-for-profit charity that worked with disadvantaged youths and sought to place them in good accommodation and suitable employment. It had a number of small offices throughout the UK, and John had been the manager of his office in Manchester for some 10 years. The charity had a good record of placement, and John had made an outstanding contribution to the aims of the organisation in his time with Betterlife.

Like many in his team, he had been attracted to Betterlife because he associated with its aims and the values that informed its work among people less fortunate than himself. The work culture within Betterlife was characterised by informality, and there was little emphasis on hierarchy and bureaucracy. Pay was low, and Betterlife tended to hire young graduates fresh from university – an age group to whom their clients could relate – and train them up to be effective counsellors who would then move on to the bigger jobs in other organisations. For this reason Betterlife was an attractive organisation for people at the start of their working lives and who wanted to develop a career within the 'caring professions'.

The democratic work regime that was characteristic of all Betterlife's offices was attractive to employees, and the organisation was as concerned to help employees as it was their clients. It was felt that having satisfied and motivated workers was the best way to ensure that clients were cared for in the best way possible. However, John felt that the system had gone too far in addressing employee needs. Meetings like the one he was now observing were becoming more commonplace, and their discussions seemed to revolve more around their own problems and the team's interpersonal relations than client needs. At the same time employees were enthusiastic, often went beyond the call of duty in helping their clients, and frequently linked their own leisure time with that of the young people they had helped. John was very conscious of this, and appreciative of his team's work. At the same time he was aware that his team's performance was not matching that of the best of Betterlife's teams – something that had always been the case until fairly recently.

John decided to discuss the matter with a good friend of his who was studying for a Master's degree in human resource management. He was certain that his friend would be able to give him some good advice on how to deal with the situation.

Case study question

Given the above account, how would you diagnose the situation in John's office, and what advice would you give him?

BETTERLIFE: GUIDANCE

Diagnosis

John's team is clearly performing effectively in terms of the team maintenance function that all teams need to address, but its task functions are suffering. Some of the reasons for this include:

- an organisational culture that is too employee-centred and maintenance-focused
- lack of clear guidelines from John on what the team's priorities and its operating characteristics should be
- lack of control by John in monitoring the team's work and its outputs
- a team that has not passed beyond the 'forming and storming' phases, or has interpreted the 'norming and performing' stages inappropriately
- lack of appropriate training for new employees in the organisation's task-based performance needs
- lack of training for employees in team-based working by the organisation
- lack of defining a clear 'line in the sand' between organisational or client-

focused work and team members' own lives, and the consequent risks this poses.

Advice

Proposals must be based on a full understanding of the current problems with the team's working and the reasons why these have come about. Here, the root causes lie partly within the organisation and its culture and partly in John's own management style. Solutions include:

- raising awareness and bringing the current unsatisfactory levels of performance to the attention of team members
- getting the buy-in of team members to the present unsatisfactory state of affairs
- involving all team members in a review of current performance problems and needs
- addressing the reasons why the team feels it necessary to discuss team maintenance needs so much
- establishing a clear division between work and social life, and explaining the reasons why this is necessary
- involving all team members in a team-building exercise, where the requirements for effective teamworking are explored
- educating John in the idea that self-managed teams are not a reason for abdicating responsibility for controlling and evaluating the work of the team
- building consensus within the team on the needs for task requirements to be addressed while allowing the required team maintenance functions to be continued
- establishing clear performance targets for client interaction and solution-building based upon benchmarks gathered from across Betterlife's operations and the performance levels of other charities engaged in similar functions
- seeking buy-in to these targets by the team
- letting the team be self-managed, and its advantages recognised, based upon consensus within the team and with John about what the performance requirements are
- maintaining staff enthusiasm and morale through the changes proposed and agreed.

FINAL CASE STUDY

Flexibility and change

Read through the Karstadt Warenhaus AG case study in the Appendix (p.231).

Drawing on the contents of the present chapter and the information given in the case, write a memo to the Managing Director of Karstadt Warenhaus AG advising her on how people and work within the Karstadt department store chain can best be organised to achieve the company's objectives.

EXPLORE FURTHER

Armstrong, M. (2009) *Armstrong's Handbook of Human Resource Management Practice.* **11ᵗʰ Edition. London: Kogan Page.**

Chapters 23–27: 'Organizational Design and Development': A series of short chapters covering the essentials of job and role design, organizational design and development and change management.

Boxall, P. and Purcell, J. (2006) *Strategy and Human Resource Management.* **Basingstoke: Palgrave Macmillan.**

Chapter 5. 'Work systems and the changing priorities of production'. An account of how new forms of work organisation, stimulated by increased competition, have impacted on HRM.

Chapter 6. 'Linking work systems and models of employment'. See pp.133–35 for an interesting adaptation of Atkinson's model of the flexible firm.

Boxall, P., Purcell, J. and Wright, P. (eds.) (2007). *The Oxford Handbook of Human Resource Management.* **Oxford: Oxford University Press.**

Chapter 10. J. Cordery and S.K. Parker. 'Work organisation'.

CHAPTER 4

Employee resourcing

INTRODUCTION

In the opening chapter we noted that one of the key themes of HRM in the twenty-first century was the use of sophisticated HR practices in recruitment and selection. Recruitment and selection are two of the most important HRM activities in any organisation. In this chapter we will examine the general principles underlying these activities and also look at some of the most widely used techniques. Oganisations also have to manage the processes involved when employees leave the organisation, and these too are studied in this chapter. We additionally introduce the concept of 'talent management'.

These activities might be described as 'managing the human resource flow'. In the UK human resource management profession they are usually described as 'employee resourcing'. In North America the term 'staffing management' is often used.

LEARNING OUTCOMES

On completion of this chapter you should:

- understand the main models of recruitment and selection of human resources, and which of these are suitable for work organisations
- understand how recruitment and selection may be best viewed as particular stages in a larger process of 'managing and developing the human resource flow'
- have an appreciation of e-recruiting
- have an awareness of the strengths and limitations of the techniques most commonly used in selection, and an appreciation of the use of assessment centres
- have an appreciation of the issues involved in managing the exit of employees from the organisation
- have an understanding of the concept of 'talent management'
- understand the idea of diversity in human resource management
- be familiar with the concept of equal opportunities.

HR specialists often talk about recruitment and selection as separate activities – 'recruitment' meaning the process of attracting people to apply for the job, and 'selection' being the final choice of a particular applicant for a specific position. (The North American term 'hiring' covers both and is sometimes more useful.) It is important that we remember that recruitment and selection do not occur in isolation from other managerial and organisational processes. They are key stages in what Beer *et al* (1984; p.66) termed 'managing the human resource flow':

> The more dynamic the environment … the more a corporation must be concerned with managing the flow of people in, through and out of the organisation.

In the twenty-first century we can update this to say 'Managing *and developing* the human resource flow'. Table 3 illustrates the key stages in this process.

Table 3 Managing and developing the human resource flow

Strategic level		Individual job/ person level	Actions/outcomes
Talent management for high-value (core) staff	Organisational development Human resource planning	Job analysis	Identifying the task requirements and criteria for job success
		Person specification	Identifying the attributes and experience the job-holder needs to achieve job success
		Recruiting	Attracting applicants for consideration for the position
		Initial screening	Examining applications to identify those most suitable for further consideration
		Selection	Interviews, testing and obtaining other information to assess applicants' attributes
		Initial induction and training	Induction to the organisation. If necessary, additional testing, assessment and training to fit the person for the job
	Continuous improvement	Performance management	Performance appraisal
		Learning and development	Knowledge and skill enhancement and development
			Promotion/transfer
Rightsizing	Restructuring	Employee exit and/or job restructuring/ elimination	Employee job exit Employee *voluntary* organisational exit: resignation; retirement Employee *involuntary* organisational exit: redundancy; dismissal

Performance management and learning and development are dealt with in later chapters.

We can see that decisions on recruitment and selection are embedded in a process of managing and developing the human resource flow through the organisation, entailing a range of HR practices, from analysing the key aspects of the job through to managing the exit of the employee from the job or organisation. This process itself is further embedded in long-term HR decisions and actions, and HR experts often talk about 'strategic selection', at least for key employees.

In the twenty-first century it is no longer sufficient just to hire the right staff – the HR talent must be managed and developed to achieve and sustain competitive advantage. This is not bad news for HR departments: *The Economist* under the subheading 'The triumph of the HR department' could write (*A Survey of Talent*, 7–14 October 2006; p.6):

> Managing talent has become more important to a much wider range of companies than it used to be. One result has been that human resources departments which used to be quiet backwaters have gained in status. A survey by Aon, a consultancy, identified 172 HR executives who were among the five best-paid managers in their companies. That would have been unheard of a few years ago.

RECRUITMENT AND SELECTION

Before you can manage the talent of your human resources you have first to get hold of it. You must hire people with the knowledge, skills and attitudes you require. Taking the long-term aspect, you want core employees who can continue to adapt and learn, so that there is a better probability that your organisation can sustain competitive advantage in the future. And from that long-term perspective, attitude and capability or potential may be more important than current skills and knowledge.

How do organisations get the human resources they need? We might distinguish six possible theoretical models of personnel selection for organisations (as derived and developed from Bass and Barrett, 1981):

- *the trial or 'try it and see' model*, in which everyone who is interested is allowed to 'have a go' at the job or role, and only some are kept on after their performance in the role has been assessed
- *the 'lottery' model* or random selection, in which a number of people are started on a chance basis
- *the 'quota' model*, by which it is required by law, or policy, that a fixed number or percentage of post-holders should be of a specific type – eg gender or ethnic group
- *the 'common sense and experience' model*, where selection is on the basis

of the sort of people who have proved to be associated with successful job performance in the past

- *the 'matching attributes' model*, where selection is made on the basis of attempting to identify and to match attributes which the applicant possesses and which it is assumed predict job success

- *the 'competency' model* – a refinement of the matching attributes model – where emphasis is placed on the applicant's possession of certain particular traits or abilities, or the ability to perform to a specified standard (or some combination of both of these requirements).

Of course not all of these models are practicable in the real world of work.

The 'try it and see' model

No one would wish to be operated on a by a surgeon recruited under such a scheme, because he or she, however well motivated, might be completely unqualified. Clubs and voluntary organisations obviously work on this basis in acquiring new members and so there are no entrance criteria for the Girl Guides or Boy Scouts, for instance (other than age and gender). As far as paid employment is concerned, however, unless there are absolutely no skill or knowledge requirements for the job, this is a very costly method because there is no guarantee that anyone who wants to join the organisation can actually do the specified job. It is completely unrealistic for most organisations. A partial exception might be voluntary workers for charities – but even in that case there are usually some minimal requirements such as basic numeracy and literacy that not everyone in society meets.

We have to remember that ideally we want to be able to make quick and accurate decisions over whether an applicant can do the job effectively before committing the organisation to hiring them. Hiring is a costly business: the CIPD has estimated that the average cost of filling a vacancy in the UK is £4,000, rising to £6,125 when the associated labour turnover costs are also taken into account (CIPD, 2010b). A wrong hiring decision is of course even more expensive – not only do you have to do it all over again to get it right, you have to bear the consequences of incompetent performance until you do.

The 'lottery' model

This is where people are allocated by means of random selection to the posts or to the organisation. This will obviously be unsuitable for commercial and most other types of organisation for the same reasons that the 'try it and see' model is – there can be no guarantee of even minimal competence or qualification. It can be appropriate where the task or job is seen to be a necessary civic duty – eg jury duty or military service, although in the latter there will be minimum physical standards to meet.

The 'quota' model

Usually this would be dictated by law or organisational policy. For example, universities in the USA are required to take set quotas of students from specified ethnic groups. This can achieve desirable social goals but might obviously be at the cost of effectiveness in any particular instance.

The next three models are all variants on a general approach of trying to find in some systematic and objective way an individual who matches the job requirements.

The 'common sense and experience' model

Using experience would seem to be sensible but can lead to difficulties when employed crudely. For example, a highway maintenance job might involve an element of heavy manual work.. Experience and 'common sense' might seem to dictate that men should be recruited rather than women because men are usually stronger. Leaving aside issues of illegal discrimination, this is misleading. It is strength not gender that will determine whether the job can be performed properly; and although on average men are stronger than women, some women are stronger than some men, and so some good applicants would be lost to the organisation if only men were hired.

The 'matching attributes' model

This is a model in which selection is made on the basis of attributes which the applicant must possess in order to do the job properly. It is assumed that these attributes can be assessed in some way prior to employment, and that such judgements can predict job success reliably. This model should avoid the difficulties noted with the common sense and experience model because the selection of individuals should ignore factors that are not relevant to job success, such as age, race, gender, residence or occupation of parents. In the example given above, organisations following this model would find out the level of strength necessary to do the highway maintenance job, devise tests to measure the lifting ability of applicants, and then make the selection on the basis of the intrinsic abilities of individuals, not what group they belonged to. Of course, a corollary of using this approach is that the organisation has to know in some detail what is required to do the job properly – the skills, knowledge, attitudes and so forth – ie it must identify the *criteria for job success*. This approach is capable of considerable refinement and can be highly sophisticated, using, for instance, a battery of psychometric and other tests. It is sometimes referred to as the 'selection paradigm' (Keenan, 2005), implying an ideal model of selection. However, as we will see shortly, it has not been developed to the point of becoming an exact science and no selection process, however sophisticated, is infallible.

The 'competency' model

In this model a 'competency framework' is established for the job to be filled. Depending on the type of competency model used, this framework will either be a list of aptitudes or characteristics or other inputs which are required (eg 'leadership') or it will consist of specific behaviours or other outputs that are necessary for job success (eg being able to read a balance sheet). Although the former is not so very different from the selection paradigm noted above, the latter specifies actual performance which must be achieved, and not just the potential to do so.

Competency models are increasingly popular with organisations.

HRM in action

CASE STUDY

Competency work pays off for council

Westminster City Council has introduced a competency framework, attracting interest from 25 other London boroughs and councils. Described as the 'golden thread running through the people management process', the framework is being used to drive the people management agenda, Tony Reynolds, organisational development manager, told *PM*.

The model was launched in January 2005, with 16 different competencies, each split into four levels, which correspond to the organisational structure. All positions at the Council have six to eight critical role competencies. 'These are the behaviours we want to recruit, develop, manage and reward,' Reynolds said.

More than 100 staff across the Council shaped the framework. After its launch, learning and development was restructured and a bank of self-development resources created. Feedback has been positive. A staff survey recently found that 80% of staff were already aware of the framework and 51% found it useful.

The next stage of the programme is talent management. 'We don't do enough,' Reynolds said. 'We want to work with our managers on talent identification and start to invest much more energy in developing and retaining these staff.'

Source: *People Management*, 29 June 2006

REFLECTIVE ACTIVITY

Consider how people are recruited into your organisation. Which of the models above best described the process involved?

Would another model give better results? If so, why?

This text is mainly concerned with the last two models of selection because they are the most appropriate ones for professional managers to operate. One of the key points to note is that in any systematic approach to selecting personnel, the selection decision is based on the organisation's making a prediction over whether or not a particular candidate could achieve job success.

JOB ANALYSIS AND PERSONNEL SPECIFICATION

The first step in the process of managing and developing the human resource flow (Table 3) is a decision about what the job is and what qualities are needed for its effective performance. At one extreme, job analysis may reveal that the requirements of the job are such that most of the employable population are capable of performing it adequately with appropriate initial training, and if so, hardly any effort at selection is warranted. At the other extreme – for example, the selection of astronauts – the job may call for a set of qualities that are rarely found in a single person within the population, and so demand a highly sophisticated (and expensive) selection procedure.

In any event, before hiring, the organisation should have identified the criteria for job success and the characteristics required of the job-holder in order to achieve this success. This is true whether the job is stacking cans on a supermarket shelf, being a member of a multi-skilled autonomous work team or, indeed, that of an astronaut.

The 'personnel specification' for the job – the list of the various attributes which successful candidates should have in order to achieve job success – can be usefully structured to assist the decision-maker(s) at the selection phase. Two frameworks often used in the UK are the Rodger's Seven-Point Plan and the Munro Fraser Fivefold Grading System. A basic outline of both frameworks is shown below.

Alec Rodger's Seven-Point Plan	The Munro Fraser Fivefold Grading System
• physical make-up	• impact on others
• attainments	
• general intelligence	• qualifications or acquired knowledge
• special aptitudes	• innate abilities
• interests	
• disposition	• motivation
• circumstances	• adjustment or emotional balance

RECRUITMENT AND SELECTION (HIRING)

If we remember that recruitment and selection are parts of a connected system of managing and developing our human resources (Table 3), we can appreciate that decisions taken in these earlier stages will impact on later stages. For instance, if after establishing the requirements for job success we then lower the specified standards in terms of skills, knowledge or attitudes for job success, we will inevitably have either to accept a lower level of performance in the job or take some form of remedial action at a later stage – eg initial training – both of which would incur additional costs to the organisation.

Decision-makers in the recruitment and selection process must try to make rational choices, for which they need information. Decision-makers ideally should limit their information-gathering to procedures in which the usefulness of the additional information justifies the cost of gathering it. However, this is not an exact science and organisations usually have no idea whether the cost of using, say, a particular psychological test, is justified. Common sense should be applied: a poor chief executive might destroy the firm, so nobody doubts the wisdom of gathering as much useful and relevant information as possible, even if this is expensive and time-consuming. But would you really spend as much time, effort and money in choosing a new caretaker?

In essence, the information gathered in the selection process is used to predict likely success on the job if the individual is to be employed. All such predictions are liable to error, because no selection process can give wholly accurate predictions of future success.

👁 HRM DILEMMA

If we raise the bar, we reject more candidates who could do the job.

Two kinds of decision error may occur in every selection process, however constituted:

(i) 'false positives' or erroneous acceptances, where applicants are selected but prove to be inadequate, and

(ii) 'false negatives' or erroneous rejections, where applicants who would have performed adequately are rejected.

Employing organisations are more concerned about false positives because they lead to incompetent performance and expensive mistakes. Accordingly, it makes sense for such organisations to raise entry requirements to reduce the probability of false positives – even though this inevitably increases the probability of false negatives. The consequences of this is that a greater number of applicants who are actually capable of doing the job will be erroneously categorised by the selection process as not meeting the required standards and so be rejected.

In other spheres the question of false negatives may be of more significance – for example, in education where (ideally) there is concern that opportunities should be equitably distributed. Where there are no funding constraints a college might deliberately lower entrance requirements for a programme. This would result in increased failure rates overall if academic standards were kept at the same level as before, but would reduce the number of false negatives. It would give a greater number of capable applicants the educational opportunity, at the cost in this case of increased false positives – students who are accepted on the programme but who are discovered not to have the capabilities to succeed in it.

'STRATEGIC SELECTION'

The selection decision has always been important. We noted above that wrong selection decisions always incur costs to the organisation, both from the damage an incompetent employee might do, and of simply having to go through the process of hiring someone else. The more senior the employee, the greater the effects of incompetence: an office worker might lose data and even some customers, but an inept CEO could destroy the firm. The better an organisation's overall selection process, the better it should perform collectively, and this has obviously always been true. However, HRM literature suggests that the selection decision now has even greater importance for organisations.

- Changes in the labour market have brought about a more diverse workforce. This increases the pool of available talent but also raises questions of fairness and equality which must be addressed, not only to ensure legal compliance but to exploit fully the talent available in the market.

- In the light of the increasing need for multi-skilled flexible workforces and teamworking, selection becomes less a matter of matching an individual to the fixed requirements of a clearly defined job – immediate skills and experience may be less important than adaptability, willingness to learn and ability to work in a team. In a word, modern organisations typically need fewer employees, but these must be of a higher calibre than was often the case in the past. There are fewer and fewer unskilled and low-skilled jobs in advanced economies.

- The need to establish a close relationship between corporate competitive strategies and HRM has produced the concept of 'strategic selection' in which the selection system supports the overall current and future business strategies. As we saw in Chapter 1, this underpins the whole idea of HRM as an approach to managing people.

For these reasons organisations are now more likely than hitherto to use relatively costly techniques that previously would have been reserved for senior high-salary positions, such as psychometric testing or assessment centres, for selection for ordinary jobs (see the Asda example below in the next 'HRM in action' case study).

REFLECTIVE ACTIVITY

Think about how you were appointed to your present job. Clearly, the right decision was made! But as a professional manager, how would you rate the effectiveness of the process?

What could you do to make it more efficient in the future?

SOME COMMON SELECTION TECHNIQUES

The most common predictors used in the selection process are interviews, tests, information from application forms or letters, curricula vitae (CVs) or résumés, and references from previous employers.

The interview

The interview is widely used and heavily relied upon, probably because of low cost, high perceived applicability and just general familiarity. There is, however, a large body of evidence that its reliability and validity are surprisingly *un*impressive (example: Hakel, 1982). The difficulty is that although we can make real – and worthwhile – attempts to improve our effectiveness at interviews (see below), there are limits to what can be achieved. The problem is intrinsic to the technique: people are just not all that good at making decisions in such contexts.

Limitations of the selection interview process

Interviewers pay too much attention to first impressions, and information obtained early in the interview has a disproportionate effect on the final outcome. Interviewers tend to compare candidates to ideal stereotypes and are prone to falling for 'contrast effects' by which a candidate's performance is unconsciously exaggerated by the interviewer in comparison with that of a previous applicant (eg after a very good candidate the next one may look poorer than he/she actually is, or perhaps even better). Interviewers are also liable to be influenced by 'halo effects' by which one characteristic of the candidate overshadows others – eg what school or university they attended. This effect can be positive or negative.

Interviewers also make decisions very early. One classic study in Canada found that in a series of 30-minute interviews the interviewers made their decisions on the suitability of a candidate in an average of four minutes! This begs the question: what were they doing for the other 26 minutes? And the answer is almost certainly that they were seeking information to rationalise or support the decision they had already privately made.

Organisations will never abandon interviewing as a selection tool. No sensible organisation hires anyone without first seeing them in person, but many seek to improve its usefulness by using it in a more systematic way, and also by supplementing it with the use of tests or other techniques designed to obtain more relevant information about the candidate.

Some hints for interviewers

It is possible to improve the effectiveness of one's interview technique. Prior to conducting it, develop a 'game plan' for the interview to cover building rapport with the candidate, obtaining information, *providing* information (salary and other rewards, of course, but also main terms and conditions of employment; superannuation, sick pay, etc) and answering questions. This should be based on current job information. A plan is particularly important for panel interviews in which a team of people jointly conduct the interview.

- Outline the game plan to the applicant at the start of the interview.
- Try to put the applicant at ease.
- Follow a common format for all applicants.
- In general, avoid leading and closed questions.
- Provide a realistic and specific description of the job and organisation.
- The applicant should do most of the talking (aim for, say, 75%).
- Develop active listening skills.
- Develop skills to observe non-verbal communication.

- Make notes during the interview and complete your record of it immediately after it.
- Be fully informed of all relevant legal, policy and ethical issues.
- Get feedback on the subsequent job performance of successful applicants so that you have some basis for assessing the usefulness of your interviewing in predicting job success.

The information obtained from selection interviews may often be supplemented by information obtained by other means, which may include psychological tests.

Psychological testing

Psychological testing involves a varied set of instruments which are usually categorised as intelligence tests, ability and aptitude tests, and/or personality tests. The latter are the most controversial but are generally viewed as being popular, especially in the case of recruitment for 'greenfield sites' (ie completely new enterprises).

It has been estimated that there are over 5,000 psychological instruments available in the English language (Toplis et al, 1987). Pearn et al (1987) commented that the question of the usefulness of personality assessment was probably the most controversial subject in occupational psychology. A review of the available evidence in the USA (Schmitt et al, 1984) suggested that ability and aptitude tests have only a modest degree of predictive accuracy so far as job performance is concerned, personality tests being even less successful (although ability and aptitude tests could give better results than unstructured interviews).

In response to concern about the abuse of psychological tests, the Chartered Institute of Personnel and Development has issued guidance on the subject (CIPD, 2006c). This recommends the use of Chartered Psychologists to administer and interpret tests, invokes the observance of strict confidentiality, and stipulates the necessity to provide feedback for applicants.

Remember: a poor test, or a good test which is poorly administered, is much worse than no test at all.

Management assessment centres

An assessment centre is a procedure (not a location!) that uses multiple assessment techniques to evaluate employees for a variety of manpower purposes and decisions. The assessment centre approach may use techniques such as tests, questionnaires and the use of background information. Information is gathered in a standardised and controllable manner on behaviour that is representative for future job behaviour. The assessment centre method is used with particular success as a method for potential evaluation and management development.

Assessment centres typically feature:

- the use of multiple assessment techniques
- the use of simulations and work sampling

- observation by multiple observers
- assessment by trained assessors
- the separation of observation and evaluation.

SO HOW EFFECTIVE IS SELECTION?

Muchinsky (1986) summarised the effectiveness of selection techniques as follows:

- No single method was simultaneously high on validity, fairness and applicability and low on cost: so a series of trade-offs was necessary.
- The single method that came closest to the ideal was biographical information ('biodata'), but while high on validity and applicability and low on cost, it was only moderate on fairness.
- Techniques that scored highest on validity were assessment centres, work samples and biographical information.
- Interviewing was low on validity, moderate on fairness, high on applicability and low on cost.
- Personality tests were moderate on validity, high on fairness, low on applicability and moderate on cost.
- Assessment centres were high on validity, high on fairness, low on applicability (beyond management grades) and high on cost.

RECRUITMENT AND SELECTION IN PRACTICE

As noted in Chapter 1, the findings of the 2004 Workplace Employment Relations Survey in the UK reinforced the view that many organisations operated a 'flexible organisation' with a 'core' of key employees and a 'peripheral' workforce of other workers. Most (83%) of workplaces had part-time employees, and in 30% of all workplaces more than half of the workforce were part-time employees. Just under one-third (30%) of workplaces had employees on temporary contracts. The use of temporary agency staff was quite widespread, 17% of all workplaces employing 'temps'. About one-fifth (22%) of workplaces gave preference to internal applicants when recruiting, and the proportion was higher for the private sector (25%).

It is beyond the scope of the present text to offer a detailed discussion of exactly why most organisations pursue flexibility. It is the accepted economic wisdom adopted not only by national governments but also by international organisations such as the International Labour Organisation (ILO) and the Organisation for Economic Co-operation and Development (OECD and supranational entities such as the European Union (EU) that flexible labour markets are a prerequisite for economic growth in a competitive global marketplace (Eurofound, 2010).

The selection process – as monitored by the 2004 survey – usually involved the use of interviews, application forms and references. Personality or competency tests, although used less often, had gained in importance in the search for greater objectivity in selection, despite continuing debate about their validity and reliability. Among workplaces using personality tests, three-fifths (61%) of managers said that they used these tests when recruiting core employees. Performance or competency tests were routinely used in 46% of workplaces and were also more likely to be used when recruiting core employees, irrespective of their occupation. Overall, one-third (34%) of all workplaces used such tests for these recruits.

The CIPD 2009 *Recruitment, Retention and Turnover Survey* of some 755 UK organisations (CIPD, 2010b) found that:

- The average recruitment cost of filling a vacancy per employee was £4,000, rising to £6,125 when the associated labour turnover costs were also taken into account.
- The most commonly used methods for attracting candidates were i) the organisation's own corporate website (78% of all organisations surveyed), ii) recruitment agencies (76%), and iii) local newspapers (70%).
- Competency-based interviews (69%) and interviews based on the contents of the CV/résumé or application form (68%) were the most frequently used selection methods.

Recruiting online

The CIPD 2006 *Recruitment, Retention and Turnover Survey* (CIPD, 2006b) found that:

- The trend for e-recruitment is growing – almost two-thirds (64%) of the organisations surveyed used technology to aid their recruitment process during 2005.
- The greatest usage was email and online applications, advertising job vacancies and placing background information on corporate websites.
- Reducing recruitment costs was the main business objective for developing e-recruitment (71% of organisations).
- Nearly half of respondents (47%) strongly agreed that e-recruitment would replace paper-based applications in the future, *but –*
- The same number believed the trend towards e-recruitment was increasing the number of unsuitable applications.

INDUCTION

The purpose of induction is to assist new starters to integrate effectively within the organisation. Research has shown that tailor-made induction programmes increase staff retention (CIPD, 2010b). Normally, a person goes through induction only once, when first joining the organisation, at which time many organisations use the induction process to introduce new staff to their organisational culture and system of values.

A good induction programme contains the following elements:

- physical orientation, describing where the various facilities are

- organisational orientation – showing how the employee fits into the team and how their role fits with the organisation's strategy and goals

- an awareness of other functions within the organisation, and how the employee fits within that framework

- meeting key senior employees (face to face or via technology)

- health and safety information (which is a legal requirement in the UK)

- details of the organisation's history, its products and services, its culture and values

- a clear outline of the new starter's job/role requirements and an explanation of the main terms and conditions of employment.

Because of its cross-organisational aspects induction is normally coordinated and largely delivered by the central Human Resources function.

TALENT MANAGEMENT

The consultancy firm McKinsey is credited with coining the expression 'war for talent', by which it meant the increasingly competitive market for key employees in the knowledge economy. 'Talent management' combines the traditional responsibilities of recruitment and selection with development activities which include 'succession planning'. In one sense it is the twenty-first-century version of an old description of the function of personnel management: 'getting the right person in the right job at the right time' – but now the 'right person' is likely to possess key skills and knowledge, hold considerable market value and require (and demand) continuous development. Talent management is another of the HRM activities which applies to the core but probably not the periphery.

Definitions vary but within the UK HR profession the emphasis is certainly on the management development and succession planning areas, as revealed by the CIPD 2006 Learning and Development Survey (CIPD, 2006a). Respondents were asked to identify the main objectives of 'talent management'. Responses are shown in Table 4. We can see that talent management straddles both recruitment and selection, and learning and development, but is predominantly 'future-focused'.

The business case for taking a strategic approach to talent management is now seen as persuasive by many organisations. Increasingly, competitive global markets, skills shortages, demographic trends, corporate governance issues and business strategy are all seen as main drivers for increased interest in talent management (CIPD, 2010a). Its meaning has evolved to cover a range of HR areas including organisational capability, individual development, performance enhancement and succession planning.

Table 4 The objectives of talent management

Main objectives of talent management	Percentage of respondents
Developing high-potential individuals	67%
Growing future senior managers	62%
Enabling the achievement of strategic goals	42%
Meeting future skills requirements	38%
Attracting and recruiting key staff	36%
Retaining key staff	33%
Supporting changes	17%
Addressing skills shortages	16%
Assisting organisational resource planning	13%
Redeployment of staff to other roles	12%
Other	2%

Source: the CIPD 2006 *Learning and Development Survey*

The CIPD defines key terms in talent management as follows:

- Talent consists of those individuals who can make a difference to organisational performance, either through their immediate contribution or in the longer term by demonstrating the highest levels of potential.
- Talent management is the systematic attraction, identification, development, engagement/retention and deployment of those individuals who are of particular value to an organisation, either in view of their 'high potential' for the future or because they are fulfilling business/operation-critical roles.

Many organisations are also responding to the downturn which started in 2007 by adopting positive talent management practices, such as developing more in-house talent, continuing to recruit key talent and increasing their focus on employee retention (Murphy, 2009).

The CIPD 2010 *Learning and Talent Development Survey* (CIPD, 2010a) found that:

- Almost six in ten (59%) organisations undertake talent management activities. Among these, half (50%) rate them as 'effective', although only 3% consider them 'very effective'.
- Talent management activities tend to be directed at high-potential employees and senior managers.
- The main objectives of talent management activities are to develop high-potential employees (67%) and to grow future senior managers/leaders (67%). The third main objective is to meet the future skills requirements of the organisation (36%).

- The three most effective activities to manage talent are coaching (39%), in-house development programmes (32%), and high-potential development schemes (31%).

- The three most common ways to evaluate talent management activities are to obtain feedback from line managers (42%), to measure the retention of those identified as high-potential (35%), and the anecdotal observation of change (35%).

HRM in action

Online tests boost jobs at Asda

Online personality testing at Asda has led to the supermarket chain running fewer assessment centres and making more job offers.

Judith Colbert, resourcing manager at Asda, said: 'The new process has ensured that we see the top 20% of candidates at interview stage, rather than 50%, as before.' She added: 'It's more consistent and we're getting a much better fit and are filling vacancies quicker.'

The online assessment – which was introduced for graduates last October and managers in January – is designed to match candidates' personalities with Asda's brand values. It involves a personality questionnaire, ability test and further questions about their CV and previous experience. Alan Redman, business psychologist at Criterion Partnership, which worked with Asda on the online assessment, said: 'All of Asda's processes are about hiring people for attitude. Candidates who don't share their values won't enjoy working there.'

The online tests have also cut costs, he said: 'Generally, the most expensive part of recruitment is hiring assessment centres. By raising the calibre of people you are interviewing, you no longer see people who are clearly unsuitable.'

Redman added that the tool had helped to reduce HR's workload by weeding out the bottom 80% of candidates. Last year Asda had 15,000 applications for 750 manager roles and 8,500 applications for 60 graduate scheme places.

Source: *People Management*, 13 July 2006

CASE STUDY

REFLECTIVE ACTIVITY

What do you think of Asda's process of selecting people via an online personality profile, as reported in *People Management*?

Would it work for your organisation?

Why/why not?

CASE STUDY

HRM in action

Employee resourcing for the Dubai Metro

The Dubai Metro has not only broken new ground in terms of technology – it also stands out because of the recruitment and employment practices used by its operator, Serco.

With its fully automated, driverless trains, the new Dubai Metro may be a technical triumph. But its launch last year would have hit the buffers if it hadn't been for an HR team working quietly – and very quickly – behind the scenes.

'As with all transport projects that carry people, it's a customer service operation,' says Nick Brown, chief executive of Serco's Integrated Transport and Middle East division, which runs the Metro. 'So while there was a huge investment in concrete and steel and state-of-the-art systems, the thing that makes the customer experience is the people who operate the railway, and I would say that the recruitment of the people, the people themselves and their training were all world class.'

When Serco won the £500 million, 10-year contract to operate and maintain the Dubai Metro in March 2008, it was already running air traffic control operations in Dubai, Abu Dhabi and some of the smaller states in the United Arab Emirates (UAE), as well as in Bahrain. But the company, which had not been involved in constructing the Metro, had only around 700 employees in the region, and needed to recruit an additional 2,000 or so. All this had to be done by 9 September 2009, the opening date for the Metro set by Dubai's ruler, Sheikh Mohammed bin Rashid Al Maktoum.

Dubai's migrant workers

Dubai is one of the seven emirates in the United Arab Emirates. Foreign nationals make up over 90% of its population, which grew from under 200,000 in 1975 to 1.5 million in 2008. With revenues from oil – currently accounting for around 6% of GDP – in decline, Dubai's efforts to diversify its economy have fuelled a construction boom in recent years.

But reports of the exploitation of migrant workers, especially in the construction industry, have taken some of the shine off the Gulf city-state's spectacular growth. According to campaign organisation Human Rights Watch, the plight of these workers has worsened across the UAE since the global financial crisis slowed down construction, with some sent home on unpaid 'vacations' by employers wanting to avoid paying compensation for breaking their contracts. However, the international NGO's World Report 2010 also highlights positive developments, notably last year's decision by the UAE cabinet to introduce compulsory housing standards for migrant workers, although employers will have five years to comply with the new rules.

Under the terms of its contract with Dubai's Roads and Transport Authority (RTA), Serco had to ensure that 30% of all management and supervisory positions on the Metro were filled by UAE citizens. There were similar targets for other roles further down the line. But with operational railway experience in short supply in a region without an existing rail network, not all of these targets could realistically be met in the short term. So while trying to hire as many local people as possible and succeeding in filling a high proportion of senior positions with Emiratis, Serco, like other major employers in Dubai, looked further afield for the bulk of its new workforce.

Michael Donnelly, HR director for Serco Middle East, who joined the company in January 2009, describes how teams of recruiters and operational leaders flew to India, the Philippines, Thailand, Malaysia and other countries in Asia and beyond. Although they used local recruitment agencies, they took care to avoid those that would charge jobseekers for finding them work – a widespread practice that leaves many migrant workers around the world heavily indebted to agents in their home countries. 'So ahead of going out to these countries we carried out due diligence and pre-qualified these agencies to make sure that they weren't taking money from candidates,' says Donnelly. 'We came across a couple of agencies where that's what they were trying to do and we quickly dropped them because we wouldn't tolerate what we saw as an abuse of the people who were going to work for us.'

The recruiters spent a couple of weeks in each location, running daily assessment centres and testing as many as 100 people at a time. In all they tested over 5,000 candidates both for their knowledge of English – crucial in an organisation where this was the main working language – and the attention skills and other aptitudes needed in a safety-critical environment. This recruitment drive produced a workforce consisting of 22 different nationalities, including Filipinos and Indians (the two largest groups), Malaysians, Thais, Pakistanis, Lebanese, Brits and other Europeans. There are also more than 100 Emiratis.

But finding people to work on the new Metro was only the first of the challenges facing Donnelly and his team. They then had to apply for work visas and permits for the new recruits, fly them to Dubai and provide them with both practical and emotional support when they arrived at their unfamiliar destination.

Because of the tight time-scale, the company decided to outsource around 900 cleaning and security roles to other suppliers. But that still left more than 1,000 employees who needed to be found suitable accommodation. Dubai's laws also had to be considered when it came to allocating accommodation to employees. In order to comply with rules governing segregation of the sexes in this Islamic society, male and female employees were housed on separate floors in the staff accommodation blocks.

As part of their week-long induction on arriving in Dubai, employees received two days of cross-cultural training designed both to help them understand and respect colleagues from other countries and to introduce them to the local culture and what is and is not acceptable behaviour in Dubai. As Donnelly says: 'Something like showing the palm of your left hand, which may be inoffensive behaviour in your home country, can be extremely offensive here.'

Source: *People Management*, 6 May 2010

EMPLOYEE EXIT

GENERAL CONSIDERATIONS

The employee relationship may end voluntarily when the employee chooses to leave the organisation to take up a position elsewhere, or it may finish at the end of a person's career by retirement at an agreed age, or the person may have to leave involuntarily through ill-health, dismissal or redundancy. Some authorities argue (Armstrong, 2009) that employee exits are increasingly likely to be involuntary as competitive pressures from technological advances and globalisation continually force firms to reduce costs even when profitable.

All HR issues regarding employee exit must be dealt with in the framework of relevant current employment legislation. We do not deal in detail with employment law in this text but up-to-date guidance for both employees and employers in the UK may be found at the Government website http://www.tiger.gov.uk/ (TIGER stands for 'tailored interactive guidance on employment rights'). The Advisory, Conciliation and Arbitration Service (ACAS) website http://www.acas.org.uk is also helpful, especially on employee relations issues.

THE ROLE OF THE HR FUNCTION IN ORGANISATIONAL RELEASE

The HR function is normally given the task of managing organisational release. When this is dealing with involuntary release it can be a hard and stressful duty. There are ethical and professional considerations. Managers have no choice, of course, about taking part in organisational redundancy or 'downsizing' programmes, but they can make an important contribution to managing the process in such a way as to minimise both the individual distress and trauma that redundancy can cause and the organisational damage that can result from ill-considered or badly implemented dismissals. Professionally, HR managers are obliged to ensure that dismissal and redundancy policies and practices are in line with legal requirements, codes of practice and relevant company policies. They can also argue for policies and actions that minimise unnecessary redundancies, and can emphasise the need to handle dismissals and redundancies sensitively. They can advise line managers on the approach to adopt, provide training, help them communicate decisions to employees and other stakeholders, and provide counselling and outplacement services to the staff who will be affected.

DISMISSAL

Some degree of legal protection is afforded to employees in most developed economies, but the nature and degree obviously differ from country to country. One of the prime HRM functions is to ensure that the organisation is legally compliant in dealing with employee issues – and in none more so than dismissal.

Any society which allows legal protection for employees will also provide a means of redress through the courts, or quasi-legal institutions such as the UK's employment tribunals, for the employee who has been 'unfairly' or illegally dismissed. In investigating any allegation of unfair dismissal such bodies will typically seek answers to two fundamental questions: 'Was there sufficient cause for dismissal?' and 'Did the employer act reasonably in the circumstances?'

Dismissals are usually held to be fair when the employee acted in a way that constituted misconduct. Actions such as theft or fighting at work, or being drunk, are termed 'gross misconduct' and might justify summary (ie immediate) dismissal without any further warning. In most other cases, however, employers will have to show that they followed some reasonable procedure which informed the employee of his or her unacceptable misbehaviour and gave him or her some opportunity to respond positively. Poor work performance on one occasion is very unlikely ever to be regarded as reasonable grounds for dismissal, for instance. Other reasons might include the employee's being unable to fulfil his or her contract of employment by reason of incapacity – and this can cover the employee's skill, aptitude and health (either physical or mental). This most often occurs when some change in a person's health renders incapable a previously

We should then turn to the role of the salesperson, the duties to be performed, the conditions under which the job is expected to be performed, and the KSAs needed. After that, the criteria for job success must be established and appropriate performance indicators developed. This job analysis should lead to the production of a job description and person specification.

We must then establish a systematic recruitment process that will be either the 'matching attributes' model, or the 'competency' model as defined earlier in this chapter.

Of course, the above procedure would be relevant for new staff we wished to employ. For the existing sales staff we should carry out other HR functions to help ensure that the high-performers stayed and that the lower-performers were brought up to acceptable levels of performance. Both types of performance will be required here (see Chapter 7). Stabilising the existing sales workforce would be a first priority, because that would then give us an indication of the staff-resourcing issues that remain.

GETTING THE BEST FROM ALL YOUR PEOPLE

People are not alike. Everyone is different. Diversity therefore consists of visible and non-visible factors, which include personal characteristics such as sex, race, age, background, culture, disability, personality and work-style. Harnessing these differences will create a productive environment in which everybody feels valued, their talents are fully utilised and organisational goals are met (CIPD, 2010c).

In many developed countries concerns about equal opportunities for women and for racial and ethnic minority groups started to find legal expression in the 1960s when governments passed laws that required employers not to discriminate on grounds of sex or race in employment matters, including pay. Other grounds such as disability or age or sexual orientation came to be included once a culture of acceptance of equal opportunities began to grow in society.

It became obvious that although a legal framework for equal opportunities was essential and achieved real progress in reducing discrimination, it had inevitable limitations in terms of producing equality of outcome.

Although the business case against discrimination was always a sound one, the original impetus for equal opportunities legislation was largely moral and social: to make a fairer and better world. These concerns are still with us, of course, and as the limitations of legislation became apparent there were calls for organisations to go beyond legislative minimum standards. Because the economy has become increasingly globalised over the past 25 years – workforces, customers and other stakeholders all becoming more diverse – organisations are now urged to positively adopt diversity in their human resource management.

And it seems that no matter how big your organisation is, you really do have to take issues of diversity seriously.

In February 2007 Wal-Mart – the world's biggest retailer and owner of the Asda supermarket chain – faced the biggest sexual discrimination case in US history when an appeal court ruled that the firm had to face a class-action lawsuit involving around 1.5 million women, who claimed that the retailer discriminated against them in terms of pay and promotion.

First, we will consider equal opportunities, and then we will proceed to discuss the somewhat wider issue of diversity.

EQUAL OPPORTUNITIES

THE DEFINITION OF DISCRIMINATION

Discrimination literally means distinguishing between people and therefore treating some differently from others. This is not always unlawful or bad management practice – for example, people are paid different wages depending on their status and skills. However, there are certain grounds on which an employer cannot lawfully discriminate against an employee. There are also other areas such as harassment and bullying of employees which might fall short of illegality but which are nonetheless both unethical and inefficient management.

If an employer treats an employee less favourably than another for an unlawful reason, the employee can take action against the employer. If an employer treats the employee unfairly for any other reason, this is not unlawful discrimination, just bad management.

TYPES OF DISCRIMINATION

Legislation protects employees from discrimination of different types.

Direct discrimination

Direct discrimination happens when an employer treats an employee less favourably because of, for example, their gender or race. (So it would be direct discrimination if an ordinary driving job was open only to male applicants.) In the UK there is legal protection on the basis of the 'protected characteristics' of age, disability, gender reassignment, marriage and civil partnership, pregnancy and maternity, race, religion or belief, sex, and sexual orientation.

Associative discrimination is an aspect of direct discrimination in which someone is discriminated against because they have an association with someone with a particular protected characteristic – for example, discriminating against someone because they are a carer for a disabled person.

Perceptive discrimination occurs another aspect of direct discrimination where the discrimination is because the discriminator thinks a person possesses a protected characteristic even if they do not. For example, if a manager discriminates against an employee because he or she thinks the person holds certain religious beliefs, this is perceptive discrimination even if in fact the person does not hold those beliefs.

Indirect discrimination

Indirect discrimination is when a condition that disadvantages one group of people more than another is applied to a job. For example, saying that applicants for a job must be clean-shaven puts members of some religious groups at a disadvantage. However, the law does allow employers to discriminate indirectly if they can show a good reason for retaining the condition. For example, the condition that applicants must be clean-shaven might be justified if the job involved handling food and it could be shown that having a beard or moustache was a genuine hygiene risk.

Harassment and victimisation

Harassment means offensive or intimidating behaviour – sexist language or racial abuse, for example – which aims to humiliate, undermine or injure its target.

Victimisation means persistently treating somebody less favourably than others through spite or in a spirit of revenge – perhaps because they tried to make a discrimination complaint.

WHY BOTHER ABOUT DIVERSITY?

There are three reasons why managers should be concerned with issues of equality and diversity at work: the moral case, the legal case, and the business case.

The moral case

Managers have a moral obligation to treat all employees fairly and equally as fellow human beings. Managers are in a position of some power over their staff and they should not abuse it by showing favouritism or prejudice. Most managers (though perhaps not all) would subscribe to this, and no organisation would wish to acquire a reputation for being immoral or unethical towards its own employees.

The legal case

Most countries have legal obligations not to discriminate on grounds of gender, race or religion. Other criteria are also often specified. For example, at the time of writing employees in the UK had legal protection against discrimination on the basis of the 'protected characteristics' noted above, namely age, disability, gender reassignment, marriage and civil partnership, pregnancy and maternity, race, religion or belief, sex, and sexual orientation. The Equality Act of 2010 consolidated nine previously specific pieces of anti-discrimination legislation.

Additionally, there was also legal protection for workers to prevent them being dismissed or treated less favourably than other workers because of working part-time or on a fixed-term contract.

This degree of protection for employees is fairly typical of most developed economies but may be untypical of some developing ones.

The business case

Any instance of discrimination means that the optimum use of the organisation's human resources has been impaired. Another consideration, noted above in connection with the moral case, is that quite apart from any legal sanction that might be applied, if a firm gets a reputation for discrimination, not only will that seriously affect the morale of its own employees who will fear being discriminated against personally, it will hurt its standing with customers and other stakeholders, including investors, and with potential recruits.

THE LIMITS OF LEGISLATION

Although legislation is recognised as essential in achieving equality at work, it has been found to be not sufficient and its limitations have become increasingly evident.

For example, according to the UK Government's Women and Equality Unit [website accessed 4 October 2007], in late 2006 – more than 30 years after legislation was passed outlawing pay discrimination in the UK – there was still a 'gender gap' between the pay of the sexes, men being paid on average some 13% more than women.

CASE STUDY

THE UK NEEDS MORE WOMEN AT TOP LEVEL

The UK needs more women at top level – but enforced boardroom quotas aren't the answer, says Ruth Spellman

This article by Ruth Spellman, Chief Executive of the Chartered Management Institute (CMI), appeared in People Management Online *at the beginning of November 2010.*

A recent report from the Equality and Human Rights Commission (EHRC), which echoed the findings of the CMI's research into gender pay, painted a stark picture of women's employment. It noted that women earned on average 16 per cent less than men – rising to 27 per cent once they reach 40 years of age – and that progress toward gender pay equality in the UK is 'grinding to a halt'.

Trevor Phillips, head of the EHRC, said: 'It shows that we are a people who have moved light years in our attitudes to all kinds of human difference, and in our desire to be a truly fair society, but that we are still a country where our achievements haven't yet caught up with our aspirations.'

Mr Phillips has a point. In a society that values tolerance and equality so highly, it is counter-intuitive to think that in 2010 women are denied the same pay as men for doing the same job, or struggle to be appointed into top boardroom positions purely because of their sex.

I was further struck by another recent report, of the top 300 European companies. Only 11.7 per cent of board seats were held by women – a staggering disparity.

So what's the answer? Here in the UK numerous initiatives have been launched to try and get more women into top jobs, but while progress has been made, there is much still to do.

There are some areas of business that continue to seem a closed shop to many women – mining and engineering spring to mind – while in other areas, the creative industries being one, women are comparatively well represented.

Some are calling for quotas at national and EU level to make sure that women are properly represented at the highest level. In Spain, where quotas were introduced in 2006, there was a 67 per cent increase in women being employed at board level.

All very well, but it's worth remembering that the UK, where no such quotas exist, is still fifth in the Europe-wide league table of female board members.

Personally, I have little time for quotas. I believe firmly in equality, but binding business up in unnecessary legislation seems heavy-handed and has the potential to create division that could hamper legitimate progress to the top for many women.

Businesses would be better off ensuring that their working practices and culture make women feel valued and respected at work while knowing their employer is supportive in terms of bringing up a family. In my experience, this is the dichotomy that many women face.

We live in a time where politicians squabble loudly over the very meaning of 'fairness'. Employers that support women to deliver the best they can professionally can take huge steps to defining that word themselves.

MANAGING DIVERSITY

Employers should follow a three-stage process to provide equality of opportunity:

- Formulate an explicit equal opportunities policy.
- Implement the policy.
- Monitor the policy to ensure its effectiveness in practice.

In the UK the Equality and Human Rights Commission publishes advice for employers on how to comply with their legal responsibilities.

Empirical evidence from the UK

The 2004 WERS survey found that 73% of UK workplaces (and 98% of public sector workplaces) had a written, formal equal opportunities policy or a policy on managing diversity, and 88% of UK employees in establishments were covered by such a policy – but 72% of workplaces neither negotiated, consulted nor informed employee representatives over equal opportunities.

Only 26% of workplaces reviewed selection and other procedures to identify indirect discrimination.

UK workplaces were revealed to be pretty bad at monitoring their equal opportunities practices, some 63% of workplaces doing no reviewing or monitoring at all. So it perhaps remains an open question whether the equal opportunities legislation would have a greater impact in the UK if employers exerted more effort to monitor and review their own stated policies.

JOB EVALUATION

Job evaluation schemes are used by employers to help ensure that pay and grading systems at the workplace fairly reflect the skill requirements (Chapter 7). There are a number of different types of job evaluation but there are two main classes: analytical and non-analytical. Non-analytical job evaluation seeks to compare whole jobs and to use relatively simple techniques such as job ranking. Analytical schemes compare jobs on a range of common factors – eg the level of skill, the amount of physical effort needed, the degree of responsibility, etc, each of which may be rated differently from job to job. Each factor can be weighted and then scored for each job, the total points rating for the job determining its relative position in the whole jobs hierarchy. Different jobs with the same overall points ratings are regarded as demanding an equal amount of work however different the actual tasks might be. For instance, a canteen server and a cleaner undertake different physical tasks but an analytical rating scheme might place both jobs in the same band of points and thus the jobs would attract the same basic pay.

The persistence of job evaluation schemes in the twenty-first century may seem something of a mystery in the present age of flat and flexible organisational structures and more individualised performance-related pay systems – it has a flavour of personnel management about it rather than human resource management. In fact, although the first three WERS surveys asked questions about job evaluation at the workplace, this was dropped from the 1998 survey and only reinstated for the 2004 one. The main reason it is still so important, at least for large employers, is that only an analytical job evaluation scheme can provide a legal defence against an equal pay claim at a tribunal.

The 2004 WERS survey (Kersley *et al*, 2006; pp244–7) found that 20% of all workplaces had job evaluation schemes, but the percentage rose significantly with size of the workplace as measured by number of employees: 35% of those with 100 to 199 employees had one; 36% of those with 200 to 499; and a majority – 54% – of those workplaces with 500 or more employees used job evaluation. The reason is quite clear: larger employers are more vulnerable to equal pay claims, which are often supported by trade unions. Job evaluation is also more prevalent in the public sector, 42% of all organisations in that sector operating a scheme, as opposed to 16% in the private sector. This probably reflects both size and trade union influence.

KEY ISSUES

In this chapter we have been concerned with 'employee flow' through the organisation; in particular, with how the organisation obtains the human resources it needs and how it manages the exit of employees. We first discussed some basic underlying principles involved in recruitment and selection, and two important findings soon emerged. First, that recruitment and selection should be seen as stages in a wider process of managing the human resource flow. This is because decisions made at the recruitment or selection stages will inevitably impact on later activities such as need for training and level of job performance. Second, that organisations should recruit using a model based on initially identifying the criteria for job success and then systematically seeking applicants with the necessary qualities to achieve that success. We noted that in the twenty-first century capability and attitude were often more important than the possession of particular knowledge or skills at the time of recruitment. A competency framework is often useful in recruitment and selection. Some of the most commonly used selection techniques were examined. We introduced the concept of talent management which in a sense bridges recruitment and selection and employee development.

The 'war for talent' – the increasingly competitive market for key employees – has become an important aspect of employee resourcing. Many organisations now employ 'talent management' strategies, at least for their core employees, which combine the traditional responsibilities of recruitment and selection with development activities and succession planning.

All employees will eventually leave the organisation, and this process also has to be managed. After some general considerations of the question of dismissal we examined some of the issues surrounding redundancy and how that can be managed.

Legal compliance with discrimination legislation is obviously obligatory and is a key responsibility of the HRM function, which should take a corporate lead on the issue. But day-to-day compliance demands that line managers and supervisors are aware of company polices and procedures and must be trained accordingly.

Compliance is necessary but is not enough. You are not going to win the war for talent if potential key employees shun you because they believe that they will be discriminated against in any way. Organisations that want to succeed must ruthlessly eliminate any discrimination in the workplace and build a genuine culture of valuing diversity.

EXPLORE FURTHER

Armstrong, M. (2009) *Armstrong's Handbook of Human Resource Management Practice*. 11th Edition. London: Kogan Page.

Chapters 28 to 37: 'People Resourcing'. Useful outlines of resourcing strategy, human resource planning, recruitment, selection, talent and career management, induction and organisational exit.

Boxall, P., Purcell, J. and Wright, P. (eds) (2007). *The Oxford Handbook of Human Resource Management*. Oxford: Oxford University Press.

Chapter 14. M. Orlitzky. 'Recruitment strategy'.

Chapter 15. N. Schmitt and B. Kim. 'Selection decision-making'.

Kersley, B., Alpin, C., Forth, J., Bryson, A., Bewley, H., Dix, G. and Oxenbridge, S. (2006) *Inside the Workplace: Findings from the 2004 Workplace Employment Relations Survey*. Abingdon: Routledge.

Chapter 4 'Recruitment, training and work organisation'

Storey, J. (ed.) (2007) *Human Resource Management: A critical text*, 3rd edition. London: Thomson Learning

Chapter 6. P. Iles. 'Employee resourcing and talent management'.

CHAPTER 5

Human resource development

INTRODUCTION

In the HRM paradigm there is much greater emphasis on development than in the personnel management paradigm, and this is extended to cover all core employees. The terms 'employee development' (ED) and 'human resource development' (HRD) are often preferred to the earlier terms of 'training' and 'management development', and they cover both sorts of activity. Recently, 'talent development' (TD) has become a preferred term among HR professionals to describe the 'high end' of HRD. TD has been defined as a set of processes which 'aim to ensure that those who are identified with potential receive the right experience and learn the right skills required to progress' (CIPD, 2010a; p.1).

Learning and development interventions can span external education and in-house activities, both formal and informal. There has been a cultural change in most developed economies over the past few decades in that the intention in HRD/TD now is often to facilitate learning and personal development rather than to impose formal training on individuals.

There is also greater emphasis on informal learning at all levels, including self-development, which formerly might have been occurring in many instances but was virtually never recognised. There are limits to this, of course, and it would be wrong to suppose that conventional structured training has no place in the twenty-first-century workplace.

Two other fashionable HRD initiatives are coaching, which is a non-directive form of development aimed at improving workplace performance, and mentoring, which aims to transmit knowledge, skills and experience in a broader sense than simply improving job performance.

In the CIPD 2010 Learning and Talent Development Survey (CIPD, 2010a) 65% of responding organisations stated that the skills they needed most to focus on to meet their business objectives in two years' time were leadership skills.

Traditionally, and for very obvious reasons, development activities are among the most vulnerable to cutbacks when organisations need to reduce their costs.

LEARNING OUTCOMES

On completion of this chapter you should:

- understand the definitions of 'training' and 'learning'
- know how to undertake a training needs analysis, and its purpose
- appreciate the necessity to identify learning objectives
- understand the importance of the principles of learning
- have an appreciation of the main learning and development methods used in organisations
- understand the Kirkpatrick model of training evaluation
- understand the concepts of single- and double-loop learning
- know what is meant by the term 'learning organisation'
- understand the idea of talent development
- appreciate the nature and importance of coaching in development
- understand the importance of mentoring.

Conventionally, in the personnel management paradigm (Chapter 1), learning at work was generally divided into more-or-less mutually exclusive domains for (i) managers (including other professionals) who might receive 'development', and (ii) non-managers, who were 'trained' (see Table 5). Traditionally in the UK firms did minimal training and development anyway, fearing that the money spent would be wasted because the employees would undoubtedly be 'poached' by competitors. Although there were some striking exceptions, until the late 1980s most UK firms did little or no management development at all, and – as noted above – the self-development that was in many cases occurring was virtually never recognised (see Table 5).

Table 5 The nature and scope of learning interventions under personnel management (PM) and human resource management (HRM)

People management paradigm	Class of employee	Nature of learning intervention/activity			
		Formal, external	*Formal, in-house*	*Informal, in-house*	*Self-development*
Personnel management	Non-managerial employees	Educational courses, usually vocational	Off-the-job training	On-the-job training	(ignored)
	Managers and other professionals	Development			(ignored)
Human resource management	All (core) employees	Learning and development			

Table 6 Types and natures of learning interventions and activities

Nature	Type	
	Formal	*Informal*
Off-the-job	Externally provided accredited education – eg MBAs, NVQs, professional qualifications	Voluntary accredited education
	Externally provided training courses	Voluntarily attended training courses

On-the-job		Learning partnerships
		    Coaching
		    Mentoring
		    Peer relationships
		Action Learning
		Self-development
		    Self-development groups
		    Learning logs

DEFINITIONS

Training is defined as a set of planned activities on the part of an organisation to increase job knowledge and skills, or to modify attitudes and social behaviour, to achieve specific ends which are related to a particular job or role.

Learning is a relatively permanent change in knowledge, skills, attitudes or behaviour that comes through experience. We may say that learning happens inside the person whereas training is something that is given to a person in the sense that it is a planned experience that is expected to lead to learning.

Development describes the continuing improvement of an individual's effectiveness in terms of their role or profession beyond the immediate task or job.

Education means the process of personal growth in abilities and attitudes which might take place independently of its application to work, and is therefore a broader experience than training or work-related learning and development (Morris, 1978).

The phrase *learning intervention* is now often used in the HRM literature to cover both training and work-related learning, reflecting the increased emphasis on active learning in the workplace.

Definitions of *management development* are given in the section on that subject later in this chapter.

A BRIEF OVERVIEW OF LEARNING PRINCIPLES

Detailed discussion of learning theory is outside the scope of the present text. The interested reader is referred to the relevant chapters of Landy and Conte (2007) for further reading.

On the basis of the research that has been conducted on the various theories of learning, certain rules or guidelines have emerged regarding efficient learning. These include:

- the principle of 'distributed practice' – ie breaking the learning experience up into manageable chunks for the learner
- praising the learner for correct responses, so reinforcing the learning
- training individuals to perform entire task units as a whole
- giving results of the training performance to the learners
- providing opportunities for practising the skills developed during training.

LEVELS OF LEARNING

There seem to be two levels of learning that occur in the modern organisation.

The first relates to obtaining knowledge in order to solve specific problems based on existing premises. The second is concerned with establishing new paradigms, mental models or perspectives. These two levels of learning have been termed 'single-loop' and 'double-loop' learning respectively (Argyris and Schön, 1978; after Ashby, 1940). The metaphor is drawn from the field of cybernetics. Single-loop learning is compared to the action of a thermostat which is used to control temperature (eg of a refrigerator), where the thermostat scans and monitors the environment (the temperature inside the refrigerator), compares the information it obtains with operating norms (the range of acceptable temperatures inside the refrigerator), and initiates any appropriate action (if the temperature is too high, the thermostat switches on the refrigeration unit to reduce the internal temperature until it is within the acceptable range). The thermostat then proceeds to scan the environment again setting up a continuous loop of activity. In double-loop learning a 'single loop' operates as before, but here the 'operating norms' themselves are questioned and if necessary altered, thus creating a 'double loop'.

For example, firms should be constantly seeking to improve their product offerings, whether these are physical goods or intangible services (see Chapter 4 on work design). Quality circles and autonomous work teams encourage workers to seek improvements continually in production and design as they deal with the everyday problems of production and delivery. This should encourage continuous learning and result in steady, incremental improvements which we can think of as the outcomes of single-loop learning – basically, learning how to do the same things better and better. Every so often, however, a worker, or a team of workers collectively, might have a sudden flash of insight which leads not to an incremental refinement but to a radical rethinking of a process or feature of the product. This discontinuous change would be an example of 'double-loop' learning.

Radical innovation relies on double-loop learning, and in the 'knowledge economy' one of the key goals of the HRD function is to help a build a culture in which double-loop learning can flourish.

KOLB'S LEARNING CYCLE

Kolb and his colleagues (1971) identified a four-stage learning cycle which has been hugely influential in people development in HRM, especially in management development. The four stages are:

1 Concrete experience

2 Observations and reflection

3 Formation of abstract concepts and generalisations

4 Testing the implications of the concepts in new situations.

The learning experience runs in sequence from 1 through to 4 (see Figure 3).

1 The individual takes note of some concrete experience. This could be part of a planned learning intervention such as a skills demonstration, or it might be accidental – he or she may suddenly realise that something has occurred.

2 The individual thinks about, or reflects upon, the experience and its significance.

3 The individual constructs some mental model to explain what happened and why. This will allow the individual to generalise about where and how the experience may recur.

4 The explanation is tested out in some new situation.

Figure 3 The Kolb learning cycle

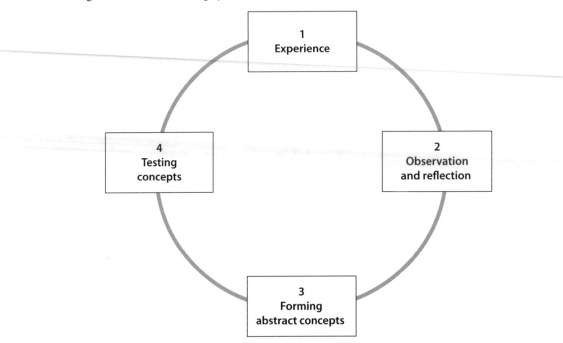

Of course, Kolb's work has not been without its critics. For instance, Holman *et al* (1997), Vince (1998) and Reynolds (1999) have argued that the emphasis on experiential learning is at the expense of psychodynamic, social, and institutional aspects of learning. It remains, however, one the most influential models of experiential management learning.

LEARNING STYLES

The effectiveness of learning will vary from stage to stage of Kolb's cycle among different people. Some will learn most effectively at the first stage; others at the second, third or fourth. This has led to the concept of *learning styles*. Honey and Mumford (1989) identified a set of four learning styles, each of which suggested a preference for a particular stage of the Kolb cycle. The cycle should always be completed by the learner but the learning style will dictate which part of the cycle is most important for a particular person. These learning styles are:

- 'Activists' tend to learn best from the experience stage: they prefer to take action – eg hands-on learning or role-playing.

- 'Reflectors' tend to learn most from the second stage, observation and reflection.

- For 'Theorists' learning is most effective at the third, abstract conceptualisation stage.

- 'Pragmatists' learn best from trying out the new skill or knowledge in actual work situations, so they benefit most from the fourth stage of the Kolb cycle.

The theory of learning styles implies that, ideally, a trainer might design each learning intervention according to the learning style of the individual learner. Clearly, there are limits to this in practice, but learners can be encouraged to identify their learning style and thus increase awareness of the strengths and weaknesses in their own learning processes. Activists, for example, can be alerted to the fact that they may tend to skip abstract conceptualisation and might neglect full testing of their new skills or knowledge in the workplace. Theorists can be reminded to get 'hands on' in the learning intervention, and so on. Honey and Mumford have produced a questionnaire which helps learners to identify their own particular learning style.

The theory of learning styles is not unproblematic: Coffield *et al* (2004) identified 71 different models of learning styles, 13 of which were judged to be influential. So caution is indicated, but the Honey and Mumford set of learning styles, as linked to the Kolb learning cycle, is certainly widely used and frequently cited in the HRD literature.

TRANSFER OF LEARNING

From the organisation's perspective, by far the most important issue is that of transfer of learning – ie whether the knowledge, skills, attitudes or behaviours learned will be available and used 'back on the job'. This is a critical issue in the evaluation of the effectiveness and utility of a learning programme, and for formal learning interventions such as conventional skills training where the intention is to impart specific knowledge or skills, or to develop certain attitudes, there can be little value from the organisation's point of view in learning which does not carry over to the job situation.

Some general rules have been established to increase the probability of transfer of learning:

- Maximise the similarity between the learning situation and the job situation.
- Provide as much experience as possible with the task being taught.
- Provide for a variety of examples when teaching concepts or skills.
- Label or identify important features of a task.
- Make sure the general principles are understood.
- Make sure that the learned behaviours and ideas are rewarded in the job situation.
- Design the learning content so that the learners can see its applicability.

EXPLICIT AND TACIT KNOWLEDGE

In almost all occupations, there are skills that will be picked up in the course of performing the job which cannot be acquired through training, only through experience. When training new staff it is important to distinguish what can be trained – such as the use of equipment and a fixed knowledge base – from what cannot. For example, medical students can be trained in how to take a patient's blood pressure correctly and effectively, but a good 'bedside manner' can only come with experience and observing skilled doctors dealing with their patients. To use the current jargon, we can train people by imparting 'explicit knowledge' but we cannot easily train people in 'tacit knowledge'. We discuss this later in this chapter in a section on knowledge management.

SOME COMMON LEARNING AND DEVELOPMENT METHODS

Action Learning was originally introduced for management development but is now widely used at all organisational levels. Groups of people work together to find practical solutions to real work problems. Instructors act as facilitators, encouraging participants to learn from each other and reflect on the experience.

Blended learning is a combination of multiple approaches to learning. Typically, a combination of technology-based materials and face-to-face sessions are used together to deliver instruction.

Case studies are detailed examinations of real-life situations written up and presented for educational purposes. Students typically work in groups to analyse each case and then to answer set tasks. They are very commonly used in management development.

Coaching is a non-directive form of development which focuses on improving performance and developing individuals' skills and giving feedback on a person's performance. Coaching should be delivered by trained personnel, who usually are drawn from outside the organisation.

Continuing professional development (CPD) is a continuous process of personal growth by which individuals improve their capability at work and realise their full potential. It is achieved by developing a range of knowledge, skills and experience which go beyond initial training or qualification, and which maintain and develop professional competence. Many professional bodies such as the CIPD now insist on CPD as a condition of continued membership.

'*Corporate universities*' have been established by some large companies for the delivery of management education. They are more than just in-company training departments and have been defined (Meister, 1998; p.38) as a

> centralized strategic umbrella for the education and development of employees ... [that] is the chief vehicle for disseminating an organisation's culture and fostering the development of not only job skills but also such core workplace skills as learning-to-learn, leadership, creative thinking and problem-solving.

E-learning is learning that is delivered, enabled or mediated using electronic technology for the explicit purpose of learning and development in organisations.

Instruction may be defined as the use of a highly structured teaching method to teach specific skills. Usually its format corresponds to a physical demonstration followed by supervised practice of the skills concerned.

Joint development activities are collaborations between employing organisations and academic institutions. They can include project work by which managers deal with work problems while receiving consultation/tutoring from the institution; consortia of companies running programmes with schools (eg 'company MBAs'); and reciprocal secondments between institutes and industry.

Lecturing is giving a structured talk, usually longer and more formal than a presentation, normally accompanied by visual aids and handouts of key points. A lecture may be combined with audience participation in a discussion, a question-and-answer session and/or group exercises/activities.

Mentoring is similar to coaching but the mentor is usually an experienced senior member of staff, though not the person's line manager. The emphasis in mentoring is less focused on the person's current job or role than in coaching, but more on his or her future development and career within the organisation.

Outdoor training comprises team exercises involving physical and mental tasks in challenging external environments. They are very popular in corporate team-building, believed by advocates to teach leadership and team- and self-development skills in addition to teamworking.

Role-playing is the enactment of roles in a structured context. This method is very useful for practising interpersonal skills.

Self-development is concerned with helping people to understand their own personal learning and development processes, and by doing so to assume greater control of, and responsibility for, their own development. There is an emphasis on longer-term development, as distinct from specific study or learning, and a stress on setting one's own goals and methods of achieving them. This technique can be applied to groups in which participants are encouraged to support each other. Self-development is frequently, but not exclusively, applied to managers and professionals.

Simulations/business games are group exercises or case studies, usually now computerised, in which the participants are asked to make certain choices and the computerised system gives them the 'result' of their decisions.

REFLECTIVE ACTIVITY

Outline a leadership programme for managers in a corporate university for a large organisation in your industry or economic sector.

CASE STUDY

AN EXAMPLE OF A 'CORPORATE UNIVERSITY': THE BOEING COMPANY

The Boeing Company provides education for its employees through its Leadership Centre, and executive learning features highly in its curriculum. Newly promoted supervisory personnel must complete a computerised curriculum within 30 days. This training includes topics on company polices and procedures, finding and using resources, and understanding legal responsibilities. Entry-level managers spend one week at a local training site studying performance management, reviewing organisational structure and learning about regulatory issues for their industry. Managers are also required to take core leadership courses at the Centre at five specific turning points in their careers: when they receive their first management assignments; when they become managers of managers; to prepare them for executive responsibilities; when starting an executive role; and when they assume global leadership responsibilities.

Boeing's primary means of evaluating the success of its Leadership Centre is by conducting employee surveys on an annual basis.

Source: Vitiello (2001; p.42)

CASE STUDY

HRM in action

Tesco and coaching: transformational coaching brings Tesco HR 'even closer to the business'

Retail giant Tesco has boosted HR's strategic impact following a transformational coaching programme for its personnel managers.

Hayley Tatum, UK and ROI Operations Personnel Director at Tesco, told *People Management* that the programme had brought HR 'even closer to the priorities of the business'.

The employer had run previous coaching programmes to master capability coaching. But Tatum said the new approach was for HR coaches to 'stretch and grow managers' via instant feedback on the shop floor.

'Before, we'd gone for personnel managers who were building capability across their management team,' she said. But the new programme aims to train strong, confident transformational coaches.

Tatum explained that by advancing management performance, employee engagement also improved, which in turn boosts customer service.

'Of course, in this climate it's difficult to attribute such benefits directly because we don't run anything in isolation.

'But we are seeing better staff retention, attendance levels and more qualified members of staff. We're also seeing more of our management population on development programmes to skill themselves for the next level. We are currently running at our best ever levels for all three indicators.'

Tatum said she hopes that transformation coaching 'will become a trend' because of the positive impact it has had.

'I think it makes HR really interesting as a function, because it continually develops us as professionals and keeps us far closer to the priorities of the business,' she said.

Tatum said that Tesco's has no plans to merge the role of HR director and customer services director like their rivals Sainsbury's, which recently appointed Gwyn Burr as customer service and colleague director.

'In some stores we've merged HR and customer roles, but it's not a strategy going forward. I think two heads are better than one for us.'

Tatum said Customer Service Director Natasha Adams, who previously worked in HR, would continue to work closely with the HR department on training.

Tesco's programme was provided by the Full Potential Group, a transformational coaching specialist.

Source: article by Claire Churchard, *People Management* Online, 3 August 2010

THE PROCESS OF FORMAL LEARNING INTERVENTIONS

By 'formal' we mean a learning intervention that is wholly or mainly planned and structured. Of course, such an intervention may include areas in which informal learning is to be encouraged – eg managers may be encouraged to keep learning logs and CPD plans within a structured management development programme – but the overall intervention will be organised from the start with clearly identified learning objectives in terms of the knowledge, skills, attitudes or behaviours to be attained as a result of the intervention.

To assess the impact of a learning intervention we usually need to know something about the status of the learners' relevant knowledge, skills or attitudes (KSAs) before development takes place, so we should obtain baseline pre-intervention information. Similarly, after the intervention has taken place we need some post-intervention information. Finally, since the purpose of the intervention is to improve job performance, we should also seek information about how the learning and development has transferred to on-the-job behaviour.

There is thus a four-stage process for any formal learning intervention:

1 Identifying the development need

2 Designing the development activity

3 Undertaking the development activity

4 Evaluating the development intervention.

This process is sometimes termed the training cycle.

The stages in the process are described in more detail below.

NEEDS ANALYSIS

We need to know the requirements of a job or role before we can know what constitutes good performance in doing it. In learning and development a particular form of job analysis is used which by convention used to be termed *training needs analysis*. In the light of the changes in people development already referred to in this chapter, in this text we will use the terms 'needs analysis' (NA) or 'learning needs analysis' (LNA) to describe this activity.

The needs analysis provides a set of learning objectives for the development programme. These objectives might include adding *knowledge*, developing specific *skills* or helping to form specific *abilities*. 'Knowledge' is the information needed to perform the work, 'skills' are attributes which are required, and 'ability' refers to the physical, emotional, intellectual and psychological aptitudes necessary to perform the work.

The objectives have a double role. Firstly, they guide us towards what learning principles and training methods should be used. Secondly, they provide a means for assessing whether the learning intervention has been successful.

The impetus for training is usually an identification of a need for improvement.

A job, task or occupational needs analysis is an examination of the actual duties and responsibilities that compose the job/task/occupation concerned. The question asked is 'What KSAs are required for successful performance of the duties?' In practice, a needs analysis consists of a combination of activities. Often there is a job description based on some earlier and perhaps less systematic job analysis. After reading this and any other relevant documentation relating to the job, the analyst will discuss the job with a supervisor or manager responsible for the staff concerned. This will allow the analyst to identify critical terminology, qualify important job dimensions, develop questions for interview and identify things to look for when observing the job. The analyst will typically observe several employees undertaking the task or job. Finally, the analyst may arrange interviews with other job-holders and/or distribute questionnaires for them to complete.

WHO NEEDS THE LEARNING INTERVENTION? PERSON ANALYSIS

There are usually two possible groups:

- present job-holders who are performing below standard
- new appointees who are about to take up the job or role.

For the first group the most obvious method for identifying weaknesses in job performance is via job appraisal or performance management.

? REFLECTIVE ACTIVITY

Consider this: training current staff and training new staff are likely to be very different processes. Why is that?

ACTIVITY ANSWER GUIDANCE

Training new starters usually provides opportunities for new learning, but training experienced workers often involves eliminating old habits. So in addition to learning, the experienced incumbent often has to unlearn old methods or attitudes. When the Japanese car manufacture Nissan built a car plant in the UK in the late 1980s, its recruitment policy was aimed at hiring people who had never worked in a British car factory.

THE IMPORTANCE OF LEARNING OBJECTIVES

On the basis of the needs analysis it should be possible to specify some objectives or goals for the training programme: what levels of KSAs would you like the trainees to have after the training intervention that they did not have before? Learning objectives for job incumbents are usually tailored to identified specific deficiencies in the employees' performance and they are often negotiated with the individual employee as a result of a performance appraisal. Learning objectives have several important uses. They represent information for both the learner and the facilitator about what is to be learned; they help to motivate the learner; and they allow evaluation of whether the learning intervention has been completed satisfactorily.

EVALUATING THE LEARNING INTERVENTION

The best-known model for evaluating a learning intervention is that developed by Kirkpatrick (1967). This operates at four levels: trainee reactions, learning reactions, behavioural change, and results.

Trainee reactions correspond to participants' evaluations of the usefulness of the learning intervention. It will be familiar to many readers from the ubiquitous 'happy sheet' or questionnaire doled out after company training events. The questionnaire typically asks the participant to rate their overall impression of the event, their perceptions of the trainer, and the extent to which the course and the trainee's own objectives have been met. Such an exercise clearly tells us nothing about how much has been learned, or whether what has been learned will be translated into better job performance, but it is not without some usefulness and is inexpensive and easy to obtain.

Learning reactions represents a level of evaluation that seeks to assess how much knowledge has been imparted to the trainee as a result of the intervention. This might be assessed by a written test, and again this can be inexpensive and relatively quick and easy to obtain.

Behavioural change is the third level of evaluation in Kirkpatrick's model. Specifically, the question is whether the training or learning intervention has resulted in observable changes in the trainee's behaviour in on the job. Such assessment cannot be quick, cheap or easy, although an effective performance management system should obtain the information required. Of course, changed behaviour will not always equate with improved job performance.

Results is the final level of evaluation. Has there been a measurable improvement in the trainee's job performance? This is the ultimate measure of the effectiveness of the learning intervention but it is often difficult to obtain, especially when the intervention has been in complex areas such as managerial or professional effectiveness. Even in more straightforward cases such as physical skills training it is often difficult to isolate the effects of the intervention from those of other extraneous factors.

INFORMAL LEARNING

So far we have discussed formal, structured learning interventions where the objective is to facilitate the acquisition of specific knowledge or skills, or the particular modification of abilities. Informal or experiential learning is quite different in nature, being unplanned and indeed unplannable in detail. It is the learning that the individual himself or herself acquires from the experiences of doing the job, from working in the organisation and from just thinking and reflecting on the work done. Informal learning may sound somewhat airy-fairy, but a US Bureau of Labor report found that people learned 70% of what they know about their jobs informally through processes which were not structured or sponsored by their employing organisation.

To be effective, informal learning requires a level of employee motivation, confidence and capability. Employers who wish to encourage informal learning strive to create a climate which is supportive and to impart basic learning skills ('learning how to learn') to their people.

ORGANISATIONAL LEARNING AND KNOWLEDGE MANAGEMENT

The manufacturing-based industrial society of the postwar period has been evolving towards a more service-based society and, more recently, an 'information society'. The leading management thinkers of the late 1990s agreed that the manufacturing, service and information sectors would be based on knowledge in the future and that business organisations will evolve into knowledge-creators in many ways. Peter Drucker was one of the earliest writers to foresee this transformation, and he is credited with inventing the terms 'knowledge-work' and 'knowledge-worker' in the early 1960s. We are entering the 'knowledge society' in which the basic economic resource is no longer capital, or natural resources, or labour, but is knowledge, and in which knowledge-workers will play a central role (Drucker, 1993). The organisation has to be prepared to abandon knowledge that has become obsolete and learn to create new things through (i) continuous improvement of every activity; (ii) the development of new applications from its own successes; and (iii) continuous innovation as an organised process. Drucker (1993; p.24) recognised the importance of tacit knowledge when he argued that a skill (*technē* in ancient Greek) could not be explained in words but could only be demonstrated through apprenticeship and experience.

ORGANISATIONAL LEARNING

Theorists have long argued for the need for organisations to change continuously (see Dodgson, 1993) and to undertake 'organisational learning'.

The concept of the 'learning organisation' was defined by Pedler, Boydell and Burgoyne (1988) as:

> An organisation which facilitates the learning of all of its members and continuously transforms itself.

This leads to a continuous process of organisational transformation, the end-points of which cannot be planned with any certainty. The cumulative learning of individuals leads, over time, to fundamental changes in assumptions, goals, norms, and operating procedures, not simply as a reaction to external pressures but based on the organic growth in knowledge of the people who compose the organisation.

Senge (1990) proposed the 'learning organisation' to overcome 'organisational learning disabilities'. To build a learning organisation managers had to (i) adopt 'systems thinking'; (ii) encourage 'personal mastery' of their own lives; (iii) bring to the surface mental models and challenge them; (iv) build a 'shared vision'; and (v) facilitate 'team learning'. Systems thinking was the key integrating 'discipline' of the five.

Nonaka and Takeuchi (1995; p.45) argued that Western organisational learning theories still used the metaphor of individual learning and failed to deal adequately with the idea of knowledge creation. They also considered that rather than relying on 'artificial' interventions such as organisational development programmes to implement double-loop learning, it should be a continuous activity of the organisation – not a special and difficult task that requires outside intervention.

In their theory of knowledge Nonaka and Takeuchi adopt the traditional definition of knowledge as 'justified true belief', but they add that whereas traditional Western epistemology has focused on 'truthfulness' as the essential attribute of knowledge and emphasises the absolute, static and non-human form of knowledge, they consider knowledge 'a dynamic human process of justifying personal belief towards the "truth"'(Nonaka and Takeuchi, 1995; p.58).

Most writers on knowledge management draw on Polanyi's (1966) distinction between tacit knowledge and explicit knowledge. Tacit knowledge is personal and context-specific and therefore hard to formalise and communicate. Explicit or 'codified' knowledge refers to knowledge that can be transmitted in formal, systematic language. Polanyi contends that human beings acquire knowledge by actively creating and organising their own experiences, and that knowledge that can be expressed in words and numbers thus represents only the tip of the iceberg of the entire body of knowledge: 'We can know more than we can tell,' as Polanyi famously put it (1966; p.4). In traditional epistemology knowledge derives from the separation of the subject and the object of perception: human beings as the subject of perception acquire knowledge by analysing external objects. In contrast, Polanyi contends that human beings create knowledge by involving themselves with objects – that through self-involvement and commitment, or what Polanyi called 'indwelling', scientific objectivity is not the sole source of knowledge, and much of our knowledge is the fruit of our own purposeful endeavours in dealing with the world.

Such arguments may not convince everybody, but it is certainly the case that the ideas of knowledge management have had an enormous influence on management thinking.

KNOWLEDGE CONVERSION: INTERACTIONS BETWEEN TACIT AND EXPLICIT KNOWLEDGE

Nonaka and Takeuchi assume that human knowledge is created and expanded through social interaction between tacit knowledge and explicit knowledge, a process they call 'knowledge conversion' (1995; p.59). They postulated four modes of knowledge conversion as these two types of knowledge are combined, which they termed respectively 'socialisation', 'externalisation', 'combination', and 'internalisation'.

Socialisation: from tacit knowledge to tacit knowledge

Socialisation is a process of sharing experiences and thereby creating tacit knowledge such as shared mental models and technical skills. An individual can acquire tacit knowledge directly from others without using language. Apprentices learn their trades from their masters, and on-the-job training uses much the same principle in business and management. Experience is thus the key to acquiring tacit knowledge.

Externalisation: from tacit knowledge to explicit knowledge

Externalisation is a process of articulating tacit knowledge into explicit concepts by means of metaphors, analogies, concepts, hypotheses or models. This utilises metaphor following Nisbet's (1969) argument that what Polanyi terms tacit knowledge may be expressible, to a degree, by means of metaphor. Successful creative design seems usually to work this way; Nonaka and Takeuchi give a number of interesting industrial design examples (1995; pp64–7).

Combination: from explicit knowledge to explicit knowledge

Combination is a process of systematising concepts into a knowledge system, combining different bodies of explicit knowledge. Nonaka and Takeuchi thought an MBA education one of the best examples of this (1995; p.67).

Internalisation: from explicit knowledge to tacit knowledge

Internalisation is a process of embodying explicit knowledge into tacit knowledge and is closely related to 'learning by doing'. When experiences through socialisation, externalisation and combination are internalised into individuals' tacit knowledge bases in the form of shared mental models or technical know-how they become valuable assets.

LEARNING AND DEVELOPMENT IN ACTION: ROADMAP TO SUCCESS

Training programme leaves US mortgage company with $4 million worth of improvements

A programme to develop future high-performing leaders has resulted in improvements worth $4 million for one of America's major mortgage-lending companies.

Washington Mutual's (WaMu) Home Loans division developed the programme 'Roadmap' to address the issue of a shrinking internal talent pool during a time of significant growth and increasing competition within the industry. It was also hoped that the new learning opportunities would attract the best talent from outside the organisation.

'Learning opportunities became a competitive advantage for us,' Marian Anderson, Assistant Vice President of Leadership Development at WaMu Home Loans, told the ASTD Conference.

The nine-month programme involves a mixture of customised workshops, structured experiential job activity, Action Learning projects to solve real business problems, virtual meetings, 360-degree feedback and coaching from participants' managers.

Anderson described it as a 'holistic approach'.

Although the division, which has almost 14,000 employees, had previously offered many of the components as individual training sessions, Roadmap combined them in a more focused and cost-effective approach.

Participants, both managers of individual contributors and managers of managers, are selected for the programme based on their potential and talent. Key areas of focus during the training include self-awareness and job accountabilities, such as managing customer experience and deepening relationships. It also involves managing employees' performance and building sales and managing the business to ensure efficiency.

On top of the significant saving in operational costs after three years, the company has achieved its goal of hiring 70% internally, also saving money on recruitment costs.

Anderson also said that one of the most crucial aspects to the initiative is the 'coaches' kick-off', a pre-programme session with all managers of participants to ensure that they understand their role as a coach.

'The manager has a key role in the programme. We will not take a participant if the manager does not attend our coaches' kick-off programme. The coach as manager is an opportunity to help people apply lessons in their daily job,' she said.

Source: ASTD Conference report, Atlanta, USA, *People Management*, 11 June 2007

MANAGEMENT DEVELOPMENT

The distinction between the development of managers and of non-managers is becoming increasingly blurred. The CIPD defines (CIPD, 2007b) 'management development' as:

> The entire structured process by which managers learn and improve their skills for their employing organisations.

Managers learn in many ways, including experientially, and many organisations combine formal and informal approaches. Handy *et al* (1988; p.12) proposed a clear distinction between 'business education' and 'management development'. By 'business education' is meant the formal or academic knowledge-base required for management, as is typically provided by an external source such as a university, business school or commercial college. The attainment of such education is primarily the responsibility of the individual manager. Business education cannot by itself qualify one for management but can only be a prelude to it. 'Management development' largely takes place within the organisation and should be seen as a combination of experience, training and education which, although usually initiated by the organisation, requires the active co-operation of the individual, and for which both organisation and manager share joint responsibility. Twenty years on, Handy's distinction still has much to commend it, although organisations are very much more likely now to actively support their managers in acquiring business education, either paying the fees for external MBAs and the like or setting up their own 'corporate universities'.

One of the key changes in management development in the UK and in many other countries in the past 20 years has been the growth in management education at university level. In North America this provision was evident for most of the twentieth century, but it was only in the latter decades of the century that most other countries took the academic education of managers as seriously as did the North Americans. Indeed, it was mainly the continuing success of the US managerial and entrepreneurial culture which brought about this change. The CIPD estimates that by 2006 there were over 100 higher-education institutions in the UK that offered undergraduate and postgraduate courses, around 20,000 first degrees and 11,000 higher degrees (mainly MBAs) being awarded every year. Over 80% of MBAs were awarded for distance-learning or part-time study. Some of these MBA graduates will have been sponsored by their employers, but others will have decided to study for themselves as part of their own programme of career development. Edinburgh Business School currently offers one of the largest distance-learning MBA programmes in the world with, to date, over 10,500 graduates working in over 150 countries (http://www.ebsglobal.net/).

Some large UK companies have followed the US lead in setting up 'corporate universities' which supply in-house many of the formal courses and programmes for their people development, including management development, which previously would have been supplied by external academic institutions (CIPD, 2007b).

THE OBJECTIVES OF MANAGEMENT DEVELOPMENT

The choice of management development approach and methods will depend on the strategic outcomes that the organisation is pursuing, such as performance, attitude and adaptability.

Improving managers' expertise in specific areas such as marketing, finance, production or HRM is usually highest on most companies' agendas for management development, followed by giving individuals experience to prepare them for senior management positions. Management development is also used either as a catalyst for organisational change or to help build a new culture following a major change, such as a large-scale merger or acquisition. Management development can also be a key factor in building a learning organisation in which there is a climate for continual learning. In this case the emphasis is away from structured programmes and taught courses and towards enhancing opportunities for self-development via methods such as Action Learning, on-the-job training, career breaks, secondment to temporary 'taskforces' and e-learning.

METHODS OF MANAGEMENT DEVELOPMENT

It is recognised that a good deal of management development takes place on the job and that planned job experience and career succession can play vital roles in the process. Line managers should be involved in the development of their subordinates.

In the UK the most common formal methods of management development are external courses, attending seminars and conferences, attending in-company training to develop individual skills, attending in-company training to develop organisational skills, and pursuing external formal qualifications such as MBAs (Thomson *et al*, 2001; p.144).

The most popular informal methods in the UK are in-company job rotation, job observation, on-the-job training, mentoring, and coaching (Thomson *et al*, 2001; p.149).

CONDITIONS FOR SUCCESSFUL MANAGEMENT DEVELOPMENT

There is a consensus in the literature (Storey *et al*, 1997; p.43) that management development is most effective when:

- it is recognised by the organisation as a strategic business activity
- the design of management development programmes recognises the nature of managerial work
- the programme is tailored to fit the needs of the individual managers on it
- education, training, selection, career planning, reward systems and managerial evaluation are recognised as all being part of a connected system
- evaluation is itself a vital part of the system of development.

Mabey and Thomson (2000a) found encouraging signs of continuing progress in British management development. Compared to the findings of Thomson *et al* (1997), the fieldwork for which had been carried out in 1996, there was an increase in the number of organisations with a formal written policy for management development, from 43% in 1996 to 51% in 2000; and in those having a specific budget for management development, from 40% to 49%. Formal training had risen to an average of to 6.5 days per manager per year for larger firms (up 18%), and to 6.4 in small firms (up 25%). There was also found to be an average of 8.1 days for informal training. Half the organisations had or were pursuing Investor in People (IiP) status, and 63% confirmed their commitment to national vocational qualifications (NVQs) in management. However, only 14% were committed to Management Standards (MCI). It was found that 72% of firms were attempting to review management development (up 5% since 1996).

Mabey and Thomson (2000a) concluded that there was evidence that organisations were moving along a spectrum from 'weak' to 'strong' management development systems in which 'strong' systems were typified by planned structures, policy frameworks and effective management development processes. The authors also claimed that they had found evidence that firms with a strong policy framework (ie high amounts of formal training and a centralised management development policy) had better current benchmarked performance.

HRM in action

CASE STUDY

Tailoring management development

A structured development programme has been the key to developing a culture that puts people first at West Sussex County Council, delegates were told.

Kieran Stigant, in charge of community engagement and organisational development at the Council, said that the organisation realised that its managers were seen as 'superior technicians' who could solve problems, rather than as developers of people who could unlock the potential of employees.

As a result, the Council put in place a management-development ladder aimed at 'achieving a focus on our communities – developing the organisation to be capable of delivering the services our communities need', Stigant said.

The four-stage programme begins with a basic 'Introduction to management' and finishes with 'Journey into the future', which focuses on behavioural change.

Implementing the development programme has required heavy investment from the Council – and high levels of commitment from the staff involved. The advanced management development stage of the programme, which is based on self-managed learning, costs £1,500 for each participant. Individual managers are required to put in around 600 hours over 18 months – and many put in twice that amount of time.

'When we started, I didn't have a clue whether it would work out or not,' admitted Stigant, who said that the response from managers had been outstanding.

Source: article by David Burt, Management Development Manager, Safeway, and Kieran Stigant, Assistant Chief Executive, West Sussex County Council, in *People Management,* 16 April 2002

DEVELOPING PEOPLE IN PRACTICE

The CIPD 2010 *Learning and Talent Development Survey* (CIPD, 2010a) reported that the most effective learning and talent development practices in the UK were (i) in-house development programmes (56% of responding organisations) and (ii) coaching by line managers (51%).

E-learning was the learning and talent development practice that had increased the most since the 2009 Survey, 62% of organisations saying they used it more than in 2009. In-house development programmes were also used more by 58% of organisations, and coaching by line managers was used more by 56%. Attendance at external conferences, workshops and events had decreased the most, one-quarter (26%) of organisations using it less – an indication, perhaps, of the impact of the recession.

Nearly two-thirds of responding organisations (65%) reported that their economic circumstances had declined in the previous 12 months: more than the 46% which reported this in the 2009 survey. So it is not surprising that funds available for learning and development had decreased in the previous 12 months for over half (52%) of organisations, while only one in ten employers (11%) expected such funds to increase in the year to come. Still, nearly 80% of organisations had a training budget, and this was over £200,000 for half of them. The survey found a median figure of four training/development days on average per employee. So despite the continuing recession, UK plc is still training and developing its employees.

Specialists were most likely to have responsibility for employees' learning and talent development (53% of organisations), followed by senior managers (33%), the HR department (30%) and line managers (29%). Most employers expected their employees/learners to show 'some' involvement in their learning and development, but relatively few (17%) expected them to be mainly responsible for their own learning.

The main gaps in skills identified by organisations were, as in previous years, business skills/acumen and commercial awareness, and management/leadership skills.

The skills which employers said they needed to focus on to meet their business objectives in two years' time were leadership skills (65%), front-line people management skills (55%), and business acumen/awareness (51%).

Under leadership skills, the main skills gaps which employers identified were performance management (and specifically setting standards for performance and dealing with under-performance), and leading and managing change.

CASE STUDY

A LEARNING INTERVENTION FOR THE TRUST RETAIL GROUP

Background information

The following information has been extracted from the TRUST Group's website.

'TRUST is the UK's leading convenience store group with over 1,000 stores throughout the country. And we're still expanding! TRUST stores provide the ultimate in convenience shopping, trusted throughout the UK for our selection, quality and value. From a great range of fresh foods through to wine, beer, household products and store-cupboard essentials, our stores go far beyond providing for our customers' top-up shopping needs. One of our most attractive assets is the TRUST own-brand range. This excellent quality label encompasses nearly 900 different products, from the innovative to traditional favourites, and we're constantly enhancing and enlarging the choices. Independent research reveals that 75% of our customers prefer to buy TRUST brand products.

'Because every TRUST store is at the heart of its community, delivering an essential service to the local area is our top priority. Each element is tailored to the needs of local shoppers – services, selection and facilities.

'TRUST stores may come in a range of sizes and formats, but every one is designed and laid out with local customers' preferences in mind, to make the shopping experience altogether easier and more enjoyable. Our aim is to provide the very best products at value-for-money prices. In particular, we focus on fresh, quality produce. Personal, friendly service is also very much part of the TRUST shopping experience. Add our range of convenient additional services such as hot food to go, fresh coffee, in-store cash machines, the National Lottery and electronic mobile top-ups, and you'll find everything you need at your local TRUST store!

'The first TRUST store opened in 1947, realising founder Adrian Wilson's vision to bring independent retailers together to benefit from increased buying power as a group. His vision has never been more relevant today in the face of tough competition from many quarters.

'Six regional distribution centres supply products and services to every one of our TRUST UK stores. The TRUST central office handles national marketing and buying services for the group, not only supporting our retailers with innovative and award-winning point-of-sale multi-media advertising and promotional campaigns, but also ensuring the best deals for our stores and our customers.

'Today, more than ever, independent retailers who affiliate themselves to TRUST benefit from an industry-leading and highly successful package. By helping our stores to compete and stay at the forefront, TRUST also ensures that each of our retailers can deliver the high standards and value discerning customers now demand.'

TRUST at a glance – key facts

TRUST is a 'symbol group', meaning that individual TRUST members remain independent but enjoy access to collective buying and marketing power and all the added benefits of operating under a strong corporate brand with back-up resources.

UK turnover is in excess of £2.7 billion and it is a market leader within the convenience store sector.

It has over 1,000 UK stores and is the employer of over 50,000 people.

Average store size is 130 square metres/1,400 square feet.

TRUST owners have won more than 100 major industry awards in the past three years.

The TRUST Group can offer retailers financial packages and credit terms, equipment/leasing loans and licensing equipment/franchising agreements, and many other services.

'Our retailers have access to the latest industry developments, including professional merchandising and category management, store refurbishment, and training and development for both managers and staff.'

The following is list of competencies which a TRUST Group store supervisor is expected to possess. Each supervisor is responsible for the work of up to 10 sales assistants and reports directly to the store manager.

- Motivating, developing, and directing people as they work, identifying the best people for the job
- Active listening, giving full attention to what other people are saying, taking time to understand the points being made, asking questions as appropriate, and not interrupting at inappropriate times
- Service orientation: actively looking for ways to help people
- Managing one's own time and the time of others

- Teaching others how to do things

- Monitoring/assessing the performance of oneself, other individuals, or organisations to make improvements or take corrective action

- Understanding written sentences and paragraphs in work-related documents

- Judgement and decision-making: considering the relative costs and benefits of potential actions to choose the most appropriate one

- Active learning: understanding the implications of new information for both current and future problem-solving and decision-making

- Critical thinking: using logic and reasoning to identify the strengths and weaknesses of alternative solutions, conclusions or approaches to problems.

REFLECTIVE ACTIVITY

Scenario:

Following an analysis of the annual performance appraisals of store assistants, management identified a persistent pattern of complaints of poor working relationships with the store supervisors to whom they reported. Supervisors were often described as being bad at communicating, poor at encouraging ideas and innovations, and insensitive in their relations with staff.

After careful consideration of these findings and further interviews with store assistants, supervisors and managers it was concluded that there was substance to the assistants' complaints. HRD were tasked with developing and implementing a skills improvement programme for store supervisors to alleviate the problems that had been identified.

Outline a formal learning intervention to deliver the required skills improvement programme.

ACTIVITY ANSWER GUIDANCE

Needs analysis

A needs analysis was conducted by analysing the job descriptions for store assistants, supervisors and managers, by interviewing a sample of assistants, supervisors and managers, and by observing work in a sample of stores.

It was concluded that there was a requirement for a programme of interpersonal skills training for store supervisors. A person analysis concluded that all existing store supervisors should participate in the proposed learning intervention, and that this should also become part of the entry-level management development programme.

The learning objectives were identified as follows.

Interpersonal skills programme for TRUST store supervisors

After completing the learning intervention the participants should be competent in the following areas:

- Developing and maintaining rapport with others

- Listening to others
- Dealing sensitively with others
- Encouraging ideas from others
- Giving feedback to others.

Designing the skills programme

A set of five one-day workshops, one day for each of the five themes identified. A maximum of 25 supervisors could attend any workshop. The total resources needed to cater for all of the Group's store supervisors will have to be calculated and approved.

Methods:

- Instruction
- Video presentations
- Case studies
- Role-plays
- In-basket exercises.

Resources:

- One facilitator for each day
- Lecture theatre and break-out rooms in the company's central Development Facility
- Audiovisual PC equipment in the Development Facility
- Pre-programme written material for distribution to the learners prior to the programme
- Pre-intervention questionnaire on existing knowledge and skills levels
- Learning materials: videos, role-play materials, cases, materials for in-basket exercises
- Learners' feedback sheets for evaluation
- Test materials for evaluation
- Attendance certificates
- Completion certificates.

Evaluation

Trainees' reactions – questionnaires distributed at end of each day's workshop

Knowledge tests to be administered at end of the programme

Analysis of performance management appraisals

Staff attitude surveys.

FINAL CASE STUDY

Read through the Karstadt Warenhaus AG case study in the Appendix (p.231).

Outline a management development programme for the Karstadt department store chain.

KEY ISSUES

There is greater emphasis on employee development in the HRM paradigm than in personnel management, and also greater scope in that development usually covers all core employees.

The terms 'employee development' (ED) or 'human resource development' (HRD) have replaced older terms such as 'training' and 'management development'.

Recently Talent Development (TD) has become a preferred term among HR professionals to describe the "high end" of HRD.

Learning and development interventions cover external education and in-house activities, both formal and informal.

The intention in HRD now is often to facilitate learning and personal development rather than to impose formal training on individuals.

There is also greater emphasis on informal learning at all levels, including self-development.

Coaching and mentoring are currently fashionable HRD initiatives.

One point of vulnerability of HRD is that development activities are among the most exposed to cutbacks when organisations need to reduce costs.

EXPLORE FURTHER

Armstrong, M. (2009) *Armstrong's Handbook of Human Resource Management Practice*. 11th Edition. London: Kogan Page.

Chapters 40–45: 'Learning and Development'. The basics on individual and organisational learning and development, plus management development...

Storey, J. (ed.) (2007) *Human Resource Management: A critical text*, 3rd edition. London: Thomson Learning

Chapter 7. A. Felstead 'Measure for measure: mapping the terrain of the training, learning and skills debate'.

CHAPTER 6

Employee relations

INTRODUCTION

'Employee relations' is the term now normally used to describe the policies and practices an organisation uses in dealing with its employees, and the systems of rules and mechanisms by which organisations and employees interact with each other. The term usually implies collective relations such as collective bargaining with trade unions (TUs) or staff associations (SAs), and the resulting agreements, but it also includes policies and procedures which operate at small-group or individual level – eg disciplinary and grievance procedures.

LEARNING OUTCOMES

On completion of this chapter you should:

- understand the nature and importance of conflict in employee relations
- understand the nature of negotiations in the context of employee relations
- understand the purpose and nature of both grievance and disciplinary procedures
- be able to describe the process of traditional collective bargaining and agreements
- be familiar with the main forms of industrial action
- understand the nature of 'new employee relations'
- understand the concepts of employee engagement and employee voice.

In Chapter 1 we introduced the idea of 'perspective' in people management and outlined the three most important for our purposes – namely, unitarist, pluralist, and radical or critical. We noted that the HRM model is really unitarist in its culture but that it is often successfully applied in a pluralist milieu. There is no doubt, however, that in countries such as the UK and the USA where trade union power has declined, employee relations are significantly less collectivised than was the case several decades ago. As we also saw in Chapter 1, as early as 1990 the Workplace Employment Relations Survey reported a significant decline in trade unionism in the UK, accompanied by a considerable increase in HRM-style initiatives in participation and communication, such as team briefings, quality circles and newsletters, replacing the more traditional collective methods. There was also evidence of the increasing involvement of line managers in HR activities which had previously been reserved for specialist personnel management departments. The later Workplace Employment Relations Surveys have confirmed these trends in the UK.

Most countries have legal frameworks which give statutory rights to employees, both individual – eg protection against unfair dismissal – and collective – eg the right to trade union membership and recognition, and ensuring legal compliance on the part of the organisation is a vital responsibility for HR managers. The actual rights and responsibilities of both parties may vary widely from country to country – a point that multinational companies have to bear in mind when framing their HR strategies and policies.

Where traditional formal employee relations processes such as collective bargaining have declined, HRM initiatives in such areas as teamworking and more direct methods of communication between management and workers have often taken their place.

DEALING WITH CONFLICT

We use the term 'conflict' widely in employee relations. It does not always mean a breakdown in the working relationship, although that can be a consequence of conflict. We mean any situation where there is a significant difference in objectives or interests between management and the workforce, whether it is a collective difference about pay rates or major terms of employment, or individual differences about a particular work situation.

So the issue of conflict and how to deal with it is important for managers, both at the level of the individual or small group – eg by means of disciplinary and grievance procedures – and at the larger-scale handling disputes with trade unions or staff associations which represent collectively some significant section of the workforce.

The adoption of more sophisticated management models such as human resource management (HRM) has had implications for the conduct of employee relations.

GRIEVANCE AND DISCIPLINARY PROCEDURES

The 2004 Workplace Employment Relations Survey (WERS) found that nearly half (47%) of UK workplaces reported having had a formal grievance from employees in 2004. The most common types of grievance raised were those on pay and conditions (18% of workplaces), unfair treatment by a supervisor or line manager (16%), and work practices, work allocation or pace of work (12%).

The same survey found that 55% of managers reported using at least one disciplinary sanction in 2004, and 28% of workplaces had made at least one dismissal on disciplinary grounds (Kersley *et al*, 2006; p.229).

Most managers would agree that it is inevitable that there are issues of grievance- and discipline-handling in most organisations. Notwithstanding the unitarist culture of most HRM models, few managers really expect that the interests of both employers and employees will always coincide. These interests are expressed in the parties' respective legal rights and responsibilities, but also in the informal expectations they have of each other.

Employees expect that employers will treat them reasonably, fairly and consistently, and that action will be taken against them only on the basis of just cause and after proper and thorough investigation. Employees will feel they have a right to pursue a grievance if these expectations are not met.

Employers expect employees to perform their duties and tasks in a satisfactory manner in accordance with their legal obligations and organisational policies and procedures. If the employees' performance is not satisfactory, employers will consider that they have the right to apply disciplinary action.

HR has an important role in resolving such differences and so assisting the effective running of the organisation. Apart from ethical and legal considerations, if grievance and discipline cases are dealt with properly, we assume that employee dissatisfaction should be reduced and motivation increased, with consequent improvements in individual, team and organisational performance. If the employment relationship is working in any sort of reasonable fashion to begin with, it is usually seen by both sides as an ongoing relationship that should survive the resolution of any one dispute whether individual or collective.

As we saw in Chapter 1, a key characteristic of HRM is the devolution to the line manager of most day-to-day people management. This includes handling grievance and discipline with minimum HR specialist input, at least initially, so it is now perceived as crucial that all line managers be trained to handle grievance and disciplinary cases properly.

If an employment tribunal investigates the dismissal of an employee, it will test the issues of fairness and reasonableness by considering whether the procedures that were applied by the employer conformed to the concepts of natural justice. From the employer's point of view the main purpose of procedures is to ensure that standards are maintained and legal compliance is adhered to.

Good grievance and disciplinary procedures typically are set in stages, and on the principle that issues should be dealt with as close to their origin as possible. Not all actions have to go through all these steps, however, since the first instance of severe misconduct may merit disciplinary action much more punitive than that of, say, a verbal warning. For example, fighting in the workplace and being drunk at work are both classed in almost all circumstances as 'gross misconduct' deserving immediate dismissal, as may be the refusal to carry out a reasonable and legitimate instruction from a superior. But the general principle is always to deal with issues at the lowest level possible given the nature of the inappropriate behviour.

It may be surprising but it is a fact that in the UK employment tribunals still report cases in which the employer has failed to conduct a proper and fair investigation before taking disciplinary action against an employee (Earnshaw and Cooper, 1998; p.15). It is the employer's responsibility to ensure that any disciplinary action is taken only after a full and proper investigation of the facts has been conducted. Line managers need appropriate training in handling grievance and disciplinary matters. HR experts are still usually involved in both, but not necessarily in person, at least at initial stages. The line managers will need access to expert HR advice, however, whether or not HR personnel themselves are present.

REFLECTIVE ACTIVITY

Find out what the disciplinary and grievance procedures are which operate at your place of employment (or some other workplace with which you are familiar). If there are neither, outline what you think the procedure(s) should be.

ACTIVITY ANSWER GUIDANCE

If an organisation lands in court or in some legal sub-forum (such as the UK system of employment tribunals) to defend its actions in respect of any grievance or disciplinary matter, there are five tests that will be applied to the employer's actions: fairness, reasonableness, consistency, operating with just cause, and operating within the law. Grievance and disciplinary issues are usually regarded as linked and often share common procedures to avoid the perception that one is being given greater status or importance than the other by the organisation. Useful advice on the handling of grievance and disciplinary matters, both from the employee's point of view and that of the employer, and also advice on employee relations issues more generally, can be found at the Advisory, Conciliation and Arbitration Service (ACAS) website: http://www.acas.org.uk/. ACAS is a publicly funded body whose remit is to 'improve organisations and working life through better employment relations'. It has produced a Code of Practice for Disciplinary and Grievance Procedures, aspects of which feature in the case study below.

performers. Supervisors are forced to address performance problems before they become too costly and cannot be remedied.

- Supervisors' views of performance are communicated more clearly. There is greater accountability in how managers discuss performance expectations and provide feedback. When managers possess these competencies, subordinates receive useful information about how their performance is seen by their supervisor.

- Organisational goals are made clear. The goals of the unit and the organisation are made clear, and the employee understands the link between what he or she does and organisational success.

- Organisational change is facilitated. Performance management systems can be a useful tool to drive organisational change. Performance management provides tools and motivation for individuals to change, which, in turn, helps drive organisational change.

THE COMPONENTS OF PERFORMANCE MANAGEMENT

We can think of effective performance management as comprising three distinct but related components:

- planning for performance
- supporting performance
- assessing performance.

PLANNING FOR PERFORMANCE

It is obvious that if a manager is made responsible for managing the performance of another employee, he or she must be thoroughly familiar with the task or job that the employee is undertaking. He or she must be able to tell whether the task or job has been done properly or not. In other words, the manager must know *the criteria for success or failure* in order to assess performance.

More specifically, we say that the manager must be aware of the knowledge, skills and abilities (KSA) needed to do the job competently. 'Knowledge' here means having the information needed to perform the work. 'Skills' are attributes which are required. These usually have been gained by having done the work in the past. 'Ability' refers to having the physical, emotional, intellectual and psychological aptitudes to perform the work. It is a prime responsibility of the manager to ensure that the employee possesses the KSA required and, if there are any deficiencies in them, to take steps to remedy them.

The KSA and criteria for job success should be explicit in the relevant job description which should summarise the duties and responsibilities – the KSAs – that are required, and the working conditions for the particular job or task.

As an illustration, see the job description that is the case study 'Personnel recruiter for Tartan Bank' below.

This job description includes information about what tasks are performed (eg 'Interview applicants to obtain information on work history, training, education, and job skills'). It also includes information about required knowledge (eg of the organisation's principles and procedures for personnel recruitment, selection, training, compensation and benefits, employee relations and negotiation, and personnel information systems), skills (eg 'active listening'), and abilities (eg 'to communicate effectively').

CASE STUDY

PERSONNEL RECRUITER FOR TARTAN BANK

Job role: To seek out, interview, and screen applicants to fill existing and future job openings and promote career opportunities within Tartan Bank.

Reporting relationship: The post-holder will work as a member of a team of up to six HR specialists and will report directly to a human resources manager.

Work activities: The primary activities of the position are recruiting, interviewing, selecting, and hiring of employees in various parts of Tartan Bank. To do this the post-holder must communicate with, and provide information for, supervisors, co-workers and other peers, and in some cases, subordinates. She or he must be competent at gathering relevant information and establishing and maintaining interpersonal relationships with these fellow-employees, and also be able to communicate effectively with people outside the organisations, such as recruitment agencies, media, customers, members of the public and industry agencies. On a personal level, the post-holder must be able to organise, plan and prioritise her or his own work, analyse information effectively and be capable in solving problems and making decisions. A very important part of the job is to ensure organisational compliance with both relevant legal/regulatory requirements and appropriate company policies on hiring staff.

Key tasks

Establish and maintain relationships with hiring managers to stay abreast of current and future hiring and business needs.

Interview applicants to obtain information on work history, training, education, and job skills.

Maintain current knowledge of relevant employment legislation and policies.

Perform searches for qualified candidates according to relevant job criteria, using computer databases, networking, Internet recruiting resources, cold calls, media, recruiting firms, and employee referrals.

Prepare and maintain employment records.

Contact applicants to inform them of employment possibilities, consideration, and selection.

Inform potential applicants about facilities, operations, benefits, and job or career opportunities in organisations.

Screen and refer applicants to hiring personnel in the organisation, making hiring recommendations when appropriate.

Arrange for interviews and provide travel arrangements as necessary.

Advise managers and employees on staffing policies and procedures.

Required competencies
(i) Knowledge requirements

Administration and management: Knowledge of business and management principles involved in strategic planning, resource allocation, human resources modelling, leadership techniques, and coordination of people and resources.

Personnel and human resources: Knowledge of principles and procedures for personnel recruitment, selection, training, compensation and benefits, employee relations and negotiation, and personnel information systems.

English language: Knowledge of the structure and content of the English language including the meaning and spelling of words, rules of composition, and grammar.

Clerical: Knowledge of administrative and clerical procedures and systems such as word processing, managing files and records, designing forms, and other office procedures and terminology.

Communications and media: Knowledge of media production, communication, and dissemination techniques and methods. This includes alternative ways to inform and entertain via written, oral, and visual media.

Customer and personal service: Knowledge of principles and processes for providing customer and personal services. This includes customer needs assessment, meeting quality standards for services, and evaluation of customer satisfaction.

(ii) Skills requirements

Active listening: Giving full attention to what other people are saying, taking time to understand the points being made, asking questions as appropriate, and not interrupting at inappropriate times.

Reading comprehension: Understanding written sentences and paragraphs in work-related documents.

Speaking: Talking to others to convey information effectively.

Service orientation: Actively looking for ways to help people.

Time management: Managing her or his own time.

Writing: Communicating effectively in writing as appropriate for the needs of the audience.

Judgement and decision-making: Considering the relative costs and benefits of potential actions to choose the most appropriate one.

Critical thinking: Using logic and reasoning to identify the strengths and weaknesses of alternative solutions, conclusions or approaches to problems.

If a current job description is not available, it will be necessary to create one using the process of job analysis which determines the key components of a particular job, including activities, tasks, products, services and processes. It will not normally be the responsibility of a general or line manager to undertake personally a job analysis or to produce a job description. Such tasks are typically undertaken by a job analyst or HR specialist, although the supervising manager will have a vital role in providing information.

For existing jobs, job analysis can be conducted using observation, standard questionnaires, or interviews. Data may be collected from job incumbents (ie those doing the job at present) and their supervisors. Alternatively, if the job is yet to be created, data can be gathered from the individual(s) responsible for creating the new position and from those who will supervise individuals in the new position.

Generic job descriptions can be obtained from the Occupational Informational Network (O*NET, http://online.onetcenter.org/find/). O*NET is a comprehensive database of worker attributes and job characteristics, and provides a common language for defining and describing occupations. The descriptions available via O*NET can serve as a foundation for a job description. O*NET descriptions can be easily adapted and changed to accommodate specific local characteristics.

Job descriptions are a prerequisite for any performance management system because they provide the criteria (ie yardsticks) to be used in measuring performance. Criteria can correspond to behaviours (ie how to perform) or to results (ie what outcomes should result from performance).

In relation to our personnel recruiter example, a behavioural criterion could involve the skill of interviewing job applicants. A supervisor could rate the extent to which the personnel recruiter effectively obtains information on work history, training, education, and job skills.

In order to manage someone's performance we need to be able to identify the results of their activities. To establish these we must be clear about the key accountabilities or broad areas of a job for which the employee is responsible. We also need to specify objectives we can understand as 'statements of important and measurable outcomes'. Finally, we need to establish performance standards. A performance standard provides a measure of how well employees have achieved each objective.

To summarise, planning for performance entails the supervising manager:

- knowing the knowledge, skills and abilities required on the part of the employee doing the job in question, and ensuring that the employee concerned possesses them; and

- knowing the key accountabilities of the job, the specific objectives that have to be achieved as part of each accountability, and the performance standards of each objective; and ensuring that the employee knows them also.

SUPPORTING PERFORMANCE

Managing the performance of other employees entails evaluating job performance in two complementary ways. First, by maintaining a more-or-less continuous awareness of how the employee is performing, and making suitable responses to this on a mainly informal basis. Second, by operating a formal performance appraisal system, which is documented and may be linked to performance-related pay and is typically part of the organisation's performance management system. The first is part of what we describe in this text as 'supporting performance', and is dealt within the present section. The second covers what we term here 'assessing performance' and is described in the section below.

Both supporting and assessing the performance of others requires that the supervising manager is aware of the level of performance of those for whom he or she is held accountable. In assessing performance this will require documenting as part of the formal appraisal of performance (see below), but in supporting performance often this is unrecorded and is mainly a matter of observation and discussion on a day-to-day basis.

Because the organisation's goals may change over time, the supervising manager has to be able to update or revise initial objectives, standards, key accountabilities and competency areas as required without waiting for scheduled formal performance appraisal meetings.

Even the most capable and motivated individual can only do a good job if the organisation provides the resources that are required. These may be physical – the tools and equipment, hardware and software needed – but they may also be informational and/or human resources. It is the responsibility of the supervising manager to ensure that the employees obtain the resources they need to perform in their jobs as required.

Feedback on how an employee is performing in relation to his or her goals is essential to allow the employee both to understand clearly what is required and to let him or her know how the standard of his or her performance is perceived by the line manager or supervisor.

We also know from the study of organisational psychology that feedback on performance is essential to motivation, and in supporting performance a manager must regularly provide informal feedback on performance. Giving feedback allows the supervising manager to reinforce effective behaviours and progress towards goals, and conversely to discourage behaviours that are ineffective.

An employee's personal development plan is a vital part of any good performance management system because it specifies courses of action to be taken to improve performance.

ASSESSING PERFORMANCE

Here we are concerned with the formal appraisal of performance, which typically is based on a regular, periodic performance review. 'Performance appraisal' is the term usually given to the process of assessing individual performance in a formal, regular and systematic way.

Formal appraisal systems typically have the following characteristics:

- They are set systems with rules and guidelines which must be followed. For example, the intervals between appraisals will be specified (eg six or twelve months), as will be the person(s) who are to conduct the appraisal.

- Traditionally, the appraiser is the direct supervisor or line manager, although it is now common for organisations to involve self-assessment from the appraisee and also input from other players such as peers, subordinates and customers (including 'internal customers') to give what is termed '360-degree' appraisal. Even with 360-degree appraisal, however, the input of the direct supervisor is still usually the most important single factor.

- The main intention of performance appraisal is to provide the organisation with a comprehensive assessment of all relevant aspects of performance. The information collected is recorded, usually in the form of a written report, or in the ratings of individual aspects of performance.

- The basis of the typical formal performance appraisal system is a review of past performance – ie in the period since the previous formal appraisal.

- There will be feedback to the appraisee on their performance, usually by means of an interview but confirmed in writing. The interview will typically include a discussion not only of past performance but also of what might be done to improve performance in the future.

Although we are concerned here with the responsibilities of the manager, the employee who is being managed has certain important responsibilities himself or herself that are worth bearing in mind. The employee should be committed to achieving the agreed goals and objectives and must be willing to communicate with managers about his or her performance and to supply any information required. He or she must also be ready to receive feedback on performance constructively. Of course, all this can be reinforced by training, and the manager must always be clear about the respective responsibilities of both supervisor and employee in the assessment of performance.

Most authorities caution that it is important to distinguish the use of appraisal for training and development purposes on the one hand from its use for rewards (including promotion) on the other, on the grounds that self-interest can corrupt the process of appraisal when tangible rewards are at stake (see the 'HRM dilemma' below).

The process of formal appraisal has the following elements:

- self-appraisal by the employee of his or her performance against agreed goals and objectives

- appraisal by the employee's supervisor/manager of the employee's performance against agreed goals and objectives

- appraisal by others of the employee's performance against agreed goals and objectives (for 360-degree appraisal)

- a regular periodic performance review interview following the above three appraisals at which the appraisals are discussed by the supervisor/manager with the employee

- a formal written report on the performance review interview signed by the supervisor/manager and the employee

- a development plan incorporated within the formal written report.

Formal appraisal relies on a record – usually known as an 'appraisal form' – being kept of the assessment of an employee's performance. Effective appraisal forms should be simple, relevant, clear and comprehensive.

Where a rating of performance is included in the appraisal, the organisation must be aware of the potential for raters to over- or under-rate performance. Mis-rating may occur intentionally or unintentionally. Managers may deliberately overrate an employee's performance to avoid confrontation or as a result of favouritism. A manager might overrate all of the employees for whom he or she is accountable in order to improve the perception of his own performance as manager. Or a manager may consciously underrate an employee out of spite or as a result of favouritism towards one or more other employees in the same team. Where peer assessment is operated, groups of peers might be motivated to overrate each other.

Unintentional rating errors can occur because of the psychological complexity of the task. Psychologists have identified the phenomenon of the 'halo effect' whereby one attribute of the person being appraised obscures other aspects and unconsciously leads the appraiser to distort the overall assessment of the person's performance. The halo effect may operate either to increase or decrease rating wrongly. For example, a halo effect may occur when the appraisee and the appraiser share a common background such as going to the same school or coming from the same town. In such instances the halo effect would probably lead to overrating. However, significant dissimilarities may trigger a negative halo effect – eg if the appraiser and appraisee belong to different cultural, national or ethnic groups which have traditional conflicts with each other – and in such cases underrating would be the probable outcome.

Another source of error or bias is what is termed 'central tendency', which is where raters avoid the extremes of the scale and rate most or all employees at the mid-point regardless of their actual performance. They may perhaps do this to avoid making difficult or controversial decisions about the performance of any particular employee. Some authorities recommend the use of an even number of points on the rating scale to avoid this. Others reject this solution on two grounds: (i) eliminating a precise mid-point does not in itself prevent the same sort of bias occurring – a biased rater would simply tend to rate everyone at the first available point above the central area (ie the third point on a four-point scale or the fourth on a six-point one); and (ii) there will be some instances where an employee's performance truly lies at the mid-point between the extremes of the scale.

Another solution sometimes recommended to avoid rating errors is to have a policy whereby everyone's performance is rated as 'acceptable' unless there are good reasons which can be documented to justify a higher or lower rating. This has the advantage of requiring raters to furnish proof of exceptional performance whether good or bad. Critics suggest that this results in few people being rated as other than acceptable performers and can result in the appraisal system being rather too much of a blunt instrument.

Both intentional and unintentional distortion in performance ratings can be minimised by providing raters with appropriate training.

Teams are ever-present in modern organisations, and it would be difficult to find an organisation without some type of work done by teams. Including team performance as part of the performance management system is a natural extension of a system that focuses on individual performance only. The general principles we have discussed above still apply. However, teams differ on the basis of the tasks they perform (from routine to non-routine) and on membership configuration (from static to dynamic).

👁 HRM DILEMMA

Should pay be linked to appraisal of performance ?

It seems obvious that if people know that assessment of their performance will impact on their rewards, they will have an incentive to enhance their accounts of their own performance. '360-degree' appraisal may go some way to reducing this possibility, but even then peers may conspire tacitly to overrate each other.

This is why standard advice to managers from social psychologists was never to link rewards directly to performance assessment.

On the other hand, one senior manager told the present author that when his firm started to link rewards to performance explicitly, 'At least then everyone wanted their regular performance appraisal interview. Before that, both employees and managers gave it very low priority and Human Resources were always tearing their hair out trying to get people to do them.'

✳ HRM in action

CASE STUDY

Local authority seeks to raise standards after Khyra Ishaq case

Six social workers have been sacked from Birmingham City Council for failing to meet performance standards, it has been revealed.

Colin Tucker, Director of Children's Services at the Council, claimed the dismissed staff showed 'no sign whatsoever' of meeting expected levels of competence.

Tucker – who was brought in to head up the department after it was severely criticised by Ofsted – told the BBC that the staff in question were not doing their jobs properly

He said: 'There is a clear indication we are serious about our standards. We are not appointing some staff, and as well as that, we have dismissed six staff in the last year. They did not adhere to standards and expectations that we laid down. They showed no sign whatsoever that they were keen to do so, so we dismissed them.'

Birmingham social services were censured over the death of seven-year-old Khyra Ishaq, who died from starvation in May 2008, despite being known to social workers. The child's mother and stepfather were thereafter jailed for manslaughter, and the city council is currently conducting a serious review of the case.

While the recent sackings were not said to be directly linked to the Ishaq case, eight other children known to social services have died in the city in the past three years. Tucker said he was aware of 'one situation where a child died of neglect' in Birmingham in the past seven months.

Tucker also revealed that 120 vacant posts had been filled with agency staff, but that he was seeking to reduce this to between 40 and 50, filling the remaining roles through training and the recruitment of permanent workers. The department currently employs 750 social workers overall.
Source: article by Michelle Stevens, *People Management* Online, 19 March 2010

Point for reflection:

This is a particularly tragic case but it raises the question: just how can you measure the performance of social workers?

PERFORMANCE MANAGEMENT AT MID-SCOTLAND DISTRICT COUNCIL

Mid-Scotland District Council provides local government services for a population of approximately 500,000 people. One of these services is the provision of libraries for the general public under the management of the Council's Leisure and Communities Department. The Department also provides three other main services: Community learning and development; Parks, sports and leisure; and Development and support (which provides financial support for independent leisure and arts groups within the District).

The Council's Strategic Plan for 2010–2015 states that:

> Library services provision will be enhanced throughout Mid-Scotland and a target has been set to increase readers' use of the library facilities by an average 5% overall per annum and with a specific target of 10% for young people (14 to 18).

This is the only reference to the Library Service in the Strategic Plan.

The Leisure and Communities Department has the following statements of vision and mission, although there are no specific statements for the Library service.

Our Vision is:

We believe in the right of everyone to:

- be heard
- become an active, informed citizen
- develop their knowledge, skills and critical awareness
- influence and achieve change
- realise their potential.

Our Mission is to:

- encourage greater access, participation and creative expression through the promotion of a wide range of lifelong learning opportunities
- promote social, educational, cultural and recreational opportunities which build self-confidence and raise aspirations
- assist in the creation of sustainable, healthier communities, which people feel they belong to and have a sense of pride in
- improve quality of life in the city through the delivery of quality services
- contribute to the continuing development of Mid-Scotland as a vibrant cultural, leisure and visitor destination.

Three of the key positions within the Library Service are those of Senior Librarian, Librarian and Library Technician. Job descriptions for each post are given below.

Senior Librarian

Job role: To administer libraries and perform related professional library services within the Council's Public Library Service.

Responsibilities include:

- administering a library
- managing one or more teams of up to 12 staff, comprising librarians and library technicians
- selecting, acquiring, cataloguing, classifying, circulating, and maintaining library materials
- furnishing reference, bibliographical, and readers' advisory services
- performing in-depth, strategic research, synthesising, analysing, editing, and filtering information
- setting up and working with databases and information systems to catalogue and access information.

Reporting relationship: Senior Librarians report directly to the Director of Library Services.

Key tasks:

Manage a library team comprising librarian and library technicians, including supervising personnel activities, budgeting, and planning.

Assist the Director of Library Services in creating and implementing a Library Strategy.

Assist in the professional development of librarians and librarian technicians.

Search standard reference materials, including online sources and the Internet, to answer patrons' reference questions.

Analyse patrons' requests to determine needed information, and assist in furnishing or locating that information.

Teach library patrons to search for information using databases.

Keep records of circulation and materials.

Check books in and out of the library.

Explain the use of library facilities, resources, equipment, and services, and provide information about library policies.

Review and evaluate resource materials such as book reviews and catalogues, in order to select and order print, audiovisual, and electronic resources.

Code, classify, and catalogue books, publications, films, audiovisual aids, and other library materials based on subject matter or standard library classification systems.

Locate unusual or unique information in response to specific requests.

Post-holders must be educated to Bachelor's degree level and hold a professional qualification in librarianship, and will be expected to have a minimum of five years' professional experience as a librarian or in a similar position.

Librarian

Job role: To provide professional library services and to assist in administering libraries, within the Council's Public Library Service.

Responsibilities include:

- selecting, acquiring, cataloguing, classifying, circulating, and maintaining library materials
- furnishing reference, bibliographical, and readers' advisory services
- performing in-depth, strategic research, synthesising, analysing, editing, and filtering information
- setting up and working with databases and information systems to catalogue and access information.

Reporting relationship: Librarians work in library teams which comprise a number of Librarians and Library Technicians, and they report directly to a Senior Librarian.

Key tasks:

Assist the Senior Librarian in managing a library team comprising Librarians and Library Technicians. This may include supervising personnel activities, and helping with budgeting and planning,

Assist the Senior Librarian in the development of Librarian Technicians.

Search standard reference materials, including online sources and the Internet, to answer patrons' reference questions.

Analyse patrons' requests to determine needed information, and assist in furnishing or locating that information.

Teach library patrons to search for information using databases.

Keep records of circulation and materials.

Check books in and out of the library.

Explain the use of library facilities, resources, equipment, and services, and provide information about library policies.

Review and evaluate resource material, such as book reviews and catalogues, in order to select and order print, audiovisual, and electronic resources.

Code, classify, and catalogue books, publications, films, audiovisual aids, and other library materials based on subject matter or standard library classification systems.

Locate unusual or unique information in response to specific requests.

Applicants must be educated to Bachelor's degree level and hold a professional qualification in librarianship, and will be expected to have minimum of two years' professional experience as a librarian or in a similar position.

Library Technician

Job role: To assist Librarians by helping readers in the use of library catalogues, databases, and indexes to locate books and other materials; and by answering questions that require only brief consultation of standard reference. To compile records; sort and shelve books; remove or repair damaged books; register patrons; and check materials in and out of the circulation process. To replace materials in shelving area (stacks) or files.

Reporting relationship: Library Technicians work in library teams which comprise a number of Technicians and Librarians. All library team members report directly to a Senior Librarian who heads the team.

Key tasks:

Reserve, circulate, renew, and discharge books and other materials.

Enter and update patrons' records on computers.

Provide assistance for teachers and students by locating materials and helping to complete special projects.

Answer routine reference inquiries, and refer patrons needing further assistance to Librarians.

Guide patrons in finding and using library resources, including reference materials, audiovisual equipment, computers, and electronic resources.

Sort books, publications, and other items according to procedure and return them to shelves, files, or other designated storage areas.

Deliver and retrieve items throughout the library by hand or using pushcart.

Post-holders should be educated to high-school level with qualification suitable for entrance to college/university Bachelor degree programmes.

Case study questions:

Your services as an HR consultant have been engaged by Mid-Scotland District Council to assist the Director of Library Services in improving the performance management of her staff.

1 The Director of Library Services has announced that she wishes to pursue a results-oriented approach to performance management within the Library Service. What recommendations would you make on measuring results and behaviours for (i) Senior Librarians, (ii) Librarians, and (iii) Library Technicians?

2 At his last performance review meeting with Sheila, the Senior Librarian, Bill – one of the Library Technicians – admitted that his job performance was suffering because he had not really got to grips with new digital technology. Bill is the designated Visual Arts (VA) Technician and his main job for many years has been to look after the library's extensive

collection of photographic slides and other images of artworks. Local students and schoolteachers are the main users of this facility, and many have been complaining that they cannot use the visual resources of the library because they cannot access images in digital form. Feedback from Bill's co-workers also indicates that that a number of the younger members of staff have found him a bit uncooperative and 'difficult to work with'. Older team members who have worked with Bill for a number of years are less critical, but when asked directly by Sheila they admit that Bill is 'not a team player'. When Sheila discussed this with Bill, he replied that he had been the VA Technician for 20 years, 'long before we had these teams', and that he was used to working on his own. He admitted that he found working in a team difficult and did not really know how to handle it.

On the basis of the above, what would you recommend for Bill's personal development plan?

MID-SCOTLAND DISTRICT COUNCIL: GUIDANCE

1 Measuring results and behaviours

In measuring performance when pursuing a results approach to performance management, the first step is to identify accountabilities, which are the particular areas in which an individual is expected to focus.

Examples of appropriate objectives might be:

- *Senior Librarian*: effective and efficient administration of his/her library.
- *Librarian*: provision of professional library service to patrons.
- *Librarian Technician*: provision of support library service to patrons.

Once all key accountabilities are identified, the second step is to set objectives for each accountability. These should be (a) specific and clear, (b) challenging, (c) agreed, (d) significant, (e) prioritised, (f) bound by time, (g) achievable, (h) fully communicated, (i) flexible, and (j) limited in number.

For example, one of the objectives for the Senior Librarian could be *to increase book borrowing by the 14 to 16 age group*.

Similarly appropriate objectives can be set for the Librarians and Librarian Technicians from their job descriptions.

The third step is to determine performance standards. Good standards are (a) related to the position, (b) concrete, specific, and measurable, (c) practical to measure, (d) meaningful, (e) realistic and achievable, and (f) reviewed regularly.

For example, the performance standards for the objective specified above for the Senior Librarian could be to increase book borrowing by the 14 to 16 age group *by 5% in the following 12 months without increasing costs*.

Again, performance standards for the objectives that will have been offered for Librarians and Library Technicians can be outlined in a similar fashion.

2 Bill's personal development plan

Personal development plans form a key component of a performance management system because they specify courses of action to be taken to improve performance. A good development plan allows employees to fully address two major objectives:

- to do better in the future

- to avoid performance problems faced in the past.

The two main problems with Bill's current job performance, and on which development should focus, are clearly his present deficiencies in (i) working with new technology, familiarity with which would enable him to replace the outmoded slides with electronically stored images of artworks which library users now desire; and (ii) teamworking skills, which, given the nature and functions of the library, will probably be in the context of service teams but might also include project teams.

Development plans should include a description of the specific development objectives and of the specific steps to be taken to achieve them. A good plan therefore includes information on (a) the development objectives, (b) how the new skills or knowledge will be acquired, (c) a time-line regarding the acquisition of the new skills or knowledge, and (d) standards and measures that will be used to assess whether the objectives have indeed been achieved.

Sheila and Bill should agree specific learning and development objectives for both technology and teamworking skills, and these should take into account the needs of both the individual and the organisation.

As direct supervisor, Sheila has a key role in helping Bill define the scope of the development plan and in explaining the relationship between the development objectives and strategic priorities for the Library and the Council. Sheila will also have direct responsibility for checking on Bill's progress towards achieving the agreed learning and development objectives, and for providing resources so that Bill will be able to engage in the appropriate activities. Supervisors must reinforce an employee's accomplishments towards completing a development plan so that the employee remains motivated. Supervisors themselves must be motivated to perform all these functions in support of their employees' development plans, and so Sheila's own performance review by the Director of Library Services should include reference to Bill's ongoing development (and that of the rest of her staff in the library).

MANAGING REWARDS

Rewards, both financial and other, are of obvious importance to employees and employers. One of the central changes which HRM has brought about in management thinking is that it is no longer enough for employers to think in terms of the old common-law principle of 'a fair day's pay for a fair day's work'. Employee commitment and motivation are so important in today's competitive, knowledge-based world that rewards have to be actively managed to secure the maximum utilisation of human assets, and to attract, motivate and retain core employees. HRM has introduced the term 'reward management' to replace simple 'wage and salary administration'.

Probably the single most significant change in reward management in the UK in the last 20 years has been the extension of performance-related pay beyond the shop floor to white-collar and professional staff, who traditionally were paid straightforward salaries.

Both employees and employers are always concerned about issues of reward and performance. So far as rewards are concerned, employees are most concerned about perceived fairness. Employers seek control and minimisation of costs combined with capacity to offer attractive packages to core staff. These objectives are not incompatible with an HRM viewpoint from management: performance-related pay, at least in principle, should allow reward and motivation for the employee and cost-control at the same time.

This section reviews traditional and more contemporary pay systems and discusses fringe benefits and cafeteria systems.

PAY SYSTEMS

In considering the payment system for any part of their workforce, management will normally seek one that they believe will give the greatest degree of cost and supervisory control, and provide the best incentive for employees.

There is no perfect payment system for any situation, and no payment system will continue to operate satisfactorily indefinitely. Anomalies will develop over time and employees will come to regard bonuses as entitlements to be consolidated into basic pay.

MONEY MATTERS

Despite some interpretations of motivation theory (see Chapter 3) which seem to play down money as a motivating factor at work, most organisations behave as if they believe that money certainly does motivate people. Even Frederick Herzberg – usually viewed as the leading advocate of the view that money is not a motivator – is reported as having admitted that 'It sure as hell helps me sort out my priorities!' (Child, 1984; p.188). Most people appear to be interested in making money if they have the opportunity to do so. This would seem to apply just as much to those who are fortunate enough to have jobs which are already high in financial and intrinsic rewards as to those who face genuine hardship. For example, hospital consultants and dentists working for the NHS in the UK are often keen to increase their earnings by taking private patients, and the remuneration of top executives in industry and commerce regularly causes

REFLECTIVE ACTIVITY

Outline a reward system for:

- casual agricultural workers employed seasonally to pick fruit
- skilled electricians employed on maintenance duties in a power station
- university lecturers.

Note that we return to this Activity at the end of the chapter, where guidance to possible answers is also presented.

scandals in both the USA and the UK because many seem to reward themselves excessively. Pay and fringe benefits remain central features in contracts of employment and are always prominent issues in collective bargaining.

The value that individuals put on pay compared to other rewards can vary according to personal circumstances over which management have no control. An employee's domestic situation may dictate the extent to which he or she would be willing to trade off pay against other benefits, for example.

Pay is expressed in monetary terms which make it easy to calculate. This gives a clear scale of measurement and a link to measures of performance or output. It also means that it can be easily costed.

Until relatively recently, the management of pay in Britain tended to focus narrowly on the issues of pay and job performance. However, in the twenty-first century 'reward management' is seen as an integral part of HRM with an interest in wider motivational issues of attraction, retention, employee expectations, skill development, and the reinforcement of organisational culture and business strategy. We should always remember that rewards can include pay and non-monetary benefits.

FAIRNESS

Any pay system will fail if it is perceived to be unfair by the employees.

Fairness of pay is a comparative concept, not an absolute one, and it may vary from society to society and workplace to workplace. It is concerned with the relationship between the pay of different individuals and different groups, and it reflects perceptions of esteem and self-esteem. People tend to take comparisons, as we might expect, more seriously with those physically and socially closer, rather than with those who are distant. Convention seems to be the usual basis for accepting the fairness of a pay differential, and so changes in the status quo always provoke most anxieties about unfairness (Wootton, 1955).

Collective bargaining, by which management and trade unions jointly agree pay rates, usually reinforces the perception of fairness because the use of traditional comparisons provides both employers and trade unions with a basis that is seen to be reasonable.

TYPES OF PAYMENT SYSTEM

Payment systems may be classified broadly as either:

- *payment by time* schemes, in which the amount of pay awarded is principally determined by the time spent at work – eg an hourly rate or a monthly salary

or

- *performance-related pay* (PRP) or 'incentive pay schemes', in which some element of the total pay is variable. Two types of PRP system are popular:
  - *payment by results* (PBR), in which the variable element is determined by some objective measure of the work done or its value.

    – *merit-based systems* in which the variable element is related to an assessment of overall job performance by a supervisor or manager.

The 2004 WERS survey found that 40% of UK workplaces had incentive pay schemes (Kersley *et al*, 2006). These were more popular in the private sector than in the public, and there were significant variations from industry to industry. For example, 82% of workplaces in the financial services sector used incentive pay schemes. Incentive schemes were more common generally where product market competition was higher (*ibid*, p. 190). There appears to be a rising trend: PRP schemes were much more likely to be used in UK workplaces in 2004 than in 1998.

In the HRM approach, pay policy is based on three principles which move away from earlier perceptions of simply 'a fair day's pay for a fair day's work':

- Pay policy should reflect and support the business objectives and strategies of the firm.
- Pay should be part of a wider human resources strategy.
- Pay policy and practices should help reinforce the dominant culture of the organisation.

NON-PAY BENEFITS

'Non-pay benefits', which are also called 'fringe benefits' or 'employee benefits', are elements of remuneration that are additional to cash pay.

The main objectives of offering employees non-pay benefits are:

- to ensure that a competitive total remuneration package is provided to attract, retain and motivate staff
- to increase the employees' commitment to the organisation
- to take advantage of tax-efficient methods of rewarding employees (ie where the employer can reduce its tax liability by offering some benefit instead of cash).

PRINCIPAL TYPES OF NON-PAY BENEFITS

The main types of non-pay benefits are:

- *pension schemes*, generally regarded by employees as the most important employee benefit
- *personal security*, which includes extra-statutory sick pay; death in service benefits; personal accident cover; medical insurance; health screening; permanent health insurance (long-term disability cover); business travel insurance; and career counselling (outplacement service)
- *financial assistance*, which includes company loans, season ticket (travel loans); house purchase assistance; relocation assistance; discounts; and fees to professional bodies
- *personal needs*, which includes holidays, compassionate leave, extra-statutory

maternity leave and pay; paternity pay; child care; career breaks; counselling; fitness and recreational facilities; and other forms of leave

- *company car and petrol*
- *other (tangible) benefits* such as subsidised meals, clothing allowance, telephone costs, and credit card facilities
- *intangible benefits*, such as status; power; recognition of achievement; training opportunities; career progression; good working conditions; recognition of the need to balance work and family responsibilities; and flexibility.

Note that all *tangible* non-pay benefits have a cash value: they can be costed and a cash equivalent could be offered.

PUTTING IT ALL TOGETHER: THE 'CAFETERIA' APPROACH TO MANAGING REWARDS

This allows employees a degree of choice in their total remuneration package – for example, by permitting them to take fewer fringe benefits and more pay, or vice versa. The total overall value of their compensation remains the same whatever choices they make. This allows individuals to tailor their rewards to their particular needs and, importantly, allows them to alter their rewards as their needs change. For example, a working mother might choose to reduce her superannuation contributions in favour of more take-home pay for a number of years, whereas a middle-aged employee might wish to increase his superannuation payment to improve his eventual retirement package.

Typically, a cafeteria system features a core package of benefits topped up by a percentage of gross pay available for additional components.

The principle advantages of cafeteria systems are:

- employee satisfaction
- the communication of the real costs of benefits to employees and employers
- the identification of the popularity of various benefits.

The disadvantages are:

- the complexity of costing out non-pay benefits
- potentially greater administrative costs
- potentially considerable tax complications for employees.

JOB EVALUATION

As Rosabeth Moss Kanter has put it, the basis for determining pay is changing 'from position to performance, from status to contribution' (Kanter, 1988).

This would seem to be inevitable for organisations operating in increasingly uncertain and competitive markets. In fact, we should expect employees' pay to be determined by the market worth of their skills, knowledge and experience, and their actual performance in the job. Increasingly, these factors are becoming important in the UK, but the fact remains that many employers feel the need for some method of establishing the relative internal value of jobs. There are two main reasons for this:

- If a hierarchy of jobs can be determined in as independent and objective a manner as possible, decisions about actual grades – and so, pay rates – should be more consistent and defensible.

- In many countries equal-value pay legislation decrees that women are entitled to equal pay with men (and vice versa) where the work is of equal value in terms of demands made in areas such as effort, skill and decisions. In Britain the case of *Bromley v H&J Quick Ltd* (1988, IRLR 249 CA) established that a job evaluation scheme can only provide a defence in an equal-value claim if it is analytical in nature. This implies that it should be a points scheme based on factor comparisons (see below). So employers who feel that they may be vulnerable to equal-value claims are easily persuaded that such schemes are essential. Above all, Article 119 of the Treaty of Rome provides that member states of the European Union shall maintain the application of the principle that men and women should receive equal pay for equal work.

  Whereas under UK law the burden of proof lies on an applicant to show that on the balance of probabilities she or he is not receiving equal pay, a decision of the European Court in *Handels- og Kontorfunktionaerernes Forbund i Danmark v Dansk Arbejdsgiverforening* (the 'Danfoss case') indicates that if a pay system manifestly produces inequalities of pay between the sexes, the burden of proof lies with the employers to show that the criteria used which produce these inequalities are not discriminatory.

THE JOB EVALUATION PROCESS

A job evaluation scheme has to be carried out with a view to evaluating jobs in terms of demands made of a worker under various headings such as effort, skill, decision-making, etc, so as to lead to a fair comparison with a comparator's job. This is termed the 'analytical' approach and is to be preferred to the 'felt-fair' or 'whole-job' approach.

There are some general points to note:

- Job evaluation is intended to determine the relative positions of jobs within a hierarchy. It is a comparative process which determines grades but *not* actual rates of pay. These must be established by some other mechanism.

- Job evaluation is normally conducted by a panel on the basis of information obtained by means of job analysis. It is a systematic but not infallible process.

- The performance of individuals in the jobs being evaluated should play no part in the evaluation process: it is the job not the job-holder that is being evaluated. This important general principle is easily applied in most situations but it should be noted that in complex, specialist jobs it can be more difficult to separate individuals' performance from their job requirements since, as jobs become more complicated and innovative, they are more likely to become constructed around the personal strengths and capabilities of the job-holder. This can be the case with, for example, highly specialised technical jobs or senior managerial ones.

- Job analysis provides the raw material for job evaluation.

JOB EVALUATION SYSTEMS

The three conventional categories of job evaluation are:

- job ranking
- job classification
- points-factor schemes.

Job ranking

The most simple form of job evaluation, job ranking is non-analytical in that it considers the job as a whole, and does not attempt to assess different aspects of the job separately. Job ranking determines the relative value of jobs in a hierarchy by placing them in rank order according to the worth of each job as established by job analysis.

The advantages of job ranking are that it is simple to undertake, easily understood and relatively inexpensive.

The disadvantages are (i) that there are no defined standards for judging relative values and this can lead to inconsistencies; (ii) that it can be difficult to establish ranking order between broadly similar jobs – the technique of paired-comparisons is sometimes used to alleviate both these problems; and (iii) that it does not equate to a defence in 'equal value' cases.

Job classification

Job classification is a non-analytical technique in which the grades to be used are first defined, and then jobs are allocated to grades by comparing the job description (produced by job analysis) with the grade definitions.

The advantages of job classification are that it is simple to introduce and use, and that the grade definitions provide some standards for judgement.

The disadvantages are (i) that grade definitions are usually so general that they are not terribly helpful in assessing borderline cases; (ii) that it is not very applicable to senior or complex jobs; and (iii) that it does not equate to a defence in 'equal value' cases.

Managing the performance of others is a continuous process. At the level of the individual manager (as opposed to the organisation), it comprises three closely related components or sub-competencies: (a) planning for performance, (b) supporting performance, and (c) assessing performance. Each of the three sub-competencies plays an important role. If any one of these is implemented poorly, the entire process of managing performance suffers.

Job descriptions provide vital information needed to manage performance, particularly the criteria for job success and failure, whether these are measured in terms of behaviour or in terms of results.

Rewards have to be actively managed to secure the maximum utilisation of human assets, and to attract, motivate and retain core employees. Despite some interpretations of motivational theory, we cannot ignore the importance of money in rewards packages. Payment systems may be based on time, or may be variable where an element of total pay is dependent on some measure of output or an assessment of overall performance.

A 'cafeteria system' of rewards allows employees the flexibility, within limits, to decide the particular make-up of their total rewards package, and gives them scope to alter it as their personal needs and requirements change. This can be very attractive to core employees but such schemes are administratively complex.

Performance management is really a management philosophy rather than just a set of techniques. It is a more comprehensive concept than simply performance-related pay or performance appraisal, and uses goals, measurement, feedback and recognition as a means of motivating people to achieve.

Job evaluation is in some ways a bureaucratic throwback to the days of traditional personnel management, but because only an analytical job evaluation scheme can provide an employer with a legal defence in 'equal value/pay' cases, its importance is actually growing in the twenty-first century.

JOB EVALUATION IN SCOTTISH SOFTRONICS PLC

Background information

Scottish Softronics is a small high-technology engineering firm located in a greenfield site in the Scottish Central Belt, which specialises in providing complex electronic/mechanical engineering products that interface with state-of-the-art software engineering. Its major clients are leading software producers in the financial services industry. It has grown in size rapidly in the last few years after creating a number of new product lines. The firm prides itself on its reputation for being a well-managed, technologically competent, high-quality supplier. The firm recently won its first Queen's Award for Exports. Trade unions are not recognised by the firm, but management acknowledge the importance of employee relations and there is a staff association which employees are encouraged to join and with which management regularly consult over pay and main conditions of employment.

Concerns about equal pay issues in the industry, combined with more general worries that the pay/grading structure is becoming unwieldy as a result of rapid growth and fast-changing work practices, have prompted the managing director to ask the human resources director to brief him on the advisability of using job evaluation in the firm.

The HR director responded with a confidential memorandum the contents of which may be summarised as follows.

Job evaluation (JE) is widely used in British industry, partly – as the MD perceived – to protect employers against 'equal value' claims from employees at tribunals.

Job evaluation has a tendency to become bureaucratic and to encourage a multiplicity of rigid grades. Such developments would not be helpful to Scottish Softronics which has invested considerable time, effort and expense in introducing flexible work practices on the shopfloor and lower management. If JE is to be introduced, every effort should be made to avoid these potential difficulties.

Job evaluation should not be used to set the actual pay rates far each grade, but rather to set the general structure.

Scottish Softronics has recently introduced performance-related pay (PRP) for all employees. The company would have to ensure that any JE scheme it adopted would not interfere with PRP. The HR director added that through his membership of the Chartered Institute of Personnel and Development he was acquainted with several organisations which shared Scottish Softronics' general business philosophy and which appeared to be able to combine JE and PRP successfully. The HR director's recommendation was that JE should be adopted.

If this was accepted, a small steering committee should be formed, consisting of seven working members – four from management and three nominated from the staff association. The HR director would chair the committee and report to the MD on progress.

The MD responded that the board accepted the HR director's recommendation, and he instructed the director to proceed.

The job evaluation exercise

Scottish Softronics employs approximately 400 people, of whom just over 300 are shopfloor staff.

At the first meeting of the steering committee it was agreed that there should be no more than four general grades: associate (ie shopfloor), senior associate, administration, and management. An inspection of the payroll and personnel records revealed that there were something like 80 different jobs. The HR director indicated that although he would expect to see that number reduced, he was not too concerned about job titles or the number of jobs in total so long as the proposed system of four grades could be made to work.

At two further meetings of the committee, 10 existing jobs were selected as benchmarks. A list of ten factors was drawn up: skill, effort, job complexity, responsibility, diplomacy, job conditions, supervision received, contact, dexterity, training.

Case study questions:

Consider the ten factors listed above.

Would you make any changes to them?

Would you weight any of them – and if you would, how?

concluded that some factors overlapped and others were hard to define clearly. The factors were redesigned working on the basis of four generic factors: skill, effort, responsibility, and job conditions. The factors were then reweighted.

Generic factors	Job factors	Points range	Weighting
SKILL	Education	1–5	3
	Experience	1–5	3
	Initiative	1–5	3
EFFORT	Physical demands	1–5	1
	Mental demands	1–5	3
RESPONSIBILITY	Process/equipment demands	1–5	1
	Material/product demands	1–5	1
	Responsibility for the work of others	1–5	3
	Responsibility for the safety of others	1–5	3
JOB CONDITIONS	Working conditions	1–5	1
	Unavoidable hazards	1–5	2

The benchmark jobs were then re-evaluated. The committee agreed that the results gave an acceptable grading structure and that the process should be applied to the remaining jobs in the firm.

FINAL CASE STUDY

Read through the Karstadt Warenhaus AG case study in the Appendix (p.231).

Drawing on the contents of the present chapter and the information given in the case study, write a memo to the Managing Director of Karstadt Warenhaus AG advising her on a performance management system for employees of the Karstadt department store chain. Your answer should build on your earlier answer to the question on this case given at the end of Chapter 3.

EXPLORE FURTHER

Armstrong, M. (2009) *Armstrong's Handbook of Human Resource Management Practice*. 11ᵗʰ Edition. London: Kogan Page.

Chapters 38, 'The process of performance management' and 39, '360-degree feedback'; also Chapters 46–53 'Rewarding people'.

Boxall, P., Purcell, J. and Wright, P. (eds) (2007). *The Oxford Handbook of Human Resource Management*. Oxford: Oxford University Press.

Chapter 18. G. Latham, L.M. Sulsky and H. MacDonald. 'Performance Management'.

Chapter 17. J.P. Guthrie. 'Remuneration: Pay effects at work'.

Boxall, P. and Purcell, J. (2006) *Strategy and Human Resource Management*. Basingstoke: Palgrave Macmillan.

Chapter 7. 'Managing individual performance and development'.

Storey, J. (ed.) (2007) *Human Resource Management: A critical text*, 3ʳᵈ edition. London: Thomson Learning

Chapter 9. I. Kessler. 'Reward choices: strategy and equity'. A good account of the evolution of 'new pay' and its relation to HR practices.

CHAPTER 8

HRM and competency, leadership and influencing

INTRODUCTION

Armstrong (2009; p.202) defined competency-based human resource management as being 'about using the notion of competency and the results of competency analysis to inform and improve the processes of performance management, recruitment and selection, employee development and employee reward'. As he noted, the language of competency has dominated much of HR thinking and practice in recent years, largely because it is essentially about individual performance and consequently organisational effectiveness.

LEARNING OUTCOMES

On completion of this chapter you should:

- understand the concept of competency
- understand the idea of a competency framework
- appreciate the importance of leadership in twenty-first-century organisations.

GENERAL DEFINITIONS OF SKILLS AND COMPETENCIES

The *Concise Oxford English Dictionary* defines 'skill' as 'the ability to do something well; expertise or dexterity', deriving through Middle English from the Old Norse *skil*, 'discernment' or 'knowledge'. The same source defines 'competency' as the quality or extent of being 'competent', which in turn is described as 'having the necessary ability or knowledge to do something successfully', from the Latin *competere* in the sense of 'being fit and proper'. It is interesting that there is the basic notion of 'knowledge' in both terms.

Although previous usage of the term 'skill' in management literature often covered what we would now define as 'competence', the latter term is often favoured now. Statements of competence tend to be both fuller in detail and broader in scope than most descriptions of skills, and therefore give more precise meaning. They are also usually more explicitly focused on the achievement of acceptable performance in the job, rather than on mere possession of the capability to perform properly. So, for example, whereas a *skilled* bricklayer will possess the knowledge and ability required to do his or her job properly, in any particular case he or she may not actually work well, for whatever reason – but a *competent* bricklayer not only has the knowledge and ability needed but in fact performs proficiently. This use of the terms 'skill' and 'competency' may seem to be the converse of normal usage: 'skilled' normally suggests a high level of capability whereas 'competent' can imply 'mere competence' – ie the ability to achieve a minimum acceptable standard – but it reflects the managerial imperative for people actually to achieve effective performance and not just to possess the capability to do so.

The Canon Working Party Report into management education training and development in the UK (1994) gave a general description of the notion of management competency in the following way:

> The term 'competency' is taken to mean the ability to perform effectively functions associated with management in a work-related situation.

DEFINITIONS OF COMPETENCIES IN THE MANAGEMENT LITERATURE

The term 'competency' first came to widespread managerial attention in the USA following the publication of Richard Boyatzis' study *The Competent Manager* (1982), which followed earlier work by Klemp (1980). Mangham and Silver (1986), explicitly citing Boyatzis, introduced the term to the UK debate on management development, reporting that many UK organisations and managers at that time lacked even the vocabulary to describe or define properly what they meant by 'competent managerial performance'. At around the same time vocational education in the UK was undergoing a revolution in which traditional examinations and tests of work skills were transformed into 'competence-based' awards. This brings us immediately to a key point in our definitions of 'competence'.

Boyatzis described competency as the 'capacity that exists in a person that leads to behaviour that meets the job demands within the parameters of the organisation environment and that in turn brings results'. The UK Training Agency defined 'competence' as 'actions, behaviour or outcome that the person should be able demonstrate'.

These subtly different definitions actually show that there are two distinct models of competence. The first, following Boyatzis' definition, is what can be termed an 'input model'. That is, it is mainly concerned to define and describe what a competent person brings to the task or job – for example, knowledge or skill, such as the ability to read a balance sheet, or some other attribute such as a personality or character trait, like empathy or hardiness, and so forth. This model is sometimes referred to as 'person-related'. The second, exemplified by the UK Training Agency definition, is an 'output model' and is predominantly concerned with actual performance – eg undertaking the task of totting up a balance sheet correctly, thus demonstrating that the task can be competently done. This is also described as a 'work-related' model.

In practice the distinction is not always clear-cut, and descriptions of output-based competencies may include, for example, some specified knowledge requirements in addition to the observable behaviours that lead to effective demonstration of the stated tasks.

COMPETENCY-BASED HUMAN RESOURCE MANAGEMENT

As noted earlier, the language of competency has dominated much of HR thinking and practice in recent years, largely because it is essentially about individual performance and consequently organisational effectiveness. Although there is often confusion between individual and organisational competencies, these are linked, and another reason for the interest in individual competencies is undoubtedly the importance attached to organisational 'core competencies' (Hamel and Prahalad, 1994). Because these are usually dependent on the organisation's attracting, retaining and motivating key personnel, the HR profession can perhaps be forgiven for jumping on this particular bandwagon.

COMPETENCY FRAMEWORKS

A competency-framework is essentially a structured collection of competencies used by an organisation to frame and underpin activities (managerial or non-managerial). Professional bodies also may use competency frameworks to show the requirements for their qualified practitioners. The use of competency frameworks has become an increasingly accepted part of modern HR practice. Rankin (2004) reported that 76% of responding UK companies when surveyed used competency frameworks or were about to introduce them. The use of competency frameworks has also extended to senior levels of the organisation (top and middle management) in addition to clerical, administrative and non-office roles (CIPD, 2007e).

It has been found empirically that employers' competency frameworks typically contain between 10 and 20 basic competencies which relate to a spectrum of roles across the organisation (IDS, 2001). In addition, some organisations have developed role-specific or technical competencies to address the problem that occurs when the basic competencies turn out to be inadequate for particular roles or jobs. More recently, some organisations have established organisational-cultural competencies which seek to reflect the ethos of the company itself, and these are concerned with ensuring that employees work in a way that is consistent with company culture.

Competency frameworks are now widely used to help select, appraise, train and develop staff. For example, in the recruitment process competencies can contribute to the content of job or role profiles, any written or practical tests, and the job interview itself. Banks of potential interview questions can be developed which are directly linked to a role's competencies. Competencies, together with personal objectives or targets, can form the basis of the appraisal systems used by organisations. In this way, employers can measure how staff carry out their work through assessing their performance against personal objectives and the role's required competencies.

The CIPD's 2007 *Learning and Development* survey (CIPD, 2007d) found that the use of competency frameworks was well established in the workplace, 60% of the respondents having a competency framework in place, and of those who hadn't, almost half (48%) intending to introduce one. In those organisations that had a competency framework, on average almost four out of five employees (78%) were included, and 50% of those organisations had a single competency framework across the organisation.

Table 7 shows the subjects included in competency frameworks as reported by respondents (CIPD, 2007d; p.19).

Table 7 Subjects included in competency frameworks

Skills area	Percentage of respondents
Communication skills	63
People management	59
Team skills	58
Customer service skills	54
Leadership/decision-making	53
Problem-solving skills	50
Technical skills	45
Results-orientation	42
Other	9

Source: CIPD annual *Learning and Development Survey Report, 2007*

The same survey (2007d; p.19) reported the main uses of competency frameworks as in Table 8.

Table 8 Main uses of competency frameworks

Main uses	Percentage of respondents
Performance reviews/appraisals	56
Employee effectiveness	47
Organisational effectiveness	44
Training needs analysis	36
Career development	36
Recruitment	28
Customer satisfaction	26
Job design	19
Other	3

Source: CIPD annual *Learning and Development Survey Report, 2007*

Most competency frameworks (85%) were designed in-house (although often with the help of consultants). A small proportion (8%) used frameworks produced and made available by an external organisation – eg a professional association or government body.

According to the CIPD (2007e) the main benefits of a competency-based system are:

- Employees have a set of objectives to work towards and are clear about how they are expected to perform their jobs.
- The appraisal and recruitment systems are fairer and more open.
- There is a link between organisational and personal objectives.
- Processes are measurable and standardised across organisational and geographical boundaries.

The following criticisms are often made of competency-based systems:

- They can become overly elaborate and bureaucratic.
- They can become out-of-date very quickly due to the fast pace of change in organisations, and it can therefore be expensive and time-consuming to keep them up-to-date.
- Competencies are often based on what good performers have done in the past.
- Competency frameworks can institutionalise discrimination against women and minorities.

The 2010 CIPD *Learning and Talent Management Survey* found that 22% of responding organisations used a competence framework to link coaching to their overall learning and development (CIPD, 2010a; p.18).

CASE STUDY

HRM in action

A competency framework at the English Football Association

The Football Association (FA) is the governing body for football in England and has a high profile in sporting and public life. Some 290 staff are employed and the key focus is the development and regulation of the game at all levels, from international football to grassroots. The FA is a not-for-profit organisation, which means that all the surpluses it gains from its commercial activities are invested back in the game at all levels. The diversity of the organisation's remit necessitates a diverse range of skills and staff. Although everyone is driven by different motivations and needs, all share a common 'love for the game'.

Tom Harlow, who was appointed to his position as Learning and Development Manager in June 2006, made one of his top priorities the establishment of a competency framework to cover all staff. A competency framework had been in place but the system was in disrepair, with different competency categories applied in different parts of the organisation. This made the system overly elaborate, it commanded little respect, and was seen to add little value to the framework of the organisation.

New organisational priorities suggested that a unified approach to performance management was desirable. Both in employee surveys and informal feedback, the FA staff expressed a discomfort with silo working and a desire for career development across functions. A key part of the need to devise and introduce a new framework was the need to recognise the commonality of tasks across the different roles in the workplace and to ensure that these were rewarded fairly.

The new framework was delivered in October 2006. It is based on six behaviours – 'the standards that staff are required to demonstrate to achieve high performance':

- teamworking
- communication
- leadership
- customer service
- delivery, and
- fairness and inclusion.

For each of the six behaviours there are four levels of indicators that correspond to the FA's four hierarchical grades.

The framework was derived internally and Tom drew on his awareness of best practice and his experience in his previous role. The design activity was also aligned to two major business initiatives. The first was a working group looking at the strategy for football development; the second was a group supporting internal communications. The expertise of participants in both groups was used to facilitate the definition of desirable behaviours at all levels in the framework.

The tight timetable applied to complete the framework design was driven by the need to use it as the basis for the 2007 performance review process. In Harlow's view, while they are good at setting objectives, 'Managers are struggling to find a way of dealing with very good or poor performance.'

In this sense, competencies are a tool to facilitate effective performance management. There is a danger of managers' taking the indicators too literally and using them as a checklist for every individual. All managers have been briefed and given detailed support.

They are encouraged to consider 'What is important for the individual and the role?' in interpreting and applying the framework. This approach has been stressed and reinforced in a one-day workshop delivered by external consultants.

The priorities for the next stage of the framework are to audit the understanding and ensure that it is embedded effectively, to integrate it into other HR activities, and to make sure it evolves effectively. The framework will shortly be extended into recruitment activities. So far, it has been well accepted and welcomed by managers and employees, who see it as a clear and concise way of setting standards and measuring performance. They also believe it brings consistency across the organisation and gives clear goals for development. It will have to evolve further and constantly be reinforced and remain fully aligned to the changing needs of the organisation.

Source: information provided by Tom Harlow, Learning and Development Manager; CIPD, annual *Learning and Development Survey Report, 2007* (2007d)

HRM in action

CASE STUDY

The need for managerial competencies: ACME Engineering

Acme Electronics plc was founded in 1924 by Bill Hoyle, a pioneering electrical and electronic engineer, and over the last 50 years has been something of an icon of British high technology. For the period from the end of World War II to the end of the Cold War (1945 to 1989) the company was highly dependent on UK government defence contracts. Until the mid-1980s these large projects were carried out on a cost-plus basis by which the firm charged the UK Ministry of Defence the total cost of the project and then added an acceptable profit margin. This allowed the firm to pursue engineering excellence to produce the best possible defence products. One of its major achievements was the development of world-beating sea radar for UK fighter aircraft such as the Sea Harrier jump-jet, which the US Navy declared to be 'twenty years ahead of anything we have'. Much of the firm's work during that period remains classified for security reasons. The firm had a reputation for employing some of the very best engineering and science graduates in the UK, who were attracted by the technical challenges of its defence work.

The large government projects and the cost-plus basis of contracting insulated the firm from the commercial realties of a competitive, global market and the firm's reputation for management never quite equalled that for its technology. In the mid-1980s the UK government, keen to inject more efficiency into the defence industry, stopped the practice of cost-plus contracting and the market for defence contracts became much more competitive.

Acme found it difficult to compete. Its technological competencies were as impressive as ever, but increasingly it seemed to observers that the firm was lacking managerial and strategic skills. This impression was confirmed in the early 1990s when an American partner who had been brought in to sharpen up its business skills was found to have embezzled over $100 million from the company. The partner went to jail and the firm went into bankruptcy.

It was bought by the Universal Electric Company (UEC), the biggest UK engineering conglomerate, which already had a considerable presence in the defence industry. UEC had been created and was still managed by the formidable Lord Portis, who practised a particularly aggressive type of financial control which included, among other practices, his telephoning every divisional MD every month and asking for personal explanations for all discrepancies between performance and budget. Personal accountability at all levels was the keynote of the UEC managerial culture.

Acme was rationalised by its new owners (or 'ruthlessly asset-stripped', according to some company insiders) but UEC valued its core competencies which were retained in a new division called Acme Defence Solutions (ADS). After a full review of ADS' physical and human resources, UEC concluded that its new acquisition contained significant managerial potential in its engineering project managers, which, if developed could benefit UEC as a whole.

These engineering project managers were typically highly experienced in managing complex, long-term and valuable projects, but due to the culture and working structures of Acme their portfolios of management skills were somewhat lopsided. As one senior Project Engineer put it:

'I never had to deal with people issues. We worked in a matrix structure where the firm had large departments of technical specialists who were seconded to projects under people like me. Projects typically lasted for years. If someone didn't match up or fit in, I just got a replacement the next day. The performance on the project was everything, and my job was to make the project succeed physically – to get the radar or the rocket guidance systems or whatever to work. Cost or efficiency or productivity were never the issues. I suppose these did matter somewhere, but these were for what we called the "bean-counters" – the accountants – to worry about, not us. Technological excellence was our only requirement. We felt we were fighting the Russians – who were better engineers and scientists than you might think – and we simply had to beat them. Like it was real war. As long as we produced the goods, we got whatever resources and people we said we wanted.'

What the company did

A set of 20 project managers were selected as a pilot group. A tripartite agreement was established between the company (represented by UEC's training director), a local university business school and a college of further education.

Each of the 20 managers in the pilot group was assisted in drawing up a personal portfolio of his or her managerial skills and experience. Gaps in development were filled by a mixture of planned experience in the company, taught theoretical courses at a Business School and skills workshops provided by a further education college. For example, most of the managers had no direct experience in recruitment and selection of staff, so managers were invited to sit in on relevant MBA classes in HRM at the Business School as non-examined participants; the further education college put on a weekend in interviewing skills; and the company arranged for the managers to participate in selection interviews across the company. The project managers' progress in developing their competency profiles was factored into their performance management reviews and appraisals.

LEADERSHIP AND INFLUENCING

The *New Shorter Oxford English Dictionary* defines a leader as 'a person who guides others in action or opinion; a person who takes the lead in a business enterprise or movement', and leadership as 'the action of leading or influencing; ability to lead or influence'. Influencing in turn is defined as 'an action exerted imperceptibly or by indirect means, by one person or thing on another so as to cause changes in conduct, development, conditions, etc; ascendancy, moral or political power (over or with a person or group)'.

So our initial everyday definition of leadership includes the idea of taking direct action, which conjures up the picture of issuing face-to-face instructions and performing visible personal, even physical, leadership, and the more intangible and subtle concepts of indirect power, persuasion and moral authority.

ASSESSING EXISTING COMPETENCE LEVEL IN LEADERSHIP AND INFLUENCING SKILLS

Evaluate the present level of your skill in leadership and influencing by responding to the statements below in the *Leadership and influencing competency questionnaire.*

Questionnaire

Rate your agreement or disagreement with each statement below on a scale of 1 to 10 in which **1 corresponds to 'total disagreement' and 10 to 'total agreement'**.

Rating

1   When starting a new task it is my responsibility to identify its objective and tell the others who are to be involved.

2   A manager should always let others know what is expected of them.

3   I always try to find a new and better way to undertake a project.

4   I should initiate action without waiting for other people to draw my attention to it.

5   I always try to give my people instructions and information in simple, clear language.

6   I always look for new approaches to the job.

7   I keep myself and my team informed about due dates and deadlines.

8   You should discourage questions and requests for information which interfere with getting the job done.

9   A manager should provide a good example for others to follow in his or her own work habits.

10   I am open about my mistakes and encourage others to learn from them.

11   I set goals for myself and help others to set their goals.

12   I always give my team feedback on their performance.

13   When assigning tasks to others I inform them of the importance and urgency of the assignment.

14   When appropriate, I delegate tasks to others in accordance with their experience and capabilities.

15   When assigning tasks to others I help them develop by giving them new responsibilities.

16   I assign tasks to others in a way that encourages them to use their initiative as much as possible.

17 When assigning work to others I require them to accept responsibility for finishing the job. ☐

18 I hold others and myself responsible for the quantity, quality and timeliness of completed assignments. ☐

19 I provide others with immediate feedback so that it is clearly associated with the task being evaluated. ☐

20 When giving others feedback I review their actual performance in terms of assignment and responsibility. ☐

21 I think it is my responsibility to ensure that my team have everything they need to do the job. ☐

22 If my team needs additional skills, I will organise the training. ☐

23 I personally review the performance of my team. ☐

24 I personally review the development of each of my team members. ☐

25 Each of my team members should want my job some day. ☐

We will return and consider the significance of your scores a bit later.

LEADERSHIP VERSUS MANAGEMENT

Some authorities on management and leadership clearly differentiate between the two concepts (eg Kotter, 1999) – 'management' being understood to relate to what managers do under stable organisational and business conditions, and 'leadership' describing what organisations require when undergoing transformation or when operating in dynamic conditions. On this view leaders and managers make different contributions – 'leaders have followers and managers have subordinates' (Kotter, 1999). The leader is someone who develops vision and drives new initiatives; the manager is someone who monitors progress towards objects to achieve order and reliability.

Of course, this view has never precluded the two roles from being undertaken by the same individual, but the crucial point is that they require distinct sets of skills, with the implication that one might be a competent manager without being a competent leader, or vice versa. Mintzberg (1973) suggested that in practice the distinction between effective leadership and effective management is blurred: effective managers require at least some leadership qualities.

Whetton and Cameron (2005; p.16) state that

the recent research is clear that such distinctions between leadership and management, which may have been appropriate in previous decades, are no longer useful. … Managers cannot be successful without being leaders, and leaders cannot be successful without being managers.

This is the view endorsed in this text.

LEADERSHIP AND INFLUENCE IN MANAGEMENT IN THE TWENTY-FIRST CENTURY

The 'classical' school of management theory defined a manager's work in terms of planning, organising, coordinating, commanding and controlling (Fayol, 1950; Gulick and Urwick, 1937). Mintzberg (1973) famously disputed whether managers actually behaved like that, although arguably he missed the point: a normative statement of the primary functions or obligations of management is not necessarily supposed to be a description of observable behaviour. Successful managers must somehow make and implement plans however hectic their work schedule, and whether or not it is done in a calm, reflective manner or in a busy, disjointed fashion. They have to organise activities, people and knowledge effectively, even if it is often done by informal communication such as face-to-face encounters, phone or email, rather than by formal written statements or pronouncements; by influence, rather than by direct command.

This is not to say that the classic description of managerial work is adequate for the twenty-first century. Contemporary managers certainly have to plan, organise, coordinate, and ultimately be accountable for, the activities and achievements of other people. But these functions are often done 'at arms' length', especially in the increasingly common cases of the self-directed team and the empowered worker. In modern organisations managers might explicitly command people relatively rarely, although they have to be able to do so when necessary, and they sometimes may have to veto some proposals from staff. They will certainly always be concerned with influencing and motivating their people, and they need to be able to be directive when required.

Control of activities, people (including teams) and knowledge ultimately rests with designated managers – but the whole thrust of work organisation and job design over the last two decades has been to move power and decision-making down the organisation to the teams and individual workers who actually perform the tasks concerned. All organisations still necessarily exercise power and control over their employees, and this is done through the management structure, but the boundaries of control and authority are typically moved further from the individual worker or team than was previously the case, giving them a higher (although ultimately still limited) degree of power and discretion.

Consequently, there have been significant differences in the emphasis given to leadership and influence. These were always both present in work, since no organisation can operate solely on the basis of direct, formal and explicit commands for all activities, but they are much more important in the era of the knowledge-worker and the self-directed and empowered team. Twenty-first-century economies require far fewer of the sort of semi-skilled and unskilled jobs that were the staple of industrialised economies until the last quarter of the twentieth century. The 'scientific management' of Taylor and others which developed to design and control such tasks was predicated on the manager's always knowing more than the worker (which is one reason why skilled workers in particular so resented its application). In the twenty-first century it is understood that it is knowledge that ultimately gives an organisation sustained competitive advantage, and the twenty-first-century manager has to be able to lead and influence workers who often have more expert knowledge and skill at their own jobs than he or she does. So managers often have to play the role of 'coach' to empowered teams or workers, rather than that of supervisor, but even in those circumstances there are situations where workers and teams have to be directed – eg dealing with crises, or with major technological or cultural change.

As a general rule, the more skilled and knowledgeable the workers are, the less directive will be the style of the effective manager. But the reality is that managers have to possess a range of management styles from highly directive to a supportive, coaching approach. Also it is worth noting in this context that the empirical evidence suggests that although there have certainly been important changes in the traditional employment relationship between managers and workers, in practice there have been limits to the extent of empowerment given to workers, at least in the UK (Gallie *et al*, 1998; pp1–27): the genuinely self-managing team is comparatively rare.

Another important dimension of the manager's job that was not recognised in the classical school's description of managerial work is the role of manager as developer of others. Peter Drucker clearly stated some 50 years ago that a key characteristic of managerial work is that it simultaneously operates in the here-and-now by ensuring efficient and effective current activities, and in the future – trying to ensure that the organisation and its people *will* perform efficiently and effectively (hence the need for corporate strategy). A direct consequence of that proposition is that senior managers had the responsibility to develop junior managers who reported to them, to 'grow the stock of managerial talent' for the future (Drucker, 1955). Nowadays, many organisations go further than this and expect managers to support the training and development of all who report to them, whether managers or non-managers. So effective managers have to be able to support their people, both in the short and in the long term.

Thus a range of management styles is required of the twenty-first-century manager. Goleman (2000) has used the analogy of the clubs in a golf professional's bag: all golf professionals need to be competent in the use of each club, and have the knowledge and experience to know which is the right one to use in any particular situation.

HOW DO LEADERSHIP AND INFLUENCING WORK?

In the following section we break down the leadership and influencing competency into five sub-competencies or skills: (1) *actioning* – ie initiating actions that will taken by others; (2) *managing work* – planning, assigning and delegating specific activities and responsibilities to people to enable the agreed actions to be followed, and directing and coordinating these activities where required; (3) *motivating* the people who are to carry out these actions; (4) *managing performance* – monitoring performance against targets and objectives and ensuring accountability; and (5) *supporting* – ensuring that people have the resources needed to carry out their assignments, and in the longer term helping to develop people and teams.

It is in relation to these sub-competencies that we will interpret your scores on the *Leadership and influencing competency questionnaire*. Look back at your ratings, and transfer them all to the scoring matrix below, in their appropriate positions. Add and fill in the totals in their respective slots too.

Scoring matrix

Skill area (sub-competency)	Scores					Totals
Actioning	Question 1 ☐	Question 2 ☐	Question 3 ☐	Question 4 ☐	Question 5 ☐ =	
Managing work	Question 1 ☐	Question 2 ☐	Question 3 ☐	Question 4 ☐	Question 5 ☐ =	
Motivating	Question 1 ☐	Question 2 ☐	Question 3 ☐	Question 4 ☐	Question 5 ☐ =	
Managing performance	Question 1 ☐	Question 2 ☐	Question 3 ☐	Question 4 ☐	Question 5 ☐ =	
Supporting	Question 1 ☐	Question 2 ☐	Question 3 ☐	Question 4 ☐	Question 5 ☐ =	
					Total of Totals	

From this matrix, when completed, it should be possible to tell at once which sub-competencies are your best (your highest totals), and which you might concentrate on developing in the future (your lowest totals) towards overall competency in leadership and influencing. The Total of Totals figure might also give you some indication of how close you are currently to that overall competency.

THEORIES OF LEADERSHIP AND INFLUENCING

Research into leadership can be categorised into three broad approaches: the trait approach, the behavioural approach, and the situational approach.

The trait approach

Historically, it was usually assumed that individuals who rose to prominent positions in society or its institutions did so because they possessed certain characteristics or traits which distinguished them, the leaders, from ordinary people, the led. These traits by implication were wholly or largely genetic, and thus inherited (a useful theory to support an aristocratic class system). Traits such as physical characteristics, intellectual abilities, certain personality features and interpersonal skills were all identified as being defining characteristics of leaders. The efforts of the armed forces in both the United States and the UK in selecting and training officers during World War II reflected the then dominant trait approach to leadership, and this model was very influential in management selection and training in large organisations for several decades after the war.

However, the trait approach failed to explain the generally recognised empirical fact that personality traits are poorly correlated with job success. There was also recognition that context or situation was important. Winston Churchill won fame as a young army officer and war correspondent, becoming one of the most successful politicians of his generation before he was 40 years old. By late middle age he appeared to be an isolated political failure until the outbreak of World War II and the recognition that he – and possibly he alone – had the abilities to lead Britain against the threat of Nazism. Yet the British electorate rejected Churchill in the General Election of 1946 – they respected him as a great wartime leader but feared that he would start another war with Russia. The British wanted peace and they voted for the Labour Party and its 'welfare state' policies instead. Drucker was to call Churchill 'the most successful leader of this [the twentieth] century' (Drucker, 1990; p.7), but he also said, 'to every leader there is a season' (1990; p.15).

Perhaps the British electorate sensed that Churchill did not possess the motivation or softer leadership style necessary to build a welfare state. But Churchill won the next General Election and in 1951 returned as Prime Minister. Circumstances had changed once more. His party had promised to accept the welfare state that the Labour Party had created, and the Cold War between the Soviet Union and the West was under way in earnest. Churchill was once again the people's choice for leader.

The behavioural (or 'style') approach

Following disillusionment with the traits approach, research into leadership moved from the issue of selection of leaders on the basis of personality traits to that of finding appropriate behaviour patterns or styles in which managers and other leaders could be trained. Two major research programmes, the Michigan and Ohio studies, underpinned the investigations into leadership style. These research programmes independently suggested a dichotomy in leadership styles: broadly, either (a) a considerate, participative, democratic and 'involving' leadership style, or (b) an impersonal, autocratic and directive style. Most interpretations of the results of these studies were thought to demonstrate that the former was the more effective leadership style.

The main criticism of this perspective comes from the observation that one leadership style may not be the most effective in all circumstances. Subsequent studies incorporated a context-specific or contingency aspect.

The situational approach

Tannenbaum and Schmidt presented the autocratic/democratic choice as a continuum from manager-centred leadership to subordinate-centred. An influential situational model of leadership was developed by Hersey and

Blanchard (1988), in which leader behaviour is described on two dimensions: 'task behaviour' – ie the amount of direction a leader gives to subordinates, ranging from specific instructions to complete delegation – and 'supportive behaviour' – ie the amount of social back-up a leader gives to subordinates, which can range from limited communication to considerate listening.

Each of these three approaches sheds light on the complex issue of leadership, though none provides a definitive description. The approach taken in this text recognises the contribution of each of these perspectives but is influenced in particular by the situational school. Our approach is based on the assumptions that:

- Certain styles of leadership are more effective in some circumstances than others.
- Although the ultimate effectiveness of any particular individual's leadership ability may be constrained by genetic or other more-or-less permanent factors deriving from his or her personality and psychological make-up, *all individuals can improve their effectiveness in leading and influencing others.*
- No single style is intrinsically 'right' or 'wrong': different situations need different styles of leadership and influencing.
- An effective leader selects the appropriate style for the particular situation.

We argue that although few of us could ever be a Steve Jobs or a Churchill or a Martin Luther King, all of us can improve our leadership and influencing skills, and learn how and when to use these to the best effect.

LEADING AND INFLUENCING OTHERS: THE BASES OF POWER AND INFLUENCE

> The processes of power are pervasive, complex, and often disguised in our society.
>
> French and Raven (1958; p.259)

A manager has five principal 'bases of power' in exerting influence on others, each of which forms the perceptions held by the others. These bases are: (a) *reward power*, which rests on the others' perception that the manager has the ability to apply or intercede in rewards for them; (b) *coercive power*, from the perception that the manager has the ability to apply or intercede in punishments for them; (c) *legitimate power*, based on the perception by the others that the manager has a legitimate right to his or her authority over them; (d) *referent power*, founded on the others' admiration for and wish to identify with the manager as a person; and finally (e) *expert power*, based on the perception that the manager has some special knowledge which the others need or can benefit from.

Successful managers often exert more than one type of power at the same time. For example, a charismatic business leader like Steve Jobs possesses legitimate power as head of Apple and reward and coercive power over his subordinate colleagues and employees, but he also enjoys referent power because of his astounding business success which most people would love to emulate, and expert power as one of the men who changed the world of computing.

REFLECTIVE ACTIVITY

1 Think about a situation in which you influenced another person towards a goal (work or other). What type(s) of power or influence did you exert?

2 Think about about a situation in which you were influenced towards a goal (work or other) by another person. What type(s) of power or influence did they exert?

There can be no strict formula for successful leadership. As a manager you should examine the situation in which you are working and the people you are seeking to influence. Motivating a group of expert engineers to meet a business deadline for a design project will require a different approach from that needed to encourage a team of office cleaners to meet quality standards.

In the first case you cannot have all the expert knowledge the team of engineers collectively possess. (If you did, you might be designing the project yourself and the engineers wouldn't be needed!) Missing the deadline is likely to have a major business impact on your organisation. The engineers are likely to be successful professionals in their own right, commanding the sort of salary and market value this implies – so you probably could not easily afford to lose them.

In the second case you will probably know at least as much as the cleaners about how to do the tasks required in order to do their job, but they are likely to be poorly paid, unskilled, and not attaining much intrinsic job satisfaction. Deadlines do not come into it, but offices need to be cleaned efficiently and effectively. You can probably afford to lose any particular cleaner or team of cleaners because the low skill levels mean that replacements can be easily found from the local labour market – but you need to get the offices properly cleaned! Both scenarios will require encouragement and the use of authority, but in very different ways.

REFLECTIVE ACTIVITY

Look at the answers you gave to the previous Reflective Activity.

What bases of power and influence would you use in the two scenarios introduced above – the design engineers and the office cleaners?

LEADERSHIP STYLE

These considerations bring us back to the question of *leadership style*. Goleman (2000) has argued for six leadership styles: coercive, authoritative, affiliative, democratic, pace-setting, and coaching. These are based on the author's previous work on 'emotional intelligence'. The styles can be thought of as occupying positions on a continuum of leadership and influencing styles from directive through to coaching.

SELECTING THE MOST APPROPRIATE LEADERSHIP STYLE

In seeking to achieve his or her objectives the manager must first decide whether leadership and influencing skills are required. Most managers have some tasks they perform themselves, such as report-writing and some planning activities, but whenever other people are involved, leading and influencing skills will be necessary.

Choice of leadership style also depends in part on the beliefs and attitudes of the manager. Some managers feel uncomfortable with highly authoritarian styles; they tend to ask employees to participate in leadership activities. Others feel that they are responsible for issuing orders to those whom they supervise. Managers who are confident in their leadership abilities will feel more confident in conferring with employees.

Further factors that influence the choice of leadership style include the manager's assessment of his or her own competencies, the needs and competencies of the employees, the nature of the situation, and the amount of time available. If the manager believes that the employees need to be told what to do in order to complete a task, that manager may use a highly authoritarian or leader-centred style. The more direction the employees need, the more appropriate is a directive leadership style. Employees who can accept responsibility need less direction, so a less directive style is appropriate.

Often, the situation itself determines which leadership style to use. In an emergency such as a fire, it would be foolish for the leader to consult with employees on whether they should leave the building: direct ordering is clearly the most appropriate leadership approach. In situations that are not emergencies, the manager should look carefully at the task. Some tasks are better accomplished by conferring with employees; others require the use of a direct style.

Time also influences a manager's choice of leadership style. If immediate action is required, the manager may choose a highly directive style; if there is time for long-range planning, a more participatory style may produce the best results.

The organisation itself is another factor. Some organisations encourage employee participation, whereas others do not. Thus the culture of the organisation can influence the manager's selection of style.

Below (as Figure 4) is an outline process model describing the managerial selection of an appropriate leadership and influencing style.

Figure 4 A leadership and influencing process model

1 Consider:
- whether and how the team can be influenced
- the condition of the team (capability, maturity, etc)
- the nature of the task
- the nature of technology used
- the time-scale/degree of urgency

2 Consider the bases of power available:
- reward
- coercion
- reference
- expertise
- position

3 Consider leadership style on the directive–non-directive continuum:
- coercive
- authoritative
- affiliative
- democratic
- pace-setting
- coaching

4 Apply appropriate leadership and influencing skills:
- actioning
- managing work
- motivating
- managing performance
- supporting

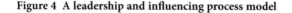

? REFLECTIVE ACTIVITY

Apply the leadership and influencing process model (Figure 4) to each of the following scenarios:

1 You are the captain of a ship facing immediate shipwreck.

2 You are the newly appointed CEO of a specialist engineering firm. Your first task is to manage downsizing the firm to enable it to be competitive.

3 You are hired to manage a traditional production line for a canned fruit producer.

4 You are leading a design project employing architects and engineers to create a 'London Eye'-type showcase structure for the London Olympics.

5 You are asked to take the role of 'product champion' for a new breakfast cereal product.

6 You are team-building in a call centre environment.

7 You are creating and implementing a management development programme in a large international bank.

For each situation you are required to:

- estimate the 'influencability' of those whom you are required to lead/influence
- estimate the maturity of the team
- establish the level of complexity of the task
- establish the level of technology required for the task
- define the time-scale and level of urgency
- identify the bases of power and influence that are likely to be most important in the circumstances
- establish which leadership style is likely to be most effective.

ACTIVITY ANSWER GUIDANCE

Compare your answers with those in the boxes below.

Situation: Captain of a ship facing immediate shipwreck	
Factor	
'Influencability' of those being led	*High – used to accepting hierarchical authority*
Maturity of team	*High*
Nature of task	*Objectives clear*
Technology	*Complex, varied*
Time-scale	*Immediate*
Urgency	*Life-or-death*
Power source	*Position* *Reward* *Coercion* *Reference* *Expertise*
Primary leadership and influencing skills required	*Actioning* *Managing work* *Motivating*
Leadership style(s)	*Coercive*

Situation: Managing the downsizing of an operation	
Factor	
'Influencability' of those being led	*Likely to be problems of poor morale*
Maturity of team	*May be mature initially, but strains of downsizing will affect team*
Nature of task	*Objectives clear*
Technology	*Generally not relevant to main situation*
Time-scale	*Short-term/immediate*
Urgency	*Usually urgent*
Power source	*Position* *Reward* *Coercion*
Primary leadership and influencing skills required	*Actioning* *Managing work* *Motivating*
Leadership style(s)	*Pace-setting*

Situation: Traditional production line management	
Factor	
'Influencability' of those being led	*Middle to high*
Maturity of team	*Probably not a team situation*
Nature of task	*Established*
Technology	*Routine*
Time-scale	*Continuous production*
Urgency	*Routine – but there will be targets on quantity and quality and frequent deadlines to meet*
Power source	*Position* *Reward* *Coercion*
Primary leadership and influencing skills required	*Actioning* *Managing work* *(Motivating)* *Managing performance*
Leadership style(s)	*Probably authoritative*

Situation: Leading a design project	
Factor	
'Influencability' of those being led	*Low – experts*
Maturity of team	*Starting from scratch*
Nature of task	*Objectives probably complex*
Technology	*Ranging from low- to high-tech from project to project*
Time-scale	*Defined time-scale*
Urgency	*Time-bound – sense of urgency increases as deadline approaches*
Power source	*Reference* *Expertise* *Reward* *Coercion*
Primary leadership and influencing skills required	*Actioning* *Managing work* *Motivating* *Managing performance* *Supporting*
Leadership style(s)	*Authoritative/affiliative/democratic as required*

Situation: Being 'product champion'	
Factor	
'Influencability' of those being led	*Say low – experts*
Maturity of team	*Starting from scratch*
Nature of task	*Complex*
Technology	*Ranging from low- to high-tech from project to project*
Time-scale	*Probably tight*
Urgency	*High degree of importance*
Power source	*Reference* *(Expertise)*
Primary leadership and influencing skills required	*Actioning* *Motivating* *Supporting*
Leadership style(s)	*Democratic*

Situation: Team-building in a call centre	
Factor	
'Influencability' of those being led	*Variable*
Maturity of team	*Starting from scratch*
Nature of task	*Complex*
Technology	*Generally not relevant*
Time-scale	*Short-term*
Urgency	*Important to complete process within reasonable time-scale*
Power source	*Position* *Reward* *Possibly coercion* *Reference* *Expertise*
Primary leadership and influencing skills required	*Motivating* *Managing work* *Managing performance* *Supporting*
Leadership style(s)	*Affiliative*

Situation: Creating/implementing a management development programme	
Factor	
'Influencability' of those being led	*High*
Maturity of team	*Not a team situation*
Nature of task	*Highly complex*
Technology	*Generally low importance*
Time-scale	*Medium to long-term*
Urgency	*No immediate urgency*
Power source	*Reference* *Expertise*
Primary leadership and influencing skills required	*Supporting*
Leadership style(s)	*Coaching*

Note that from the information in the boxes above it is evident that project management is likely to be one of the most demanding and complex leadership situations for managers.

REFLECTIVE ACTIVITY

Now fill out the *Leadership and influencing competency questionnaire* again – without looking back at your answers from the first time. The questionnaire and the scoring matrix are repeated below.

AFTERWARDS compare your responses and scores with those of your first attempt. Pay particular attention to changes in responses between the two attempts. Do you understand why your answers changed?

If you keep a management log, write down the changes you think are significant and what you feel you have learned from working through the module. Note the areas of the competency where you feel you have particular strengths and weaknesses, and identify areas you wish to work on in your job.

If you use a Professional Development Plan for your continuing professional development (CPD), you should be able to incorporate leadership and influencing competencies in your plan.

Questionnaire

Rate your agreement or disagreement with each statement below on a scale of 1 to 10 in which **1 corresponds to 'total disagreement' and 10 to 'total agreement'**.

Rating

1 When starting a new task it is my responsibility to identify its objective and tell the others who are be involved. ☐

2 A manager should always let others know what is expected of them. ☐

3 I always try to find a new and better way to undertake a project. ☐

4 I should initiate action without waiting for other people to draw my attention to it. ☐

5 I always try to give my people instructions and information in simple, clear language. ☐

6 I always look for new approaches to the job. ☐

7 I keep myself and my team informed about due dates and deadlines. ☐

8 You should discourage questions and requests for information which interfere with getting the job done. ☐

9 A manager should provide a good example for others to follow in his or her own work habits. ☐

10 I am open about my mistakes and encourage others to learn from them. ☐

11 I set goals for myself and help others to set their goals. ☐

12 I always give my team feedback on their performance. ☐

13 When assigning tasks to others I inform them of the importance and urgency of the assignment. ☐

MARKET DYNAMICS AND COMPANY CHANGES

Hennes & Mauritz launches two main collections a year, in spring and in autumn. Within these ranges are a number of subcollections that ensure that the customer always finds new goods in the stores. The stores are the main distribution channel, but in the Scandinavian market Hennes & Mauritz has also distributed goods via mail order since 1980 and via e-commerce since 1998. Although the e-commerce activities in particular are intended for continuous improvement, it is expected that the stores will remain the primary distribution channel for Hennes & Mauritz.

The most significant current challenges for Hennes & Mauritz are:

- continuous expansion
- cost-efficient production and logistics
- the reduction of lead times.

Expansion

From the beginning, Hennes & Mauritz has focused on expansion, which is regarded as one of the main drivers of competitive advantage. There is no franchising: Hennes & Mauritz owns and manages all its stores. This allows the company to maintain central control over the expansion strategy and business locations. When deciding on a new location, the department responsible for expansion selects the best sites in the current market and waits until the location becomes available rather than opening a new store in a less preferred location. Another reason the company avoids franchising is that it can maintain central control over store design and communication.

Cost-efficient production

A second driver of competitive advantage and profitability is an emphasis on the cost-effective production of goods. Hennes & Mauritz has, like many other clothing companies, gone through a major bout of switching production locations. At the very beginning, almost all production took place in Sweden. During the 1960s most production moved to other Scandinavian countries and the United Kingdom. At the end of the 1960s, production moved again, this time to southern Europe – mainly Italy and Portugal, although Hennes & Mauritz established additional production operations in Hungary, Poland and the former Yugoslavia. In the mid-1970s production moved to the Far East, where the first production unit opened in Hong Kong in 1978. Today [in 2003], Hennes & Mauritz has 21 production units, generally reflecting the location of suppliers: 10 are located in Europe, 10 in the Far East, and one in Africa.

This is the classic story of production moving to locations with a good supply of labour, low wages, and fine quality. It is simply cheaper to produce goods in the Far East because of the low wages there, while the quality of the goods produced there is of an excellent standard. This explains why in those far-flung production units the workforce is made up of local staff. These branch offices have a dual function. First and foremost, the production units mediate contact between the head office purchasing department and the independent regional suppliers. This ensures that the right order is placed with the right supplier. Second, the production branch offices are responsible for finding new suppliers and negotiating contracts with them. This also includes making sure that the suppliers conform to the Hennes & Mauritz code of conduct.

When deciding where to place an order, it is a question not only of where goods can be manufactured most cost-effectively, but also of distance to the primary market. It is evident that the transportation times from the Far East to Europe are greater than within Europe. This may have some influence on where specific goods are manufactured. A final aspect that plays a role when deciding on a manufacturer is the quota system. In common with all textile/clothing companies, Hennes & Mauritz are subject to the import regulations defined by the World Trading Organization's quota system [originally intended to give textile manufacturers in poorer countries an opportunity to compete]. However, the company is unsure whether or not the abolition of the quota system [as of 31 December 2004] will have any impact on where the company has goods manufactured. The abolition of the quota legislation may mean that more goods are manufactured in the Far East – but this is uncertain simply because the company does not know what national or international regulations, if any, will replace the quota system afterwards. In this context, more timely information on the policy decision-making process would be helpful to Hennes & Mauritz. In any case, because of the transportation time factor, Hennes & Mauritz thinks it unlikely that in the near future all production will take place in Asia.

The reduction of lead times

A final aspect, which has added positively to the company's competitive advantage, is the focus on reducing lead times and improving logistics. Lead times from manufacture to store have been reduced by 15% to 20% over the last two to three years. In competition with other fashion companies and department stores, it is crucial that there are always up-to-the-moment lines on sale in the shops, and that Hennes & Mauritz can move fast when new trends are identified. All stores must have such vital products on display and in stock at all times. Furthermore, the overall logistics department must monitor the sales progress of each individual product line in order to avoid the over-production of goods which cannot then be sold. To ensure this, the buying staff work closely with the branch production offices, making good use of information and communication technologies (ICT) to follow sales and make intelligent choices. One benefit of the company's owning the stores is that they therefore share a common ICT platform on which all sales are reported. Buyers and logistics staff can thus keep track of sales and of stock status at each individual store as well as at the regional or national warehouse.

Purchasing flexibility is central to the Hennes & Mauritz strategy. The pattern of seasonal flexibility that applies to many retail fashion stores was broken as early as in 1968. Instead, buyers set up a routine of purchasing 12 times a year, making rapid switches of fashion possible.

In its own perception, the company's strategic management committee perceives the company as being very informal in terms of decision-making processes. According to Kent Gustafsson, Director of Development, 'We know from previous experience that decision-making is based 90% on feeling and 10% on history.'

Nevertheless, company strategy is extremely visible to employees. The first CEO introduced *takten* ('the rate'; literally, 'the tempo') – an instrument that is still in place and is now supported by ICT. This is a visible list that appears weekly, showing every buyer how many of each individual product have been sold in the stores. Everyone understands the risks involved in falling short, and, according to several sources, the expression 'Shape up or ship out' is always notionally hovering in the background.

In summary, Hennes & Mauritz operates in a highly competitive fashion market in which it has to offer goods of high quality at a competitive price. In order to achieve this, it has focused on expansion (market access as well as economies of scale in terms of production) as well as improved logistics (reduced lead times from manufacturer to warehouse to store). Company management is built on a model of centralised regulation (part of the organisation from the start as a result of the personality of the founder and his emphasis on control) combined with an environment in which ideas can emerge from anywhere within the company and can circulate freely. What sets Hennes & Mauritz apart from most of its competition is its lightning-fast turnaround: a garment can move from design to hanger in just 20 days. Only Zara [part of the Spanish-owned Inditex Group] can react more rapidly (14 days) – but its prices are 30% to 50% higher than H&M's. By comparison, [the US clothing manufacturer] Gap's minimum turnaround is three months. As a result, H&M can very quickly add design elements that were not part of its original product or increase quantities if an item sells well. For example, last autumn, when miniskirts began to sell well, H&M tripled the original order on a black wool miniskirt and distributed it to all markets instead of just to a handful of key stores.

Research and development

Hennes & Mauritz thus aims to keep in step with current fashion trends and, indeed, to remain at the forefront of them. This is done via the designers, who attend many exhibitions worldwide. Furthermore, managers in the national shops are responsible for following new market trends and competitors and reporting on them to the head office in Stockholm. In these processes, H&M makes very little use of external consultants. Each store manager is encouraged to carry out market and competitor surveillance at a local level, but very little analysis of the competition is done at central level. The same goes for customer analysis.

Trial and error plays a prominent role in market strategy as practised by H&M. It is acceptable to make an error – as long as that error is not repeated. This is particularly important for the buyers because it enables them to be more innovative in their purchasing. An example of a failed strategy was an attempt by H&M to introduce shoes within its accessories departments in 1974. This had to be abandoned because of strict trade regulations and requirements for larger stocks than H&M was accustomed to.

Hennes & Mauritz is not involved in experiments with new fabrics. There has to be proof that clothing and products that make use of new textile materials have genuine commercial value before they are introduced into the collections.

ORGANISATION AND THE MARKET

Hennes & Mauritz is a global company in terms of production and market penetration. The company has over 25,000 employees worldwide. Most of these are employed in one of its more than 840 stores, while others are employed in administrative functions in either Stockholm or in one of the 21 production or 14 national branch offices. This highlights the fact that Hennes & Mauritz has no production facilities – all production is outsourced. The main argument for the company's not having its own manufacturing facilities is that capital is not tied up in machinery and equipment, thus permitting a wide degree of flexibility.

Hennes & Mauritz has roughly 90 designers located in Stockholm. These employees are responsible for identifying new fashion trends and designing new models. Hennes & Mauritz sees itself as a fashion company which is able both to follow general trends and to come up with totally new concepts when needed. The designers work closely with the buying department, which in turn communicates with the production offices. The aim is to identify the best supplier worldwide for new goods in terms of price, quality, speed, and location (transportation). The production officers report back to the buying department, which then places the order (half-and-half within and outside Europe – 'outside' usually being in Asia).

Once the goods have been manufactured, they are shipped using H&M external contract companies. This is generally to the main central warehouse in Hamburg, but it may also be to the national offices (if the goods are country-specific) or directly to an individual store if the quantities are large enough. However, the most frequent scenario is that goods are sent to Hamburg, where they are sorted and sent on to the individual stores. This transaction model is depicted in the diagram below.

Another factor contributing to Hennes & Mauritz' success is the ICT-enabled feedback loop between the individual stores, the central warehouse, and the buying department/production offices. It is possible centrally to monitor the sales of individual items in the stores and restock when necessary. This feedback loop achieves transparency between sales, stock, and production capacity, and enables intelligent procurement planning. As in other retail trade sectors, this means that employee skills relating to managerial planning processes are being taken over by ICT, whereas the requirements for customer service orientation remain unchanged.

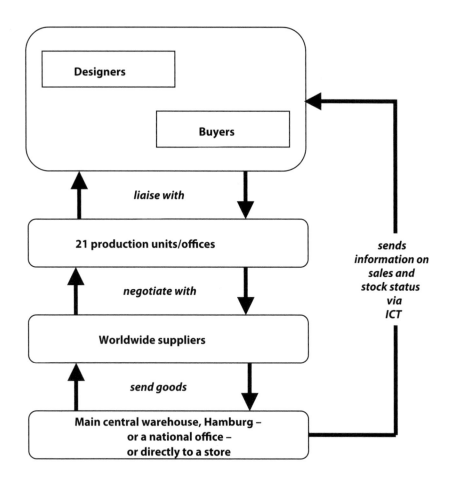

A further reason for setting up the production offices to oversee the manufacturing process is the accurate translation of the designers' models into actual goods. Discrepancies used sometimes to be noted between initial sketch and final product. Today this can be thought of as more or less a historical phenomenon: due to the long-term relationships with suppliers, it is no longer necessary to offer any 'translation' help to turn sketches into goods. Instead, the main functions of the production offices are to negotiate prices, to communicate between central functions and suppliers, and to monitor compliance with the code of conduct. This code was established as part of the Hennes & Mauritz focus on corporate social responsibility (CSR). The code includes the following conditions:

- full compliance with all legal requirements
- a ban on child labour
- safety and factory conditions commensurate with employee well-being
- acknowledgement of workers' rights and their freedom to organise
- proper housing conditions and a 'green' environmental outlook.

All suppliers have to live up to these requirements, and fulfilment of the code is frequently checked and enforced by the production office employees. Approval of a supplier by Hennes & Mauritz thus implies the creation of what is intended to be a very long-term relationship. Hennes & Mauritz is thereby often able to exploit economies of scale, and the supplier companies have a very loyal customer.

It is company policy to label all goods with the country of their origin. However, Hennes & Mauritz believes that the customer is not as interested in where the goods have been produced as in quality and price, and to some degree in whether or not the goods have been manufactured under sustainable conditions. The post-quota-system future of the European textile industry should thus be debated in the light of the trend towards production moving to the East. There is also the possibility of having not just production but also design carried out in the East. H&M management believes that the time for viewing China as the 'sweatshop of the world' is past – the Chinese are certainly able also to produce work that requires higher levels of competence.

THE WORKFORCE AND ITS CAPACITY

As previously mentioned, Hennes & Mauritz has approximately 25,000 employees (81% of them female). Most of these work in the stores as shop assistants. Only about 3,000 are in administrative functions (including production and national offices).

Hennes & Mauritz puts great emphasis on maintaining a corporate ethos – most recruitment and training is therefore carried out internally. All new store employees undergo a three-week induction course and are assigned a personal mentor. Employees for head office functions are mostly recruited internally from the stores in order to maintain the corporate spirit, and head office staff are regularly rotated to store functions in order to keep in touch with the company's customers.

H&M's outsourcing model is different from that of most of its competitors in that H&M's code of conduct is an ethical one which also applies to its global suppliers.

The fundamental intention behind Hennes & Mauritz's code of conduct is to maintain good labour relations. The code of conduct states that employees are free to organise. Furthermore, the code of conduct covers not only the 25,000 workers directly employed by Hennes & Mauritz but also those who are employed by subcontractors who produce goods for the stores. These are independent companies, but often have very long-term connections with Hennes & Mauritz. If a company wishes to become a supplier to Hennes & Mauritz, it must agree to adhere to the code of conduct: compliance with the code is continuously monitored by regional Hennes & Mauritz representatives. The code of conduct focuses not only on (for example) freedom to organise but also on establishing good working environments. Even more important, the code forbids the use of underage labour. Hennes & Mauritz can therefore be certain that employees working on the production line for its subcontractors in a far-off foreign country often enjoy far better working conditions than other employees in that country.

H&M's business model strength lies to a great extent in the centralised control of all phases from store location to inventory for display campaigns and shop windows. At the same time, however, the H&M system is based on integrative interaction between different localities and levels of management. Internal recruitment thus plays a central role in promotions.

Electronic efficiency

A central part of the Hennes & Mauritz success is the ICT system that connects the individual stores with the logistics and procurement department. As described above, the system keeps track of all sales and stock management activities. Whenever an item is sold in an individual store, it is registered in the central system, which additionally monitors any need for restocking and rebuying.

There is also ICT integration between head office in Stockholm and the 21 production units. All communication between the departments takes place electronically, including the distribution of design sketches. Such integration is expected eventually to include those suppliers with whom the most long-term relationships exist.

ICT plays an important role in Hennes & Mauritz's effort to reduce lead times. It is of the utmost competitive importance that there are always new goods on the shelves, that stores do not run out of stock lines, and that excess and unsaleable stock does not clutter up warehousing space (which corresponds also to having capital tied up in useless stock). This requires good market intelligence as well as tools for market forecasting and stock control, and for this ICT is essential.

The single ICT system common to the whole company facilitates this integration throughout the enterprise through both front-end and back-end data-sharing and integration. Hennes & Mauritz can keep track of sales and integrate this directly with buying. Very little human interaction is needed, in that data is automatically sent to the central database each time a single item is sold in a shop. This facilitates the tracking of local and regional stock and integration with the production facilities, and it provides Hennes & Mauritz with market intelligence – eg which products seem to be most popular and which are more difficult to sell.

Market intelligence can also come from other sources. In order to keep up with new trends in the fashion market, Hennes & Mauritz's representatives spend considerable time at trade shows and exhibitions, and in Europe designers attend the main design exhibitions. More information on market development comes from the countries (mainly in Asia) where production takes place. As outlined previously, Hennes & Mauritz retains local production units whose main responsibility is negotiation with subcontractors and supervision of the code of conduct. However, an additional aspect of their work is to monitor local market development and send information back to the central administration in Stockholm.

A final aspect of electronic efficiency is the new e-commerce initiative – involving online sales – which is currently being rolled out only to customers in Scandinavian countries. This is considered an additional channel of distribution, but is not expected to replace or eliminate the need for the more traditional channels: the stores remain (and will no doubt always be) regarded as the main distribution channel.

References

ADLER, N. J. (1987) 'Pacific-Basin managers: a *gaijin*, not a woman', *Human Resource Management*, Vol.26, No.2, 169–92

ADLER, N. J. (1991) *International Dimensions of Organizational Behavior*. Boston, MA: PWS-Kent

ADLER, P. S., GOLDOFTAS, B. and LEVINE, D. I. (1997) 'Ergonomics, employee involvement and the Toyota production system: a case study of NUMMI's 1993 model introduction', *Industrial and Labor Relations Review*, Vol.50, No.3, 416–37

ADVISORY, CONCILIATION AND ARBITRATION SERVICE (2009) *Disciplinary and Grievance Procedures, Code of Practice*. London: ACAS. Available online at: http://acas.org.uk/

AGUINIS, H. (2005) *Performance Management*. Edinburgh: Edinburgh Business School

AITKEN, H. G. J. (1960) *Taylorism at Watertown Arsenal*. Cambridge, MA: Harvard University Press

APPELBAUM, E., BAILEY, T., BERG, P. and KALLEBERG, A. L. (2000) *Manufacturing Advantage: Why high performance work systems pay off*. London: Cornell University Press

ARGYRIS, C. and SCHÖN, D. A. (1978) *Organizational Learning*. Reading, MA: Addison-Wesley

ARMSTRONG, M. (2009) *Armstrong's Handbook of Human Resource Management Practice*, 11th edition. London: Kogan Page

ARMSTRONG, M. and MURLIS, H. (1998) *Reward Management*, 4th edition. London: IPM/Kogan Page

ASHBY, W. R. (1940) 'Adaptiveness and equilibrium', *Journal of Mental Science*, Vol.86, 478–83

ATKINSON, J. (1984) 'Manpower strategies for flexible organizations', *Personnel Management*, August, 28–31

BAILEY, K. D. (1994) *Typologies and Taxonomies: An introduction to classification techniques*. Quantitative Applications in the Social Sciences Series, No. 02. London: Sage

BARNEY, B. (1991) 'Firm resources and sustained competitive advantage', *Journal of Management*, Vol.17, No.1, 99–120

BASS, B. M. and BARRATT, G. V. (1981) *People Work and Organizations: An introduction to industrial and organizational psychology.* Boston, MA: Allyn & Bacon

BEAUMONT, P. (1993) *Human Resource Management: Key concepts and skills.* London: Sage

BECKER, B. and GERHART, B. (1996) 'The impact of human resource management on organizational performance: progress and practice', *Academy of Management Journal*, Vol.39, No.4, 779–801

BEER, M., EISENSTAT, R. and SPECTOR, B. (1990) 'Why change programs don't produce change', *Harvard Business Review*, Nov–Dec, 158–66

BEER, M., SPECTOR, B., LAWRENCE, P. R., MILLS, D. and WALTON, R. E. (1984) *Managing Human Assets.* New York: Free Press

BELBIN, M. (1981) *Management Teams: Why they succeed or fail.* London: Heinemann

BELBIN, M. (1993) *Team Roles at Work.* Oxford: Butterworth-Heinemann

BLYTON, P. and TURNBULL, P. (1992) *Reassessing Human Resource Management.* London: Sage

BOXALL, P. and PURCELL, J. (2006) *Strategy and Human Resource Management.* Basingstoke: Palgrave Macmillan

BOXALL, P., PURCELL, J. and WRIGHT, P. (2007) *The Oxford Handbook of Human Resource Management.* Oxford: Oxford University Press

BOYATZIS, R. E. (1982) *The Competent Manager: A model for effective performance.* London: Wiley

BRAVERMAN, H. (1974) *Labour and Monopoly Capitalism: The degradation of work in the twentieth century.* New York: Monthly Review Press

BUCHANAN, D. (1994) 'Principles and practice in work design', in D. Sissons (ed.) *Personnel Management: A comprehensive guide to theory and practice in Britain.* Oxford: Blackwell

CALDWELL, R. and STOREY, J. (2007) chapter in J. Storey (ed.) *Human Resource Management: A critical text*, 3rd edition. London: Thomson Learning

CANON WORKING PARTY REPORT (1994) *Progress and Change 1987–1994.* Corby: Institute of Management

CHANDLER, A. D. (1991) *Strategy and Structure: Chapters in the history of the American industrial enterprise.* Cambridge, MA: MIT Press [first published 1962]

CHIANG, F. (2005) 'A critical examination of Hofstede's thesis and its application to international reward management', *International Journal of Human Resource Management*, Vol.16: 1545–63

CHILD, J. (1972) 'Organisational structure, environment and performance – the role of strategic choice', *Sociology*, Vol.6, 1–22

CHILD, J. (1984) *Organisation: A guide to problems and practice*, 2nd edition. London, Paul Chapman

CHILD, J. (1997) 'Strategic choice in the analysis of action, structure, organisations and environment: retrospect and prospect', *Organization Studies*, Vol.18, No.1, 43–76

CIPD (1994) *People Make the Difference*. London: CIPD

CIPD (2005) *What Is Employee Relations?* London: CIPD; also available online at: http://www.cipd.co.uk/subjects/empreltns/comconslt/empvoice

CIPD (2006a) *Learning and Development*. Survey. London: CIPD; also available online at: http://www.cipd.co.uk/onlineinfodocuments

CIPD (2006b) *Recruitment, Retention and Turnover*. Annual Survey. London: CIPD; also available online at: http://www.cipd.co.uk/onlineinfodocuments

CIPD (2006c) *Psychological Testing*. Factsheet. London: CIPD; also available online at: http://www.cipd.co.uk/onlineinfodocuments

CIPD (2007a) *Employee Engagement*. Factsheet. London: CIPD; also available online at http:www.cipd.co.uk/onlineinfodocuments

CIPD (2007b) *Management Development*, Factsheet. London: CIPD; also available online at: http://www.cipd.co.uk/onlineinfodocuments

CIPD (2007c) *Employee Voice*. Factsheet. London: CIPD; also available online at: http://www.cipd.co.uk/onlineinfodocuments

CIPD (2007d) *Learning and Development: Annual survey report 2007*. London: CIPD; also available online at: http://www.cipd.co.uk/surveys

CIPD (2007e) *Competence and Competency Frameworks*. Factsheet. London: CIPD; also available online at: http://www.cipd.co.uk/onlineinfodocuments

CIPD (2009a) *Managing Change*. Factsheet. London: CIPD; also available online at: http://www.cipd.co.uk/onlineinfodocuments

CIPD (2009b) *Corporate and Social Responsibility*. Factsheet. London: CIPD; also available online at: http://www.cipd.co.uk/onlineinfodocuments

CIPD (2010a) *Learning and Talent Development*. Survey. CIPD; also available online at: http://www.cipd.co.uk/surveys

CIPD (2010b) *2009 Survey of Recruitment, Retention and Turnover*. London: CIPD; also available online at: http://www.cipd.co.uk/onlineinfodocuments

CIPD (2010c) *Diversity in the Workplace*. Factsheet. London: CIPD; also available online at: http://www.cipd.co.uk/onlineinfodocuments

COFFIELD, F., MOSELEY, D., HALL, E. and ECCLESTONE, K. (2004) *Should We Be Using Learning Styles? What research has to say to practice.* London: Learning and Skills Research Centre

CULLY, M., WOODLAND, S., O'REILLY, A. and DIX, G. (1999) *Britain At Work: As depicted by the 1998 Workplace Employee Relations Survey.* London: Routledge

DE CERI, H. (2007) 'Transnational firms and cultural diversity', in Boxall, P., Purcell, J. and Wright, P. (eds) *The Oxford Handbook of Human Resource Management.* Oxford: Oxford University Press

DEPARTMENT OF TRADE AND INDUSTRY and CIPD (2005) *High-Performance Work Practices: Linking strategy and skills to performance outcomes.* London: HMSO; also available online at: www.dti.gov.uk

DEPARTMENT OF TRADE AND INDUSTRY and DEPARTMENT FOR EDUCATION AND EMPLOYMENT (1997) *Partnerships at Work.* London: HMSO

DESSLER, G. (2005) *Human Resource Management,* 10th (International) edition. Englewood Cliffs, NJ: Prentice-Hall

DODGSON, M. (1993) 'Organizational learning: a review of some literatures', *Organizational Studies,* Vol.14, 375–94

DRUCKER, P. F. (1955) *The Practice of Management.* London: Heinemann

DRUCKER, P. (1990) *Managing the Non-profit Organization.* New York: HarperCollins

DRUCKER, P. (1993) *Post-Capitalist Society.* Oxford: Butterworth-Heinemann

DU GAY, P. and SALAMAN, G. (1992) 'The cult(ure) of the customer', *Journal of Management Studies,* Vol.29, No.5, 615–33

DUNCAN, C. (1989) 'Pay and payment systems', in B. Towers (ed.) *A Handbook of Industrial Relations Practice.* London: Kogan Page

DYER, L. and REEVES, T. (1995) 'Human resource strategies and firm performance: what do we need to know and where do we need to go?', *International Journal of Human Resource Management,* Vol.25, No.9, 934–48

EARNSHAW, J. and COOPER, C. (1998) *Stress and Employer Liability.* London: IPD

EMERY, F. E. (1963) *Some Hypotheses About the Ways in Which Tasks May Be More Effectively Put Together to Make Jobs.* London: Tavistock Institute of Human Relations

EUROFOUND (2003) *Corporate and Social Responsibility.* London: European Foundation for the Improvement of Living and Working Conditions: http://www.eurofound.eu.int/

EUROFOUND (2010) *European Company Survey 2009*. London: European Foundation for the Improvement of Living and Working Conditions: www.eurofound.europa.eu

FARNHAM, D. (2000) *Employee Relations in Context*, 2nd edition. London: IPD

FARNHAM, D. and PIMLOTT J. (1995) *Understanding Industrial Relations*, 4th edition. London: Cassell

FAYOL, H. (1916/1950) *Administration industrielle et générale*. Paris: Dunod

FERNIE, S., METCALF, D. and WOODLAND, S. (1994) *Does HRM boost employee–management relations?* Working Paper 548. London School of Economics: Centre for Economic Performance

FISCHLMAYR, I. (2002) 'Female self-perception as a barrier to international careers?', *International Journal of Human Resource Management*, Vol.13, No.5: 773–83

FISHER, C. D., SCHOENFELDT, L. F. and SHAW, J. B. (1993) *Human Resource Management*, 2nd edition. Boston, MA: Houghton Mifflin

FOMBRUN, C. J., TICHY, N. M. and DEVANNA, M. A. (1984) *Strategic Human Resource Management*. New York: Wiley

FOULKES, F. K. (1980) *Personnel Policies in Large Non-Union Companies*. Englewood Cliffs, NJ: Prentice-Hall

FOX, A. (1966) *Royal Commission Trade Unions and Employers' Associations Research Papers 3: Industrial Sociology and Industrial Relations*. London: HMSO

FRENCH, J. and RAVEN, B. (1959) 'The bases of social power', in D. Cartwright (ed.) *Studies in Social Power*. Ann Arbor, MI: Institute of Social Research, University of Michigan

GALLIE, D., WHITE, M., CHENG, Y. and TOMLINSON, M. (1998) *Restructuring the Employment Relationship*. Oxford: Clarendon Press

GENNARD, J. (2009) 'The financial crisis and employee relations', *Employee Relations*, Vol.31, No.5: 451–4

GERHART, B. and FANG, M. (2005) 'National culture and human resource management: asumptions and evidence', *International Journal of Human Resource Management*, Vol.16: 971–86

GOLEMAN, D. (2000) 'Leadership that gets results', *Harvard Business Review*, March–April: 78–90

GUEST, D. (1987) 'Human resource management and industrial relations', *Journal of Management Studies*, Vol.24, No.5, 503–21

GUEST, D. (1989) 'Human resource management: its implications for industrial relations and trade unions', in J. Storey (ed.) *New Perspectives on Human Resource Management*. London: Routledge

GUEST, D. (1995) 'Human resource management, trade unions and industrial relations', in J. Storey (ed.) *Human Resource Management: A critical text*. London: Routledge

GUEST, D. (1996) *The State of the Psychological Contract in Employment*. London: IPD

GUEST, D. E. (1997) 'Human resource management and performance: a review and research agenda', *International Journal of Human Resource Management*, Vol.8, No.3, 263–90

GUEST, D., MICHIE, J., CONWAY, N. and SHEEHAN, M. (2003) 'Human resource management and corporate performance in the UK', *British Journal of Industrial Relations*, Vol.41, No.2, 291–314

GULICK, L. and URWICK, L. (eds) (1937) *Papers on the Science of Administration*. New York: Columbia University Press

GYLLENHAMMAR, P. G. (1977) *People at Work*. Reading, MA: Addison-Wesley

HAKEL, M. D. (1982) 'Employment interviewing', in K. M. Rowland and G. R. Ferris (eds) *Personnel Management*. Boston, MA: Allyn & Bacon

HAMEL, G. and PRAHALAD, C. K. (1994) *Competing for the Future*. Boston, MA: Harvard Business School Press

HAMMARSTRÖM, O. and LANSBURY, R. D. (1991) 'The art of building a car: the Swedish experience re-examined', *New Technology, Work and Employment*, Vol.6, No.2, 85–90

HANDY, C. (1985) *Understanding Organizations*. New York: Penguin

HANDY, C., GORDON, C., GOW, I. and RANDLESOME, C. (1988) *Making Managers*. London: Pitman

HENDERSON, I. S. and DOWLING, M. (2010) *Managing Personal Competencies*. Edinburgh: Edinburgh Business School

HERSEY, P. and BLANCHARD, K. H. (1988) *The Management of Organizational Behavior*. Englewood Cliffs, NJ: Prentice-Hall

HERZBERG, F. (1966) *Work and the Nature of Man*. Cleveland, OH: World Publishing

HOFSTEDE, G. (2001) *Culture's Consequences*, 2nd edition. London: Sage

HOLBECHE, L. (2007) 'Building high performance – the key role for HR', *Impact: Quarterly Update on CIPD Policy and Research*, No.20, 10–11

HOLLINSHEAD, G. and LEAT, M. (1995) *Human Resource Management: An international and comparative perspective*. London: Pitman

HOLMAN, D., PAVLICA, K. and THORPE, R. (1997) 'Rethinking Kolb's theory of experiential learning: the contribution of social constructivism and activity theory', *Management Learning*, Vol.28: 135–48

HONEY, P. and MUMFORD, A. (1989) *A Manual of Learning Opportunities*. Maidenhead: Peter Honey

HOUSE, R. J., HANGES, P. J., JAVIDAN, M., DORFMAN, P. W. and GUPTA, V. (2004) *Culture, Leadership and Organizations: the GLOBE Study of 62 Societies*. Thousands Oaks, CA: Sage

HUSELID, M. (1995) 'The impact of human resource management practices on turnover, productivity and corporate financial performance', *Academy of Management Journal*, Vol.38, No.3, 635–72

HUSTED, B. W. (2003) 'Globalization and cultural change in international business research', *Journal of International Management*, Vol.9: 427–33

INCOMES DATA SERVICES (1991) *Guide to Incentive Payment Schemes*. London: IDS

INCOMES DATA SERVICES (2001) *Competency Frameworks*. IDS Study 706. London: IDS

INCOMES DATA SERVICES (2010) *Employee Mobility*. IDS Study 916. April. London: IDS

INSTITUTE OF PERSONNEL AND DEVELOPMENT (1997) *The IPD Code of Professional Conduct and Disciplinary Procedures*. London: IPD

INTERNATIONAL LABOUR ORGANISATION (1984) *Payment by Results*. London/Geneva: ILO

INTERNATIONAL LABOUR ORGANISATION and IFTDO (2000) *Supporting Workplace Learning for High-Performance Working*. London/Geneva: ILO: www.ilo.org/

IRS (1993) *Multi-employer Bargaining*. IRS Employment Trends No.544, 6–8

JAVIDAN, M. and HOUSE, R. J. (2001) 'Cultural acumen for the global manager: lessons from project GLOBE', *Organizational Dynamics*, Vol. 29: 289–305

JELINEK, M. and ADLER, N. J. (1988) 'Women: world class managers for global competition', *Academy of Management Executive*, Vol.2, No.1, 11–19

JOHNSON, G. and SCHOLES, K. (1997) *Exploring Corporate Strategy*. London: Prentice-Hall

JOHNSON, H. (1971) *Business in Contemporary Society: Framework and issues*. Belmont, CA: Wadsworth

KANTER, R. Moss (1989) *When Elephants Learn to Dance*. New York: Touchstone

KEENAN, T. (2005) *Human Resource Management*. Edinburgh: Edinburgh Business School

KENNEDY, G., BENSON, J. and McMILLAN, J. (1984) *Managing Negotiations*, 2nd edition. London: Business Books

KENNEY, M. and FLORIDA, R. (1993) *Beyond Mass Production: The Japanese system and its transfer to the U.S.* Oxford: Oxford University Press

KENNOY, T. (1999) 'HRM as hologram: a polemic', *Journal of Management Studies*, Vol.36, No.1, 1–23

KERSLEY, B., ALPIN, C., FORTH, J., BRYSON, A., BEWLEY, H., DIX, G. and OXENBRIDGE, S. (2006) *Inside the Workplace: Findings from the 2004 Workplace Employment Relations Survey*. Abingdon: Routledge

KESSLER, S. and BAYLISS, F. (1992) *Contemporary British Industrial Relations*. London: Macmillan

KIRKPATRICK, D. L. (1967) 'Evaluation of training', in R. L. Craig and L. R. Bittel (eds) *Training and Development Handbook*. New York: McGraw-Hill

KLEMP, G. O. (1980) *The Assessment of Occupational Competence*. Report to the National Institute for Education. Washington DC

KOCHAN, T. A., KATZ, H. A. and McKERSIE, R. B. (1994) *The Transformation of American Industrial Relations*. New York: Basic Books

KOLB, A. and KOLB, D. A. (2002) 'Bibliography on experiential learning theory'. Available online at http:// www.learningiromexperiGnce.com/Research_Library/ELT_bibJulOl.pdf

KOLB, D. A. (1984) *Experiential Learning: Experience as the source of learning and development*. Englewood Cliffs, NJ: Prentice-Hall

KOLB, D. A., RUBIN, I. and MCINTYRE, J. M. (1971) *Organizational Psychology: An experiential approach*. Englewood Cliffs, NJ: Prentice Hall

KONZELMANN, S., CONWAY, N., TRENBERTH, L. and WILKINSON, F. (2006) 'Corporate governance and human resource management', *British Journal of Industrial Relations*, Vol.44, No.3: 541–67

KOTTER, J. (1999) *John Kotter on What Leaders Really Do*. Cambridge, MA: Harvard Business School Press

KUHN, T. S. (1970) *The Structure of Scientific Revolutions*, 2nd edition. Chicago: University of Chicago Press

LANDY, F. J. and CONTE, J. M. (2007) *Work in the Twenty-First Century: An introduction to industrial and organizational psychology*, 2nd edition. Oxford: Blackwell

LEGGE, K. (1989) 'Human resource management: a critical analysis', in J. Storey (ed.) *New Perspectives on Human Resource Management*. London: Routledge